About the author:

Read the book, and you will know me.

Writing in the first person, I have kept the words simple to appeal to everybody – no need for a dictionary.
    I hope the story encourages you in your time of difficulty – nothing is impossible.

                                                     Frances

Copyright © Frances Joseph 2023

The right of Frances Joseph to be identified as the author of this work has been asserted by her in accordance with the Copyright Designs and Patents Act

ISBN 978-0-6457517-0-3

All rights reserved. No part of this publication may be reproduced or transmitted in any form or by any means, electronic or mechanical, including photocopy, recording, or any information storage and retrieval system, without permission in writing from the author.

Scripture quotations taken from The Holy Bible, New International Version® NIV®
Copyright © 1973, 1978, 1984, 2011 by Biblica, Inc.®
Used by permission. All rights reserved worldwide.

Cover illustrations by Germancreative at Fiverr website

Printed and bound in Australia by
Ingram Spark Melbourne Australia

Crying Mummy's Tears

By

Frances Joseph

Dedication.
This book is dedicated to the memory of my mother, Emily and sister Patricia. I pray you rest peacefully in the arms of our heavenly father, Jesus.
　　　Also, to all women who have been and are suffering domestic violence, you deserve better.

Acknowledgements
My deepest gratitude goes to the love of my life, Hans, for his unending devotion and support to me in the darkest times as I wrote this book. To my bible study group, the Women of Hope, Kristyn Rostan and Annette Mace, for your friendship, love, encouragement, support and prayers on my writing journey.
To Joan Bungar for editorial help. Special thanks to the Fellowship of Australian Writers, North West Tasmania members, for your encouragement and support in writing this book.

Most importantly, to my Heavenly Father, Jesus Christ without whom I would not be where I am today.

Disclaimer:
All names are fictional, having been changed to protect the individuals' identities. Only the countries where the events took place are actual.

CONTENTS

FOREWORD I	7
FOREWORD II	9
CHAPTER 1: INTESTATE	14

Mum, Dad, Early childhood, Weddings, The courts, Looking for a new home, School days, Three life-changing days, The exam, Last day of school, Reflection

CHAPTER 2: BE IT EVER SO HUMBLE   49

Eviction, Re-homed, The flat, The boy, Community centre, Sick for a week, Leaving, Secondary school, Cathy, Farewell Cathy, New school, Live-in maid, New responsibilities, Final year, A home upgrade, Furniture, Final exams, Working life, The shop, The call, The party, First date, Exam results, Job applications, Heartbreak

CHAPTER 3: STUDENT NURSE   76

Fledgling, Gastric lavage, Home front, Second year, Third-year nursing, Graduation, First posting, Frying pan, Bread rolls, self-improvement, Modelling, Love your bride, Sam again, Moving up, Well played, Wedding bells, On our own, Regret, Why?, Lonely holidays, Decisions, On your marks, Interview, Farewell Singapore

CHAPTER 4: BACK TO SCHOOL   112

Antenatal clinic, Shopping, Postnatal experience, Christmas, New life, Birthing suite, Special Care Baby Unit, Antenatal ward, Community placement, Growing into myself, Final exams, New job, Home, Couple time, Holidays alone, King Richard, Death, Praise, Homeowner, Community midwifery, Homebirth, A very special cake, Discord, Clinical nurse specialist, Rose, Parting, The dress, The wedding, Migration dramas, Settling in, A lifetime of holidays, Fertility treatments, Sterility

CHAPTER 5: STRIPPED   153

Informing family, Waiting, Repossession, Decisions, Advice, Sleepless, Term of endearment, The blue ledger, Negotiations, Support gone, Gift, Professional overhaul, Hayfever, In court, Over, Moving, Christmas present, Resolution, Saudi, Departure

CHAPTER 6: A WHOLE NEW WORLD 172
Settling in, Orientation, Birthing, A mixed model, The Saudi father, Emergency, Domestic help, Social life, The swimming pool, Finding my way, Disappointment, Debt-free, Family matters, Darwin, Bedouin Souq, Gold Souqs, Hashing, All that glitters, Last days, One last look, Farewell England

CHAPTER 7: "DOWNUNDA" 195
The hospital, Settling in, A crisis of faith, Initiation, On the ward, Fruity Joe, Decision, Starting anew, Seeking, Challenged, Replies, Buddy, The Call, Christmas day, The drive, The visit, A perfect start, Beauty and brains, At the farm, Making a home, Sight, Made anew

CHAPTER 8: UNION 230
God's plan, Forgiving, Living my best life, Unfinished business, Workplace bullying, Toastmasters International, On air, Gideons, One last encumbrance, Intercession, He hears us, Subdivision, Trouble, Divine knowledge, Still building, Long wait, A journey

FOREWORD I

Like many others, when I open my Bible and read the testimonies within its pages, I am encouraged and inspired. In addition, I find my hope is also built up, my resolve is strengthened, and my faith is elevated to believe God will also carry me through any hardship I encounter, just as He has done for the Bible characters of old.

Our Lord is the same yesterday, today, and forever (Hebrews 13:8); therefore, the same God from the Bible who chose and called David (1 Samuel 16) and Esther (Esther 1-10) is the same God who chooses and calls each of us. The same Jesus who healed the lame man at the pool of Bethesda (John 5) and the woman with the blood disorder (Luke 8) is the same Jesus who heals us today. Likewise, the same Holy Spirit that those encountered in Acts chapter two is also present in our world today and is willing to move with the same power.

These stories are all testimonies of what the Lord has done, and the records of our lives are no different. When we survive any hardship, it is a story worth sharing that may help someone persevere through similar circumstances.

I met Frances one morning at a women's event I was speaking at, where I shared about God's miraculous intervention in my life. After the meeting was over, we sat down together. Frances shared Lilly's story of suffering and surviving, which I encouraged her to write.

Just as every story in the Bible is centred upon God's goodness, so is Lilly's story. This book is an account of a life interwoven throughout the recollections, and you will discover the presence of our Heavenly Father, constantly protecting and blessing.

You may very well shed mummy tears as you read this story. Still, I pray too that by the time you turn the last page, you will have gained a greater knowledge of who God is, a greater awareness of His immense love, and a greater openness to believe and receive the same love of the Lord you will be introduced to throughout the telling of this godly woman's life.

Annette Mace
Author, Speaker,
Spiritual Mentor & Life Coach

FOREWORD II

I have known the author for a few years now and she impresses me as someone who does not allow difficulties to deflect her from achieving her intentions. She is to be admired and her true story will leave you, as it did me, thunderstruck by how Lilly was able to bust through all the roadblocks that individuals and governments put in front of her and to come out the end to live a pleasant, peaceful life with a very compatible husband in a wonderful part of the world.

Allan Jamieson (*)

===//===

At the tender age of five, little Lilly was suddenly confronted with the huge, cold, rough World. Being a citizen of the tiny nation of Singapore was no safeguard. Until then, she had experienced a reasonably comfortable family life. The family comprised Lilly's father and mother and their five children (Lilly was the youngest), however the house was also home to the three daughters from the father's previous marriage plus a niece of his. Lilly's mother's niece came to Singapore from Malaysia to continue her schooling and she lived in the house as well. The house was owned by the father and there was a rental income available that came from a second house owned by him.

This life changed drastically when the father died – intestate! Despite having some forewarning of impending death, he chose not to write a Will. The house now accommodated twelve people, of which Lilly's mother was effectively the sole adult in charge; the three stepdaughters, who were adults in fact, were more hindrance than help and eventually two of the stepdaughters were married off; the house ended up with just Lilly's mother and her five children plus one stepdaughter who was deaf due to a bomb explosion during the War.

This change was not the worst of it, when the sons-in-law successfully forced the sale of the properties to gain access to their wives' inheritance, which being intestate was permitted. The family eventually became homeless.

Social welfare did not exist in Singapore and the family quickly discovered that charity – at least as represented by the clergy at the local Catholic Church frequented by the family, was cold and of no help at all. The $500 inheritance proceeds for each child, received by Lilly's mum, weren't going to go far and abject poverty was unavoidable. The members of the family were forever hungry and Lilly drank water to fill her belly. They were rehoused to the sixth floor of a government housing building (no lift), infested with cockroaches and bedbugs.

Lilly had been in two minds about her father. Yes, he had ruined her life by not writing a Will, but he had insisted that his children would speak English and only English in their home. A simple survey of the household would have shown Tamil to be the dominant language spoken there, but Lilly spoke English as her first language forsaking Tamil as her ethnic language. English proficiency was to be a great help to Lilly as she grew older and tried to break out of her poverty.

Lilly and her sisters were sent to Catholic schools run by British Missionaries. Lilly was fortunate in primary school because the Principal, an Australian lady, drove her car each day filled with kids who did not have the money for the bus fare. In Lilly's case, she also lacked the money to buy food at the school's tuckshop and she took to salvaging leftover food from plates before the janitor threw it out.

A problem arose at exam time. The class lessons had been held in the afternoon, but the exams would be held in the morning, thus the Principal's car would not be available. Lilly would need to walk more than 3.5 km one way to get there from home and the same distance back after the exam. Exams were to be held on three days. Lilly and a schoolmate started out each morning at 5:30 am to walk together to get to the school in time. Lilly passed with grades that allowed her to go to high school. At age 12, Lilly observed; "We had taken destiny into our own hands and did what neither of our parents had done for us."

In high school, Lilly's mother was able to give her sufficient money for the bus fare, but not for food. Once more, Lilly drank water to quieten her stomach and enable her to focus on her studies. Then, one day she heard a voice in her head; *"if you want anything in life, do it yourself – don't expect anyone to do it for you."* To any Indian female, this was a radical concept!

Her mother became a live-in maid to a wealthy family. Lilly was left to run the flat; although her sister and brother also lived there, it was Lilly who did the bulk of the work. Her mother was able to give her $5 each fortnight as 'pocket money.' This sufficed for Lilly to take a bus to high school and to buy food in the tuck shop. Eventually, the flat was condemned by the government and they had to move again, only this time they found much better accommodation.

Lilly passed her high school exams and decided to become a nurse. Her mother was not overly enthusiastic at this news, as it would entail yet more study, so she arranged for Lilly to become a sales assistant at a clothing store. The pay was $60 a month! She was invited to a party by a school friend, where she met the friend's brother, Sam, who was soon keen on Lilly, but he cooled off when Lilly asked him to introduce her to his parents; instead, he suggested they separate.

Nurse training (over three years) started just prior to Lilly's 16th birthday. She had to work shifts as part of her training. She was paid $90 a month. She became a State Registered Nurse and this would enable her to work in the UK. She also gained a large pay rise.

Sam showed an interest in Lilly once again and they bought a flat to force his parents to allow them to be married as the lease required them to show a marriage certificate within three months. Their marriage started to fail as Sam gambled heavily and was alcoholic.

Lilly started working at a private hospital and decided to focus on midwifery. A midwifery course in England would be a highly desirable career move. She flew to England and succeeded in being offered a place in a course starting a few months later. In terms of becoming a highly skilled midwife, Lilly could not have made a better decision; eventually qualifying as a midwifery sister; clinical nurse specialist.

Sam was unfortunately not the person Lilly wanted to live with; he was a typical Indian male who saw a wife as a mere chattel and he was very dismissive of her efforts. She applied for a divorce, which was granted some months later.

While working in England, Lilly met several nurses from Malaysia. They started migrating to Australia and Lilly decided to follow them, but first she needed money. She applied to be a midwife for 12 months in Saudi Arabia. Monetarily, this move was definitely of value, though life there – and the work experience too – was far from being consistently positive. The ethos of male Arabs was appalling in Lilly's eyes; some of the events she describes would be appalling to most people!

Lilly longed for the day when she could get on a plane and fly out – never to return!

Lilly's landfall "Downunda" was at Darwin, where she could not secure a job in a local hospital. She moved to a hospital in Queensland, which was somewhat better, though the work ethos was not good; the staff were very "laid back" and not interested in attaining extra skills. [In my opinion, this attitude is a serious drawback of Australian culture; one must accept this weakness if one is to continue living in Australia – AJ.]

With time, Lilly felt able to finally settle down, but she was single! She tried a dating agency and one man struck a very positive chord in her mind. They eventually met and soon it was clear they should marry. The man, Gian, worked in "IT", but he had a farm and this was very important to him. Could Lilly accept a farm life?

Throughout her life, Lilly found the Bible was her one constant support, despite her negative experience of the Catholic Church. In her story, she inserts some of the sentences and sentiments from the Bible, which gave her the strength to persist in her search for happiness.

(*) Allan Jamieson was born in Australia, but worked overseas for 17 years, living on three continents and working in over 20 countries. He returned to Australia over 40 years ago.

CHAPTER 1 -- INTESTATE

Mum screamed when Dad drew his last breath. I was five years old. I could not make out what was happening. Uncles, aunts and grandmother were all in our crowded house. Dad lay on the bed. Several people had been feeding him milk, which dribbled down his cheeks. Mum was by his side, and grandma held me close to her. Everybody was in tears. The parish priest gave Dad what I now know was his last rite -- or "extremunction", as someone close by murmured. I could not understand the scene in front of me. No one said anything to me as to what was going on. I just knew something was wrong.

I was not allowed to go to his graveside funeral, but we visited him at the graveyard a week later -- the first time I had ever been to a cemetery. We regularly went to see his grave for the first year after his death and on All Souls Day in the following years. We stopped at one of the last graves, and Mum put her bag down. Inscribed on a small marble slab at the top of the site was Dad's name. Mum told us to weed around the mound of dirt, so we got busy. She then lit candles and led everybody in prayer. Mum cried, and my sister whispered that this was Dad's grave. It did not make any sense to me at all. When I asked what she meant, she just looked at me through the tears in her eyes. I just listened as I still did not understand any of it.

Mum
Mum was just thirty-five years old when Dad died. I think Mum was sad about her lot in life. It seemed to be full of hardship and worry and no joy. I know little about the events that led to my mother's arranged marriage, as was customary in her day. The wedding photos show her and Dad in the typical wedding pose. Mum wore a saree and had a bouquet in her hands; Dad was in a suit. At six feet, he towered above her diminutive four foot ten inches. Dad was some 20 years older

than Mum, while she was just twenty-one when they were married. He had been married before and had three daughters; his first wife died giving birth to their third child during an air raid in World War II. Mum was only 15 years older than my eldest half-sister at her wedding.

Like many families during the Japanese Occupation of Singapore, theirs was an instant blended family. In addition to three stepdaughters, she lived in a household that included Dad's young niece. The latter was the child of his brother. Her parents were among the thousands who succumbed to tuberculosis in the early 1940s. The schools declined to enrol my half-sisters, claiming they were too old to commence primary school. My half-sisters did not have much schooling. My oldest half-sister, who had initiated school before the war, could read simple English. However, she lost her hearing as a child when caught in an air raid. She had not been able to reach the bomb shelter in time, and the blasts had caused irrevocable damage to her ear drums. Dad had had her seen by the doctors, who told him there was little they could do for her. Not surprisingly, she tended to speak loudly. Mum and Dad then had the five of us: my two sisters, my two brothers and finally myself. Eventually, my Mum's niece came across from Malaysia to live with us and continue her schooling, so our household numbered 12.

Mum was born in Malacca, in what was then British Malaya, in 1920. Hers was a comfortable life. Some might even describe it as a life of privilege. A younger sister soon followed. Their education was rare for Indian girls in the early 1930s, with tutoring at their homes. They learnt to read and write in English and Tamil and studied mathematics, geography, history and domestic science. Mum excelled in sewing and was known for her prowess in dressmaking, knitting and crocheting all her life. When she was a teenager, Mum's mother died, leaving Granddad with two girls to raise independently. Granddad found another wife, a stepmother to my Mum and her sister. Though she did not know it then, Mum was to repeat this family history when she was wed to a widower and became a stepmother to Dad's children.

Mum's stepmother, or Grandma as she eventually became known to me, was not kind to her stepdaughters. Mum and her sister worked in the kitchen and around the home doing the cooking, cleaning, laundry and other household tasks. Their happy childhood ended abruptly. Grandma and Grandfather had three children, so I had two uncles and another aunt. Grandma favoured her children over her stepdaughters. They played in the garden, had the best clothes and food, and attended the best schools. Mum and her sister waited on them like servants. Grandma often berated Mum and her sister for their work around the home: the potatoes in the curry were uncooked, her son's shirt was not pristine enough, or the house was untidy. Mum and her sister comforted each other through this ordeal.

As soon as they attained puberty in their mid-teens, Grandma planned to get them out of her way by marrying them off. She eventually settled on husbands for both of her stepdaughters. She arranged for both young women to marry widowers considerably older than them and had children from their first marriage. It was a fate not dissimilar to Grandma's own. Mum's education and maltreatment by her stepmother yielded an unexpected advantage: she was already skilled at keeping house, a common expectation at the time. However, while she gained a husband, Mum lost her single source of comfort, her sister. The two sisters did their best to stay in touch, but the demands of being a wife, widow and mother in the following years often made this difficult. While my aunt remained in Malacca till her marriage a few years later, Mum moved across the causeway to Singapore with Dad as soon as the wedding formalities and festivities were over.

Dad

At five years of age, I did not know my father. Someone told me that my mother would sometimes ask Dad's cousin Uncle John, who lived nearby, to drive her to the bars and clubs that she knew Dad frequented. One of the many indignities Mum suffered upon his death was making the rounds of his preferred watering holes to settle the debts he had run up drinking. Dad would often be legless and have to be carried home to bed.

It is difficult for the family to understand why he did not make a Will when the doctors told him there was nothing more, they could do for him. Things would have turned out quite differently for us had he done this. He had lain on his deathbed for nearly a month. Why had he not organised his affairs then? Perhaps, he was too sick by then to do much else. Maybe he had been paralysed by the fear of his impending demise. Perhaps? In a sense, he abdicated from his duty as husband and father. My siblings and I have spent many a day speculating about his reasons, but we will never know what had been behind this particular failure on his part.

Dad was not without redeeming qualities. I have him to thank for my grasp of the English Language. He ruled that we would not speak our mother tongue Tamil at home. Instead, we were to speak only English. This move reflected his foresight and wisdom. The British colonial administration employed him, and he would have spent time with his British bosses. Dad knew to improve his children's prospects; they must not speak English as a second language, which would severely hamper their future employment. Dad must have known that Singapore could grow into something big. English was and still is the language of government, finance and trade on the island. Dad's directive was to have a lasting impact on my professional and personal life. It was probably the best decision he made for us.

Dad had the foresight and was keen to ensure his children would succeed when they grew up. He sacrificed tradition and culture for our future in an impending modern nation-state. Dad sent my siblings and me to Catholic schools run by British Missionaries, the best in Singapore then. Mum, Dad and my half-sisters are the only ones who could speak Tamil. Mum could read and write Tamil. My siblings and I all speak, read and write good English. In addition, I love to read. Books were the only free thing in the dark days when even a meal was sometimes beyond our reach.

I borrowed them from the library and lost myself in the story. Surrounded by sadness and eventually poverty and squalor, I was transported to beautiful places and wonderful people in the books that inspired me. One pivotal book was *The Diary of Anne Frank*. If Anne could go through what had happened to her, I often thought I could cope with what was happening to me. The stories helped me forget that I was hungry and that Mum often cried in bed. She thought I couldn't hear her. We shared the same bedroom. It made me sad. I wished I could help her. She cried a great deal in the years after Dad died.

Early Childhood

My family's Catholic faith defined and dictated the milestones of our lives. My baptism as a baby was in keeping with Catholic practice. The family albums are full of photographs of babies decked in the family's christening robe and bonnet made by Mum. The next generation would eventually wear a frothy concoction of expensive lace and satin ribbons. We went to church every Sunday as a family, participating in all the relevant sacraments of Holy Communion and Confession. We fasted during Lent, prayed the rosary as a family daily with all of us on our knees in the living room and attended the lengthy Good Friday service. Parties followed attendance at mass, presents, visits to friends and relatives, and lots of good things to eat at Easter and Christmas warranted big celebrations in our household.

In school, I was taught catechism by the nuns and the parish priests in preparation for First Holy Communion and Confirmation. I knew the Ten Commandments and what Heaven, Hell, and Purgatory were. What was lacking was the encouragement to read the Bible and develop a personal relationship with Jesus Christ. This lack contributed significantly to the issues that marked my first forty years. Life took a desolate turn after Dad died without a Will, and our lives spiralled out of control into poverty. While Dad was alive, the family lived in one of two houses he owned. An Australian family rented the second house. Dad also had an excellent job from which he must have earned a good income because we lived a comfortable life, all 12 of us. In today's money, those two houses and the land would be worth over $15 million Singapore dollars.

We had a car and a driver at our disposal. My half-sisters claim that the driver was given to smoking marijuana and often drove them around under the influence. When they tell these stories, they recount them with great aplomb, and everyone roars with laughter. One of their favourite tales features me as a toddler. My second half-sister, charged with running errands, took me with her. The driver had failed to secure the car door before setting out. As the car turned a corner, the door swung open with me holding on for dear life. Then it slammed shut with me still attached when the driver turned the corner in the opposite direction. My half-sister was somehow able to secure the door, loosen my grip and settle me safely in the back seat. She says I was unscathed by the adventure. She laughed so hard that she had tears as she told the tale. Those were happy days in simpler times. Then Dad died. He left many unpaid bills for Mum to settle. The only source of income was the rental property. Mum was left with ten children to raise with Uncle John's help. In colonial Singapore, there was no social security for those in difficult financial straits.

Weddings

The family limped along for a couple of years after Dad died. Then Mum decided it was time to get my half-sisters married. According to Indian custom, girls in their late teens are ripe for marriage, and to keep such women unmarried in the home for long was unacceptable. So, finding a husband for all three of them commenced. Mum engaged a matchmaker who brought a string of suitors to our home to view their prospective brides. She consulted astrologers for the best dates to hold the weddings. As a practising Catholic, this was something that she ought not to have done, for the Bible warns us,

"Do not turn to mediums or seek out spiritists, for they will defile you. I am the Lord your God." (Lev 19:31). However, she was not to know this as reading the Bible was not something we did in our home.

With the matchmakers came suitors. The kitchen bubbled and sizzled in a cooking frenzy. On these occasions, it was customary for the bride-to-be to serve tea and cakes to the suitor allowing each party to view the other—the preparation of speciality cakes and sweetmeats was for the prospective grooms' delectation. The elders accompanying the potential groom would scrutinise the bride's demeanour and manner, expecting her to be modest and demure. The young woman would risk taking only furtive glances at her possible intended from under her lashes while she kept her gaze lowered as she served.

There was much excitement amongst the half-sisters. They peeked at the suitor from behind the lace-curtained window when he strode up the driveway. Draped in their best sarees, they giggled and nudged each other, whispering about the merits of each suitor and which one they hoped would pick them. It did not take long for the girls to choose their prospective husbands. Parents usually had the final pick from a shortlist of suitors. Unusually, Mum allowed my half-sisters to make their own choice.

My second half-sister picked a man. Mum disapproved. Mum advised her not to accept his hand because she could see he was an alcoholic. He swayed as he walked, and his eyes were bloodshot. Nicotine stains between his left hand's index and second fingers indicated that he smoked heavily. But there was no telling second half-sister otherwise. He was the one she wanted, and so it came to be. A man from Kuala Lumpur chose my third half-sister. She agreed to the match though he was at least fifteen years older. My first half-sister did not receive any offers for her hand, probably because of her deafness.

Once again, Mum consulted the astrologer to identify the most auspicious dates to hold the weddings. The girls were to marry on different days, so they would each have a special day. In keeping with the custom for the bride's parents to pay for the wedding, my mother footed the bills. Custom-required wedding invitations are delivered personally to the guests during home visits. Mum gave each invitation on a decorative silver platter along with some sweetmeats for the occasion and pre-arranged time for the call.

Indian Catholic weddings are colourful events with the womenfolk dressed in bright, elaborate sarees contrasting with the virginal white one of the brides. Indian families that converted to Christianity substituted the Hindu celebrations and customs they were obliged to leave behind with aspects of Western traditions. Hence the veil and a white saree rather than a brightly coloured one. A Hindu bride would never wear a white saree as this is the Hindu symbol of widowhood.

The church ceremony was at our local parish. The sweet scent of jasmine flowers that adorned the women's hair mingled with the rosewater sprinkled on guests as they walked into the church. The reception venue was in a nearby hall my mother had hired. The three-tier wedding cake came from a famous downtown bakery. Indian festive fares include biryani, lentil and fish curries, scented tri-coloured rice studded with raisins and cashews and many side dishes and condiments for the celebratory meal.

It was customary for the bride's parents to deck the bride and groom with jewellery. The groom was given a large signet ring with his initials and a gold chain to wear around his neck. The most important piece of jewellery was the *tali*, a semi-spherical pendant marked with the Indian symbol of marriage on a gold chain and placed around the bride's neck by the groom. The bride wore this for the rest of her life, so everyone knew she was married and only removed it if she outlived her husband. Mum paid for all of it! The couple also exchanged wedding rings and flower garlands.

Sometime after the weddings of the two half-sisters, Mum's niece got married. She and Uncle John had fallen in love. Uncle John and my cousin moved away to live in one of Singapore's new high-rise housing estates. Mother sold the car Uncle John used to drive us around, as no other family member could drive. Dad's niece went to live with Uncle John's brother's family. She had gone to school with the girls in that family, and they all got on well. Our house had more room. Only Mum, her five biological children, and our first half-sister live there now. We had more room to spread out and enjoyed the luxury. Since Dad had passed away, I shared their bed with Mum. Perhaps she did not want to be alone.

The Courts

It was not long before I sensed something was wrong. The first thing I noticed was that my mother cried again, usually after some of my uncles visited us. My half-sisters' husbands also seemed to visit frequently. I had not yet begun school, so I went everywhere with Mum. I accompanied her to the Subordinate Courts of Singapore on several occasions. My half-sisters' husbands would meet us there. They would all go into the courtroom while I was sent off with a social worker and was kept busy with crayons and colour pencils. After some time, Mum and my uncle would exit the courtroom; Mum would be in tears. The adults would continue to talk, sometimes heatedly. Separation from Mum made me cry.

"What am I supposed to do?" my mother pleaded with my brothers-in-law. "I still have five children and one stepdaughter to feed and clothe. We are living off the rental from that second property. My youngest child is too young to be left alone at home, so I can't go out to work. The sale of the properties will not raise enough to feed, house, and educate them all. Why are you doing this to us? Did I not give you a wife? Now you want the roof over my children's heads. What kind of men are you? I tried to do the right thing by you; now you want to destroy us!" Mum was weeping.

The brothers-in-law just looked at her, unmoved. Another man, a family friend, said sadly, "Your husband did not leave a Will. He should have done that when he knew he was going to die. Now he has left you in a bad state."

Mum continued weeping as we left the building, and the brothers-in-law went their way. We attended court for three days, and Mum cried all the time. While in another room trying to draw, I could hear Mum wailing in the courtroom next door. Things came to a head on the last day. With the proceedings over, I was allowed to return to Mum. She was in a state. My three brothers-in-law stalked out of the building. Mum's friend was trying to help her, but nothing he said seemed to be helping. She was weeping hysterically. Eventually, we got into a taxi and went home. She did not say much. She just continued sobbing. When she had exhausted her tears, she was reticent. We had lost the roof over our heads and the rental property, our only source of income.

Looking for a new home
A family friend took my mother to a flat at a high-rise housing estate. These were being built rapidly as Singapore's answer to affordable housing for its growing population. There was much argument and discussion. Some weeks later, we moved from our home with the large garden to another property, a terraced house. Our family now consisted of all five of my Mum's children and our first half-sister.

Relatives continued to visit us, and everything seemed normal. I started school while living at this address. We made friends with the new neighbours and attended lots of parties. Mum often cooked large amounts of food for these occasions. One day, my mother decided to tell us what happened in court. She said that because Daddy did not leave a Will, the courts could not stop our brothers-in-law from forcing the two properties to be sold so that their wives, our half-sisters, could claim their share. Having had to give the half-sisters their share of the estate, she had told them that she did not want to see them again! The court's decision forced the sale of our family home and the rental property. My siblings and I finally understood why we had to move. We were now tenants in a rental ourselves. We had each received $500 from the sale of the properties, which the Public Trustee held. Mum could draw from it for living expenses.

We lived in this terraced house for a few years, and our first half-sister married at this house. She moved into a modest home with her new husband soon after the wedding. My mother had to face another court case. My cousin, Dad's brother's daughter, claimed that she had a share in the proceeds of the sale of the family properties. This time, though, Mum prevailed. The court ruled that my cousin had no claim to an inheritance from Dad's estate.

Some years after Dad's passing, Mum said she wanted Daddy's gravesite covered with a tombstone. She planned to have our names inscribed on it. However, Mum had resolved not to include those of my two half-sisters whose husbands had taken her to court. She said they did not deserve to be remembered on Dad's tombstone. We visited the grave to inspect the simple marble slab with Dad's details and our names. Mum lit candles, and we said prayers. She seemed pleased with it. Sometime later, we heard through the family grapevine that the omission of both second and third half-sisters' names caused them to be outraged. I imagine Mum must have felt a certain satisfaction upon learning this.

There was now Mum and just the five of us. Mum found that she could no longer afford the rent for the terraced house. So, we moved to the first of three slum homes. These slum areas were known as *kampong*, a Malay word which translates loosely into "village". The houses here were largely shanty homes with communal outhouses for toilets. The excrement fell into buckets, collected and emptied by the night soil man. He was a regular feature of the dawn: a scrawny Chinese man bent under a long wooden pole at each end was a black, metal bucket of excrement. The toilets over dams were cleaner and smelt less offensive; catfish fed off the human waste that plopped into the water below.

In the 1960s, Singapore was a far cry from today's ultra-modern clean and green city-state. Dirt laneways and small open areas separated the houses. Amongst the shanty homes were terraced houses and bungalows. Wastewater ran into crude drainage systems in the kampong. These eventually connected to large open monsoon drains. They often stank because of their contents: rubbish and sewage and were often stagnant, breeding disease-bearing mosquitoes.

At first, we were all crowded into a small house. When a larger one became available, we moved into it. The Chinese landlords lived in the most prominent house at the compound's front. They treated us well. Mum and their eldest daughter became friends; they were about the same age. Mum often would cook a curry for them, and in return, they would send us something to eat.

At Chinese New Year, we had our first steamboat dinner experience. It was a treat they gave us every year, which we enjoyed. When Mum could not afford the rent for that big house, we moved to another smaller, cheaper house further down the road.

School days

Because the primary school exams were in the morning, it posed a problem for me. My principal gave me a daily lift to school for a few years. When Mum informed her that she could not afford to send me to school anymore, my principal, Mrs Cox, a kind Australian woman, offered to take me to school. It was no inconvenience, she explained, as she drove past our home daily. There were a couple of hitches.

Mrs Cox worked in the afternoon session of the school day, from about noon to 6.00 pm. She started earlier and finished later than I did. Despite this, my mother agreed to the arrangement rather than jeopardising my education. Mrs Cox also arranged a sponsorship that covered the cost of my school fees. I attended school during the afternoon session with my principal, who also picked up four other students in similar financial straits. I became a latchkey kid entrusted with a house key which I used to let myself into the empty house after school. The other siblings, all older, left for school or work during the week. Mum went out too, though I did not know where.

"How will you get to school on the exam days, Lilly? The papers are in the morning. Mrs Cox won't be picking us up then. My parents say they don't have the money for bus fare!" said Peng, fretting to me one afternoon a week before the exam dates. Like me, Peng was in Primary 6 and rode to school in Mrs Cox's car.

"I know, Peng; my mother said the same thing. I don't know what to do!" I replied.

Looking worried and close to tears, Peng said, "But we have to sit the exams. Without them, we can't go to high school, and then we'll never be able to finish school."

"I know, Peng," I repeated. "Could we walk, you think?"

"That's a long way, over three and a half miles, Lilly," Peng groaned.

"I know, Peng, but we have no choice. Can you think of another way?" I asked.

We were sitting on the concrete staircase at the back of the school. Mrs Cox had sent us to water the plants. The school took part annually in the nationwide Best School Garden Competition. All five girls who rode to school with Mrs Cox tended the gardens with her after school every day. We spent an hour or so weeding, watering, fertilising and sometimes planting new shrubs under Mrs Cox's instruction. We put away the watering cans and made our way to the car. Halfway there, Peng agreed that we would walk to and from school together on exam days.

"What time should we start?" I asked her.

"How about five-thirty in the morning? That will give us two and a half hours to get there. Hopefully, we'll have some time to rest before the exams start," Peng said.

"Yes, let's do that," I agreed.

The day before the exams, I asked my mother if there was money for the bus fare to school for the exams.

"No, Lilly, I don't have money to buy food for the six of us. How can I give you cash for bus fares?" Mum frowned.

"Ok, Mum," I murmured and returned to my school books to try and study.

Food had become scarce in the home. We were all hungry. I could not remember the last time I had eaten because my stomach growled. I went to the kitchen to fill my empty tummy with water. I remembered the look of desperation and hopelessness in my mother's eyes. I wondered how she must have felt—being unable to feed her children. I often found her on her knees, praying in front of the altar. Mum hung large pictures of the Sacred Heart of Jesus and the Blessed Virgin above the altar, which housed a figurine of the Holy Family and other Roman Catholic votive objects. Very often, I saw my mother shed tears as she prayed. She had bought a sizeable leather-bound luxury edition of the Bible. It was beautifully illustrated, but never consulted. Even at the young age of twelve, I knew something was very wrong with my family. We were getting poorer and poorer. There were no more parties or coffee visits. All the relatives that once used to come around disappeared.

Three life-changing days
Day one
Five am. I got dressed in the rays of the early morning sun. I washed in the cold water in the bathroom, finished dressing and drank a large glass of water for breakfast. It was still cool, and the rest of the family was asleep. Packing my school bags and laying out my uniform the night before meant I could quietly move around the bedroom I shared with Mum. Picking up my school bag, I stopped to say a prayer at the altar. I looked up at the Holy pictures on the wall and the statues on the altar. Then, quietly, in my mind, I prayed.

> Jesus, you have to help me for the next three days. I am hungry. There has been no food for so long at home. Now I have to walk to school to sit these exams. Please help me to pass these exams! I don't know how, but I will try my best.

Unlocking the front door, I stepped out into the early morning calm. Walking on the dirt track, I made for the road about a half kilometre away. The stench of the latrine hit me full in the face. I stepped up my pace to get away from it. I found Peng sitting on a pile of rubble, reading a textbook halfway up the main road. Last-minute revision, I thought.

"Hi, Peng," I called out; she looked up.

"Hi, Lilly," she replied.

"Ready to do this?"

"Let's go," she said, standing up.

Together we set off, two uniform-clad twelve-year-olds, doing what seemed almost impossible. Both of us were quiet, each deep in our respective thoughts. The road would become busy as the day progressed. A few cars and a truck whizzed past us. There was an industrial estate just past where we lived. To keep safe, we had to watch our step and stay close to the side of the road. A significant monsoon drain ran alongside the route. There were no safety barriers, and we had to be careful not to fall into the gutter.

"We're coming up to the main road," Peng observed. "We have to cross at the overhead bridge."

The four-lane dual carriageway was a busy arterial road that fed traffic into the industrial estate. The law required pedestrians to cross streets only at designated crossings or face hefty fines if charged with jaywalking. Two young girls in school uniform walking along the road would attract attention; neither of us wanted to draw attention to ourselves. We had to watch where we walked. When we had crossed over to the other side, I asked Peng,

"Those red marks on your legs looked like cane marks. What happened?"

"Yes," Peng admitted. "Mum and Dad argued about my low grades in school. Dad caned me about them," she confided.

I did not know what to say. We just put one foot in front of the other silently, intent on getting to school in time for the exams. I recalled the evening Peng invited me to dinner at her house after I told her there was no food at home. I felt sad for Peng, who was a kind soul. Peng's mother initially smiled at me when Peng told her mother that she had brought me home for dinner. After a few moments, she slapped Peng hard, making her cry. They were speaking in Cantonese, a local Chinese dialect. I was embarrassed.

"Peng, I think I will go home; your mother is unhappy," I whispered.

"No, no! Don't worry," Peng protested through her tears. "It's all right. Stay for dinner."

I still felt embarrassed. But I was hungry. The aromas of the food Peng's mother was preparing made my stomach growl. "Ok," I agreed.

Peng's mother served the food and waved me over to the table. Fortunately, no one else was at home. I ate as sparingly as possible, conscious that I may be taking away someone else's portion. After finishing my meal, I thanked Peng and her mother and left for home.

"Why are you late, Lilly?" Mum asked me that evening when I got home.

"Oh... I had dinner at Peng's," I explained reluctantly.

Mum just looked at me and nodded. There was still no food in the kitchen. I was thankful for what I had in my belly.

We reached the next major intersection. This section of the walk was the longest part. Thankfully we did not have to cross the road! We continued on our way.

"Oh no, Peng. We're coming to the market. Can you smell the food?"

"Yes, let's just walk faster and escape it as quickly as possible."

We walked as fast as we could and stopped when we could no longer smell the tempting aromas, sitting on a concrete bench by the roadside.

"Lilly, why is your family so poor?" Peng enquired.

"It's a long story, Peng. I think it's because my Dad died without a Will."

"Oh! Tell me how," said Peng.

"Do you want to know, Peng?" I asked, surprised.

"Yes, Lilly," she said, nodding.

"Well, if I tell you my story, will you tell me yours, Peng?"

"I don't have much to tell. My parents think I am too stupid to send to school. That is why they did not want to pay for my bus fare or give me money to buy food at recess. Dad always canes me, and Mother tries to stop him. They often fight about money. Dad gets drunk. I am going to try my hardest to pass these exams. I will show them that I am not stupid. Tell me your story," Peng said, setting her chin determinedly.

"Ok, I will tell you my story, but we'd better start walking again, or we'll be late."

We weaved through the side streets off the main road and past shopfronts to avoid drawing attention to ourselves. We were absorbed in our conversation and sometimes in our thoughts.

The Exam

I was deep in my thoughts, telling and reliving my story when Peng had to bring me back to the present. We had reached the end of the long stretch of our journey. We would have to cross over to the other side of the road before walking up the avenue that led to the school building.

"We will have to cross at the overhead bridge," Peng insisted.

"Yep, that would be best," I agreed.

"Today's exam papers will be difficult for me."

"Why Peng?"

"Because the English language is not my best subject," she groaned.

"Just do your best," I encouraged.

I did not tell her I was looking forward to it as English was my best subject. We started climbing the overhead bridge stairs and crossed the road. The school was not far ahead.

"We speak Cantonese at home," Peng confided. "That must be why I am not that good at English."

We reached the school gates and made it just in time for assembly. Wishing each other good luck, we joined our respective classes in the schoolyard. We waited for classical music to start booming across from the loudspeakers around the school, which was the cue for the rows of students to walk onto the field and take their designated place facing the flagpoles. For the morning session, vice-principal Mrs Tan addressed the assembly. She intoned the morning prayer and led the whole school to sing Singapore's national anthem *Majulah Singapura*. The senior school prefect raised the flag. We recited the national pledge and then sang the school song. Finally, Mrs Tan instructed all students sitting for exams to head to the school hall.

Students snaked their way to the hall, Peng and I among them. Our teachers led us to our seats after ensuring we left our bags behind. We were allowed to take only our pencil cases into the hall. Desks and chairs were in neat rows; the stage curtains were drawn. I remember watching my eldest sister, dressed as an Arab man, pull a camel across that stage in a school play a few years ago. Then, one of the teachers rang a bell to capture our attention. She explained that the day's exams were to be in three parts.

Part One was a test of language use with a series of multiple-choice questions. In addition, students would have to do a writing task, such as a short story. Part Two was comprehension. It entailed reading a short passage and answering questions based on it to show that we understood what we had read. There was also a short writing task where we used words from the passage to demonstrate that we understood and used them correctly. Part Three was an oral exam. Students had to read a short excerpt aloud and answer a few questions posed by the teachers. There would be a twenty-minute break between the second and third parts.

I looked for Peng and found her seated to the right, towards the front of the hall. Unfortunately, I could not catch her eye. Teachers handed out the first set of papers face down. A bell rang, signalling the start of the exam. I flipped the exam paper over and began reading. *Write a short story about a holiday.* There were thirty multiple-choice questions to get through. I finished the tasks and then went on to comprehension. After reading the question, I turned over my paper, heart-thumping, and smiled.

Holidays were unheard of in my family. Mum could barely scrape together enough to pay the rent and feed us. I would have to use my imagination and make up a fictitious holiday. I settled on the train ride to Kuala Lumpur that I took with my mother and half-sister when we accompanied her to her marital home after the wedding. I did not stop writing until the first bell rang to signal that we had another half hour to finish our essays. I quickly tied up the loose ends of my story and spent the last ten minutes reviewing it and correcting mistakes. The final bell rang, and the teachers collected the papers. We could not leave the hall but could mingle for about ten minutes before the next part of the exam. I made a beeline for Peng.

"How did you go?" I inquired.

"Oh, I think I did not do too badly. I wouldn't say I liked the multiple-choice questions. I found some of them tricky," Peng smiled.

"What did you write about in your story?"

"A trip to Penang," she said, grinning, "I've never been!"

"Mine was a trip to Kuala Lumpur," I said.

We chatted until the bell rang again, and Peng returned to her seat.

Paper Two

The question demanded that we describe a school excursion and what we'd learned from it. I had been to The National Museum of Singapore the year before and had had a wonderful time exploring Singapore's history. It was a rare occasion when my mother had the money to let me go with the class. I treasured every moment of that memory. I had plenty to write. My pen did not stop till the bell went at the end of the exam. I had forgotten to give myself time to review my work and correct mistakes. It would have to do. I was happy with my essay.

I was beginning to feel hungry. Delectable aromas from the tuck shop below the hall were causing my tummy to growl loudly, and I found it difficult not to wish for food. During the break, I would get water from the taps where we filled the watering cans during gardening. In the meantime, I had to get as far away from the tuck shop as possible. I realised that Peng had left the hall via another exit. In a way, I was glad. I did not want her to feel obliged to feed me.

On the other hand, I did not know if Peng had the money for food. I left the hall and walked to the back of the school to sit by myself. I drank as much water as I could at the garden tap. I sat on a step and waited for the bell to summon me back for the oral exam. Closing my eyes, I leaned against the wall and fell asleep. It was the best thing to do. Hunger always made sleep easy. I slept to forget my growling stomach.

I remembered how often I had fallen asleep at my desk in class. The teacher would throw chalk at me to wake me up, and all my classmates would look at me. Don't you get enough sleep at home? The teacher would demand. As punishment, I often stood in the doorway so everyone could see me. In the far recess of my mind, I heard the bell ringing. The break was over, and I hurried back to the hall to join the rest of the students. The teachers had changed the exam hall set-up. Two teachers now sat at a table; a single vacant chair faced them. I waited my turn.

When my turn came, I read a page from Enid Blyton's *The Faraway Tree*. I had read this book before and so sailed through the task. Next were the questions. The teachers wanted to know what subjects I enjoyed most and what I wanted to be when I grew up. I replied that I enjoyed English Language, Art and Needlework best. I was not sure what I wanted to do in the future. I said I would wait for my exam results and decide what to do. The teachers said the exam was over, and I could leave, pointing to the exit. I found Peng waiting for me at the entrance of the school. We set out on our return leg home.

"How did you do on the exams, Peng?" I asked.

"I struggled with the multiple-choice questions but found the comprehension easier. The reading was difficult for me, Lilly. I stammered through it. So, I don't know how well I have done," she said quietly with a frown.

"You gave it your best; that is all you can do," I said encouragingly.

It was almost one o'clock in the afternoon. We had reached the longest stretch of our journey and were getting close to the marketplace. Both of us were hungry.

"Let me ask someone for money at the bus stop," Peng suggested.

I was horrified. "You can't do that!"

"I have done it before. I'll go and ask that lady in the *samfu*."

Before I could say anything, Peng approached the lady dressed in a top with a Mandarin collar and a pair of pants. Speaking in Cantonese, she asked for just a few coins to buy food. The woman looked disapprovingly at Peng, who persisted. Eventually, the woman opened her purse and grudgingly gave Peng a few coins. I thought we were in uniform; the woman could complain to the school. However,

Peng had the money in her hand, and we were giddy with the thrill of being able to buy something to eat. The market was not very far ahead. Peng had 20 cents in her hand. We began discussing what we could buy. Ice-cold soya bean milk was an attractive choice. We were so busy walking and discussing our options that we did not notice that a car had pulled up just a little before us. Mrs Cox stepped out of her car and came towards us. "What are you two girls doing walking along the street?" She asked. We both looked at each other and then at Mrs Cox.

"We don't have money for bus fare," Peng confessed.

"Didn't your parents give you money?" She asked.

"They haven't any," I told her dully.

"Wait here," the principal instructed. She went back to her car and came back with her purse. She handed a few notes to Peng and urged us to take the bus back home, adding that there was enough for the remaining two days of the exams. We thanked Mrs Cox and watched her get back into her car, do a U-turn and continue driving to the school.

"Peng, she must have seen us from across the road. Some of the other girls she gives a lift to were in the car," I whispered, almost as if Mrs Cox could hear me.

"Yes, I know," Peng replied.

She looked at the money in her hand, which we counted together. Mrs Cox had given us $2! We now had $2.20, including Peng's coins from the *samfu*-clad woman.

"Do you want to take the bus home, Peng?" I asked.

"No, I'd rather eat!"

"Me too!" I concurred, thinking about all the food we could buy at $2.20. What a banquet! I realised we would have to spread it over the next two days if there was nothing at home.

So, I told Peng we would divide the money into three lots. We had 70 cents for that day and the next and 80 cents to celebrate the end of the exams. Walking to the market, we had our seventy-cent feast and continued home.

"It still does not make sense to me. You have educated parents, but you are still poor. How come?" Peng quizzed me again. So, I continued with the tale of my early childhood. Before too long, we were at the top of Peng's Lane. We agreed to meet at the same time here the next day. I continued but heard Peng call after me a few steps later.

"Lilly, I think you had better take the 70 cents for tomorrow in case something happens and I cannot come to school," she said, her arm outstretched with the coins in her hand.

"Oh, Peng, I hope not!" her words alarmed me. "But how would I know if you're not coming?" I asked.

"I'll still come to meet you here at 5.30 in the morning, no matter what. You'll know I'm not going to school if I'm not in uniform." Peng handed me the money and turned down her lane.

It was about three o'clock in the afternoon when I reached home. No one was home, as the front door was locked. I let myself in and locked the door on the inside as Mum had instructed me. I was also not to open the door to strangers. I was tired from all that walking in the hot afternoon sun. I took off my uniform and made for the bathroom to wash, grateful for the cold water sluicing down my back.

There was no shower. We collected water in a large ceramic tub and used a big plastic scoop held aloft to pour the water over our heads. There was no hot water. We could not afford a hot water system, and the landlord did not permit one installation. After my wash, I lay on my canvas camp bed and fell into a deep sleep. I woke up to noises in the house. It was nearly 6.30 in the evening. Ordinarily, this would be dinner time. But I guessed that there would be nothing to eat. Walking into the living room, I found my eldest brother reading and my sisters chatting in their bedroom. They informed me that my mother was visiting the neighbours.

There was nothing to eat in the kitchen. I drank a glass

of water and returned to my bedroom. Anxiety about the next day's exams sent in. There would be two parts. The first consisted of multiple-choice questions and short answers, while the second involved problem-solving with lengthy explanations. The subject –mathematics – was my worst nightmare. I was not too fond of maths and working with numbers. I could not deal with them.

My maths teacher threw me out of the class countless times because I could not work out the sums. Once, she asked me if I did not like maths. When I replied truthfully, she screamed at me to leave the class. Once again, I stood in the dreaded doorway. On one occasion, Mrs Cox walked past and asked me why I was out of the classroom. When I told her, she just nodded and walked on. On another occasion, all the students were seated on the floor at the front of the classroom. The teacher had written the times table on the board, with blanks for the answers, and students were asked to fill in the blanks. When it came to my turn, I had to work out the seven times table. I counted on my fingers but could not work out the more significant numbers. I stalled after seven times seven and could not go any further. I was conscious that the other student left the board after completing her tables. My anxiety worsened. I froze at the board. After a while, the teacher called me over. She asked me why I had not studied my multiplication tables. I remained silent. The teacher then slapped me hard across the face, making me cry. The same punishment was dealt to three other girls. All had hard slaps for not knowing their tables. One of them started to bleed from a split lip. This punishment did nothing for me. It only made me feel sick whenever I had to do any counting.

Pushing that memory to the back of my mind, I opened my math textbook to see if I could try some exercises. I could manage addition and subtraction, measurements and simple pie charts. But multiplication, division, fractions, decimals and geometry might as well have come from the moon as far as I was concerned. Almost half of my maths workbooks had red fail marks on them. I was too embarrassed to ask my brothers and sisters for help and did not want to disturb my mother. I was not looking forward to the next day. By eight-thirty in the evening, I was tired and put myself to bed, knowing I needed the rest for the next day's walk to school. It would be just as challenging, if less painful. We had money to buy food. Sleep came quickly that night despite my aching calves.

Day Two

At just a quarter to six, I met Peng at the entrance to her lane. I was pleased to see my walking mate, as I would have been nervous about doing the trek alone.

"Peng! I am so glad to see you," I cried when I'd caught up with her.

"Me too, Lilly," Peng replied. "We don't want to be caught by Mrs Cox again on the way home," Peng murmured, thinking aloud as she walked.

"Yes, I have been thinking about that too," I agreed. "What do you suggest we do?"

"The best thing to do would be to wait at school till we see Mrs Cox park her car before we leave. That way, she and the other girls would not see us on their drive to school."

"That's a good idea, Peng. We can wait behind the tuck shop."

With that problem solved, we continued walking. I returned to telling my story to Peng, who reminded me I had been telling her about my half-sisters' weddings. We soon reached the market.

"Shall we have something to eat out of the 70 cents you have?" Peng suggested.

"Yes, let's get two glasses of hot soya bean milk, the most filling of the drinks vendor's beverages. It would cost us 20 cents. That would at least keep us going for the morning," I said.

We continued on our way. Soon, we were walking into the school compound. Assembly was already over, and we filed into the exam hall with the other girls. As I took my seat, I felt my mouth go dry. I should have had a drink of water from the tap as we got into school. Too late; I will have to suffer for the next few hours. While the teachers handed out the maths papers, my anxiety levels increased steadily. I began to worry that I could not do any of the sums. The first paper had multiple-choice questions. Some were simple enough: additions and subtractions. The rest I waded through, guessing most of the answers to the sums on multiplication, fractions and decimals. I am not going to get through this exam, I thought. I can only do what I can. I spent a large part of the time doodling on scrap paper. Soon the bell rang, and we had to put our pens down. We were allowed to mingle for about ten minutes before the following exam paper. I spent the time listening to some other students talking about the questions. Unable to join in, I could not understand the bulk of the exam questions, so I walked towards Peng.

"How did you do, Lilly?" Peng enquired,

"Badly," I replied. "I am not going to get through this exam," I sighed.

"Just try your best," Peng encouraged me, squeezing me on the arm. It was a reversal of roles from the previous day.

"Yes, that's all I can do," I moaned. "I have to drink some water," 'I rasped as I left Peng. I ran down the steps to the nearest drinking fountain for a quick drink.

I returned just before the next bell and rushed to my seat. Geometry, geometric shapes and measurements danced before my eyes as I turned the pages of my exam paper. I attempted some of the questions, but the majority were left blank. One question I could do was to measure the distance between one point to another with the given scale. I pulled a hair from my scalp and used it to take measurements. Well, at least I will get one right, I mused. The bell rang, and the exam was over. This time there was no break; the following exam paper was given out immediately. I saw red: statistics and probability, pie charts. Hell had arrived on Earth. I had a flashback to when I could not do my homework and did not hand it in on time.

The teacher became very angry. Three other girls were also in trouble. We were taken to the school tuck shop at recess and made to stand on chairs placed on one long dining table. The hems of our uniforms were pinned to the top of our pinafore at the back, exposing our knickers for all to see. Many students who came to the tuck shop to eat turned their heads away when they saw what was happening. With our heads bowed in humiliation and shame, we wept. My eyes became swollen because I cried so much. It was worse for me as we had no money for store-bought knickers. Mine had been made of white cotton by Mum, and they looked like bloomers! After that incident, my math phobia was so bad that I suffered a mental block whenever I had to do any. My brain would not work. Wading through the last maths paper for the day, I tackled a couple of pie charts and a few other questions I thought manageable. When the final bell rang, I was happy to hand over my answer script and leave the hall. I had arranged to meet Peng in the tuck shop and found her sitting at the table furthest from the food stalls.

"We'll have to wait for Mrs Cox to arrive," Peng stated.

"Yes ... perhaps we could eat something small while waiting? Spend no more than 20 cents while we wait for the hour to pass. Then we can take the route around the school where she won't see us. That way, we can return earlier," I suggested.

"That's a good idea. Let's go see what we can get at one of the stalls," Peng stood up.

We found that for 10 cents, we could get a rice cake each to keep us going until we reached the marketplace, where a glass of soya bean milk would set us back another 20 cents.

That would leave us with an extra 10 cents for the last day of the exams. Having made these calculations, we bought the rice cakes and spooned as much chilli sauce as possible onto them to add more bulk to the snack. Then, taking our rice cakes to the back of the building, we sat on a step and ate our feast while looking out for Mrs Cox's car.

"How did you do on the exams, Peng?" I asked.

"I feel good about them, Lilly. I think I'll get through these papers," she said. "Maths is one of my best subjects."

"Well, I don't think I'll make it," I said. We fell silent, both of us deep in thought.

"It's been an hour," Peng broke the silence. "I think we can head home now."

I nodded my agreement and stood up. We left the school by the back gate and started on our way. We were at the first bus stop outside the school when I spotted Mrs Cox's car.

"QUICK, Peng! Just stand at the bus stop till the car is out of sight. It will look like we're waiting for our bus," I exclaimed, pulling Peng into the bus shelter and hiding behind other people at the stop. We watched the car turn down the lane and disappear. With a sigh of relief, we continued on our journey. Reaching the market, we stopped for our drink of soya bean milk and continued. We parted company, and I went home to find my mother resting on her bed.

"How was school?" She asked.

"Oh, it was ok," I replied.

"How did you do on the exams?"

"I don't like Maths. I can't count properly!" I cried.

My mother did not reply. I got out of my uniform and had a shower. Then, pulling out my canvas camp bed, I settled to sleep. I did not realise how tired I was. I could not have kept it up for much longer. I was glad the next day would be my last day of walking. I was roused from my nap by the voices of my siblings. I joined them in the kitchen. My brother and two sisters were seated at the dining table. A sliced-up loaf of bread was on the table, and everyone was eating it.

"Have some," my mother called, and I accepted the slice of bread she handed me. Along with the bread were glasses of water. I ate a couple of pieces of bread and washed them down with water.

"Where did the bread come from?" I asked.

"We brought it back from the convent," one of my sisters replied. That was all we had that evening.

My sisters had started working for the Catholic Church's sewing rooms in town, where all the clergy's vestments and articles were made. They embroidered delicate and elaborate designs onto the garments and altar cloths for a minuscule wage.

I spent the evening revising science subjects. Day three of the exams was dedicated to science. There would be two papers. The first would be a multiple-choice paper, while the second would consist of structured, open-ended questions. I felt confident that I would at least pass these two papers. After a couple of hours of study, I went to bed early.

Day Three

I met Peng, as usual, the following morning and continued with my story.

"When we were in the bigger house, Mum took in a boarder to help with the expenses. She was an old Indian woman who needed someone to look after her when her son went to work, as she was frail. We called her Granny, even though she was not our actual Granny. Granny used to save some of the watery oats that Mum made her for breakfast for me. She could see that there was not much in our house. After a while, when Granny's son paid his bills, Mum could buy us some food. We were able to have a leg of lamb for the Sunday roast. But Granny only stayed with us for a short time. When she left, we returned to having very little to eat, even though my two sisters were working. Soon after, we moved to the present house. Things got terrible there. It was seven years since my Dad had died, and the money from the Public Trustee was all used up. During Chinese New Year, my mother went to help a Chinese neighbour's family with the cooking. They didn't need help; she hoped they would give her some food to bring home for us. I went to watch for a while. There were heaps of food to be prepared. I only stayed for a short time. I was starving. Being around food I could not eat was not a good idea. Mum came home with steamed fish bones left over from their dinner table. There was also some rice. We polished it off. It tasted so good," I concluded.

I told Peng how my eldest sister met her boyfriend. He lived further down the same road. We stopped at the market for a glass of soya bean milk and continued walking.

"My mother does not like him. He wears the latest oversized bell-bottom trousers, and his shirt is tight and unbuttoned to the waist exposing his chest. He wears a lot of gold jewellery which Mum thinks makes him look cheap," I said, repeating Mum's remarks about the man.

Mum hoped that it was a passing fancy that would die away soon. Both my sisters argued all the time over boys and their clothes. Sometimes my mother had to tell them to be quiet. My mother sent my second brother to Boys' Town Boarding School as she could not afford to feed and educate him. It was a reform school for wayward boys run by the Gabrielite Brothers. This option meant he would be provided, housed and educated for free.

"We had not known that she was going to do that," I confided to Peng. My heart ached for my brother. I wondered how he'd felt about the arrangements. As far as I knew, he had not seen it coming.

We went to the hall to tackle the first science paper and chatted during the break. After the second paper, we were all dismissed. The primary school leaving exams were finally over! Peng and I met at the back of the tuck shop as usual. We were both pretty confident with our exam performance, although Peng was concerned that her grade for English would be low. Once again, we bought rice cakes doused in chilli sauce—the three successive days of walking several miles had worn us out. As it would be the last time we would have to walk, we decided to rest a bit longer before setting off. We left when we glimpsed Mrs Cox's car in the school car park.

I told Peng most of my story, so we discussed our future.

"What would you want to do, Peng, with your results?" I asked.

"I don't know. I will have to wait and see, Lilly." Peng said.

"Me too, Peng. I hope to have enough marks to stay in the same school. It won't be easy if I have to go to a vocational school. I don't think my mother will have any money for school fees. I might never finish my schooling if that happens," I sighed.

We spent much of our return journey silent and absorbed in our thoughts about an uncertain future. Eventually, Peng spoke, echoing my thoughts. Reaching the market, we bought our soya bean milk drink. We still had 20 cents left.

"Let's take the bus home for the last leg. I'm so tired," declared Peng.

"Yes, I agree," I said.

We walked to the bus stop where Peng had begged. We boarded the bus, paying the fare and considering the money well spent. We alighted at the stop closest to home, continuing on foot the rest of the way.

"Bye! I'll see you on Monday afternoon when Mrs Cox picks us up for normal school hours," Peng called, turning down her lane,

"Yes, Peng, see you then. Have a good rest. We deserve it!"

Waving, we each continued on our separate ways.

Exam Results

We continued the remaining weeks of the term as we had before the exams. It was the end of the school year. Once the results were released, school holidays would begin in December. The school posted the results outside the administration office. Some students were jumping with joy, while others were crying with disappointment. Peng and I had to wait till the crowd thinned to get to the board. Peng got there first and peered intently at the list. Then, she rushed to me on the outskirts of the crowd and hugged me.

"We passed, we passed!" she chanted, hugging me so tight that we nearly fell over.

Finally, Peng let me go. I rushed to the board to see for myself. There my name was at the bottom of the list. I had passed with just enough marks to stay in the academic stream in high school. Searching, I found Peng's name further along the list. She had been channelled into the vocational stream.

"Is that what you want, Peng?" I asked.

"Yes, I don't mind it. At least I won't have to crack my head over academic things," Peng cheered.

"This means we will be going to different schools next year, Peng," I observed.

"Yes, Lilly, this Friday will be our last day together," Peng replied. "Today is Wednesday. Two days left to have fun together."

We made the best use of those last precious moments together.

Last day of school
It was Friday afternoon. Peng, I, and the other students that Mrs Cox drove to school were watering the plants for the last time. When we gathered by her car, Mrs Cox spoke to us.

"Well, young ladies, congratulations on passing your exams. Lilly, I won't be able to take you to school anymore. Next year you will be off to secondary school in the morning. I wish you well. I hope your mother will find the money for you to continue schooling," she said.

"I know Mrs Cox. I think Mum will work something out. But I will still see you when school sessions cross over," I assured her. "Thank you, Mrs Cox, for taking me to school these last two years," I said gratefully. Mrs Cox nodded her acknowledgement.

"And you, Peng, you will be off to vocational school. We won't see you at all. I wish you all the best, Peng." Mrs Cox held her hand out to Peng and me; we each shook her hand.

"Thank you, Mrs Cox," said Peng.

We all got into Mrs Cox's car, and she turned the key. When we reached Peng's lane, she said goodbye to everybody in the car and gave us a big wave before turning and walking down towards her home. I waved hard, thinking it could be the last time I saw Peng.

"Goodbye, Mrs Cox, have a lovely holiday," I told Mrs Cox before leaving the car. I waved at Mrs Cox as she drove off. Mrs Cox waved back at me. I watched the car disappear down the road and felt a knot in my stomach. It was not hunger. It was the knowledge that this was the end of a chapter in my young life. Next year was going to be a new era: secondary school. Peng and I did not realise we had achieved something remarkable at the time. *We had taken destiny into our own hands and did what neither of our parents had done for us.* In refusing to be beaten by the odds stacked against us, we carved our future and made it possible to move forward. We had achieved this with little more than youthful determination and an intrinsic hunger for something better. We never saw each other again.

Reflection

Now in my mature years, as I write my story, I know that my Heavenly Father, Jesus Christ, was by my side all through this ordeal. He led me to do things and think far beyond my years. He put Mrs Cox onto my path and allowed my education to continue against all odds. My faith was still in its infancy. The lack of good Biblical and parental leadership harmed my life. As the Bible says, "I fed you with milk, not solid food, for you were not ready for it…" (I Corinthians 3:2).

I regret that I did not keep in touch with Peng and can only hope that life has treated her well. I could not have done my walk to the exams without her.

CHAPTER 2 – BE IT EVER SO HUMBLE

"Mum, Mum.... a man is sticking a note on our door," I observed.

As Mum approached the door, the man I'd seen was getting into a car. He was about to drive off when she caught up with him.

"Why the notice of eviction?" She asked.

"Mrs John, you've not paid your rent. I'm the court bailiff. If you don't pay up within fourteen days, we will have to sell all your furniture and evict you from this house," he told her quite bluntly. Mum started to cry. The bailiff drove off as we walked back to the house. That night, very little was said when everyone returned from work and school.

"Why is Mummy crying?' My siblings wanted to know.

When Mum went to bed, she was still in tears. I felt helpless. Over the next few days, Mum went to many relatives asking for help, but they all turned her away. They abandoned us. She came home defeated and in tears. Before going out, Mum would stop before the altar and pray. I wondered what she prayed for or why. Things did not seem to be getting better. There was still no food in the house. I took to stealing from my sisters who were working. I knew their wages were a pittance, barely enough to get to work and pay for a simple weekday lunch. I didn't know if they contributed to the household. When they were not in their bedroom, I would sneak in, take their purses from their handbags and steal five cents. I knew not to take so much that they would notice. The following day when Mum left to go on her begging rounds, I would go to the grocer's next door and buy an egg to fry. I would eat it topped with tomato sauce. That would be my meal for the day. As it was the school holidays, I was mostly alone at home.

"Mum, can I have a doll?" I asked her once.

"I have no money!" She burst out. "Go through the scrap material box and make yourself one!" She instructed. That was my school holiday project over the next few days. I made myself a rag doll. It was the only doll I had owned for a very long time.

Eviction

"Take your things and get out!" the landlord shouted at Mum.

"But my children and I don't have anywhere to go! Please, please, don't do this!" Mum was in tears, begging the owner not to do the auction.

We were all home that Saturday. A crowd of people gathered outside the house. They were walking through the house when the owner opened the door. Mum just stood there with tears streaming down her face. Strangers started removing things from our cupboards and laying them on the floor. They carried the furniture to the front door, where an auctioneer took bids. People made bids, money changed hands, and our furniture was removed from the house.

"Excuse me," a woman called to us, "Why don't you bundle up your things in the bedsheets?"

We made bundles of clothing and got boxes from the grocery shop next door for crockery and kitchen appliances. Soon, it was all over. The owner locked up the house and walked away. We stood on the veranda, and our things were strewn all over it. We continued to organise our remaining possessions as best we could. When night came, we slept on the mattresses left behind. Thankfully the veranda was all bricked up, giving us some privacy, and we still had the use of the communal toilets. We lived on that veranda for three days. We would crouch down behind the patio bricks and hide when anyone walked in front of the house so that no one would see us. Shame overcame us.

Re-homed

Mum approached the social welfare department for assistance. They could not re-house us immediately, but asked her to return the following morning. The clerk handed my mother money, and Mum bought us food. The next day she left early, and we did not see her until late that evening. She told us that the social welfare department had found us a flat in which to live. A lorry would arrive the following morning to take us there. That night, we had food to eat again. It was our third night on the veranda, and we did feel dirty as we had all not showered or cleaned our teeth for three days! At least our bellies were full.

The Flat

"Hang on!" My sister called out. We were in the back of the lorry; Mum rode in the cabin next to the driver. We had loaded our remaining belongings onto the lorry and were on our way to the flat. I watched the houses and surrounding areas disappear. I remembered my walk with Peng and felt sad that I had not said goodbye to my friend. Still, I was glad to see the last of that road and open a new chapter with my family. The following year I would start high school.

The lorry came to a stop in front of several blocks of flats. They all looked dirty and crowded.

"Wait here with the lorry," Mum instructed and took my eldest sister to find our flat. When they returned, we started to unload our belongings. We carried everything six floors up as there was no lift. We were fortunate to have only a few things left to our name. The common corridors and stairs were in the middle of the building. Flats on either side of the corridor made it dark and dingy.

"Gee, this place stinks!" my brother complained.

"That's because the toilets are opposite the stairs. We have to share them with everybody else. There are only twelve toilets for forty flats," my sister explained as she set down a box.

Still, those toilets were an improvement from the ones in the *kampung*. Mum paid the lorry driver, and we settled into our flat. There was a small room to live and sleep in, some 4 m². A veranda ran along the back of the flat, just over a metre deep at the back. It included a small enclosure which was the bathroom. Next to it was the kitchen with a gas ring on a slab. We set about cleaning and arranging our things the best we could. All the mattresses were rolled up and stacked in one corner of the flat. Everything boxed was placed along one wall. Looking out the veranda, I saw the many blocks of flats surrounding ours. They were all different in design. It was one of the first public housing estates the Singapore government built. The holidays stretched out in front of me. I would have a whole month to explore.

It soon became apparent that the flat was vermin-infested. An army of cockroaches streamed out of the drain pipes at night. They would crawl all over us as we tried to sleep at night. I felt terrible for my mother, who slept on the veranda on her rolled-out mattress. She must have had the worst of it as the pipes were closest to her. We stopped the roaches by blocking the drain pipes before settling down to sleep every night. Then we'd roll out the mattresses. Being the youngest, I was the smallest, and my "mattress" consisted of several blankets folded and placed one on top of the other at the foot of the others.

Unfortunately, it was not long before all the bedding became infested with bed bugs that went through all our clothes. The battle against vermin infestation lasted all the years we lived in that flat. Despite my sister's employment, the family income still did not stretch to cover all the bills and the cost of food. My mother approached the local parish church for help. She was given some rations and put on the charity list. The allocation of a small bag of rice, some milk powder and a packet of noodles that did not taste like any noodles we had eaten did not make sense. A decent meal could not be made out of these items. Somehow, we managed to add spices to flavour the rice and noodles and use the milk powder for coffee. We exhausted our supplies before the two weeks were out.

"Father Adam, the rations for my family have run out. It is only Monday, and our next ration day is next week. My mother begged the parish priest. Can we have some more?"

"No," Father Adam replied. "You have had your share; you just have to wait!" He barked.

"But how am I going to feed my children!" Mum begged.

"That's not my problem. Come back next week," said Father Adam, pointedly turning his back on her.

Mum and I walked to the back of the church to watch volunteers handing out rations to non-Catholics living in the *kampung* at the back of the church. We left. My mother never set foot in the parish church again except to attend someone's wedding or funeral. She felt betrayed by the church. Perhaps even by God in her hour of need. Despite all her trials, Mum had held steadfastly to her Catholic faith. Before this unfortunate turn of events with Father Adam, we travelled to the cathedral in town, the biggest one in Singapore, for Sunday mass as if attendance here could alleviate our plight. She still had no regular means of income. It was the school holidays. When school recommenced, she would have to find the money to pay for bus fares and school fees for my brother and me as we were still in school. From where was the money going to come?

The Boy

"Are you sure, Mrs John, that you'll be able to care for our son?" The man queried.

"Yes, yes," she replied quickly. I looked at the boy. He was severely crippled and needed care 24 hours a day. Lying on the floor in a tangle of limbs, he could not walk. Nor could he talk; saliva constantly dribbled from the corner of his mouth. He had to be fed and bathed, and the bedsores on his back dressed daily. A strong odour of urine and decaying flesh emanated from him.

But Mum was confident she could look after him. Perhaps she was desperate as we needed the money. We headed home in a taxi, and Mum carried the boy up the six floors to our flat. No one else was at home. Mum placed the boy on the floor on one of our mattresses. A whole heap of other things was necessary for his care. Those things took up a lot of room in the already crowded flat. All hell broke loose when the family came home from school and work.

"Just what were you thinking, Mum?" My oldest sister screamed. "There is barely enough room for us, let alone a cripple!" She cried. Everyone wanted the boy gone.

"I was trying to put food on the table! The bills are not going to pay themselves. What you contribute from your wages is not enough," Mum pointed out through tears.

"Take the boy back!" My siblings demanded.

And so, he was returned to his family. The boy had been with us for just three hours. His parents were furious with my mother. While she was very apologetic, my siblings and I were relieved.

Community Centre

"I'm going to watch TV, Mum," I called out as I left the flat, heading down the dark and dingy corridor to make my way to the community centre.

Though television had come to Singapore, it was out of the reach of most. Community centres around the island featured a television contained in a box mounted on a post outdoors. Chairs were arranged in front of it for residents to sit and watch a program. The government, keen to engender a nascent nationalist spirit, hoped this would contribute to community cohesion. The box sheltered the television from the elements. Sometimes fights broke out amongst the audience when someone shimmied up the post and changed the channel! Someone would walk off cursing and spit on a chair so no one else could sit in it. I would watch whatever channel the television was tuned to for a while and then make for a nearby playground and get on a swing. I spent a lot of time there thinking about my life. What was happening around me, where my life was heading, how it would unfurl. There was a new year in the offing with its promise of new beginnings, high school being one of them. I was preoccupied with the prospect and spent many hours worrying about it.

"How will Mum find the money to pay my school fees," I wondered as I swung. "… and the bus fares to and from school? Will there be money to buy food at the tuck shop?"

Mum received a small amount from the social welfare department every month. It was just enough for us to get along with the church rations. We ate very simply. The only meat we could afford was chicken necks made into a curry and eaten with boiled rice. We soon learned to strip all meat off the chicken necks and leave behind a pile of tiny bones. Sometimes even the bones would be eaten when they were soft enough. They filled the belly and were a good source of calcium. Otherwise, meals consisted of *rasam* and rice. *Rasam* is a watery, tangy soup. Made of spices, garlic, black pepper and tamarind, it offered little nutrition. My mother would buy a tin of luncheon meat when she could afford it. It would be curried or pan-fried. It was to become standard fare for my family.

Sick for a Week

"Mum, I don't feel well," I rasped. My throat was sore. My mother put her hand on my forehead.

"Go back to bed. You have a fever. Don't go to school today, "Mum instructed.

My sisters had left the flat for work. I unrolled the nearest mattress and went back to sleep, not knowing that I would not wake up for a week! I don't recall much. Unable to get up, my brother told me they had moved me from one spot to another in the room. I do vaguely remember hearing their voices. Sometimes, I was fed medicine. Once, I felt my mother shaking me, ordering me to get up. I recognised her voice. Another time, she kicked me when I did not do as she commanded. It was a swift kick to the belly. I was too weak to react. I just lay there and eventually drifted back into sleep. When I finally woke up, my lips were dry and cracked. I noticed that I was lying on a rattan mat. My legs wobbled like they were made of jelly when I tried to stand.

"You were mumbling and talking to yourself," my brother told me later. "What was wrong with you?" He asked.

"I don't know," I replied. And I was never to know! It was a mysterious illness that lasted about a week, perhaps a childhood fever that sorted itself out. I was left untreated because there was no money to get me to the doctor.

Leaving

"I am not staying here anymore!" My eldest sister was screaming at my mother. "I'm not giving you any more money!" She continued angrily.

Pulling out old shopping bags, my eldest sister started to stuff her things into them. Then she was out the door, slamming it behind her. Everyone was in tears. Some months later, we learned she was marrying the man my mother disliked. She did not think he would make a responsible husband. My second sister and brothers attended the wedding. In her hurt and anger, my mother refused and forbade me to attend.

Secondary School

Come January, the new school year started. My mother gave me just enough money for the bus fare to and from school. There wasn't enough to buy food as well. I continued to drink water from the taps around the school, the same fixtures I had used to fill watering cans for the garden when I tended the school garden for Mrs Cox. Walking to the back of the tuck shop, I watched the hawker throwing the leftovers from the bowls and plates into the bin. I imagined that if I could make myself invisible, I could catch the food she was pouring out of the bowls and plates and eat it before it hit the bin! Out of desperation, I came up with a plan. Walking between the tables of the tuck shop where the students were eating, I observed if they left food behind. Taking note of which bowl held the most food, I waited until the bell rang, marking the end of recess, and everybody returned to their classrooms. As students left the tuck shop, I would make a dive for that particular bowl and gulp the food down as quickly as possible while praying that no one was watching me. Then I ran to join my class. That came to be the only food I would have for the day.

Cathy

Cathy and I had met in primary school, but did not become close friends until we found ourselves in the same class in Secondary 1. She was Eurasian and very mature for her age. We spent a lot of time together. Being tall and pretty, Cathy would attract the attention of the Catholic boys' school students just down the road from ours. The girls and boys met at the bus stop when school was over. Lipsticks were whipped out to emphasise pouts, and skirts were hitched to reveal more legs! Cathy made sure she always looked her best. I became her shadow. The boys were indeed more interested in her than in me. Several times a week, I went to her place after school, spending my bus fare home on the ride to Cathy's. At Cathy's place, we did very little apart from styling each other's hair, giggling and gossiping. As the afternoon wore on, her mother would prepare dinner, inviting me to join them for the evening meal. That meal became another regular source of food for me. After dinner, I would walk home as I did not have the bus fare for the next ride. This walk was over 3km long. When I reached home, it would be around eight in the evening, and Mum would have worried herself into a temper.

"Where have you been? It's so late, and it's dark!" Mum would scream. I could never bring myself to tell Mum that I stayed at Cathy's house so that I'd get at least one meal that day. It would not have helped matters. Indeed, it would only make things worse: I'd get a beating and be forbidden to go there. During my second year of high school, my mother separated me from Cathy, whom she considered a bad influence. She transferred me to the sister school of the one which I was attending.

"She comes home after dark very often," Mum informed Reverend Mother. "She's been hanging around with this Eurasian girl leading her astray. Her grades are bad. She was just pushed to Secondary two though she failed her exams," she continued.

Reverend Mother looked at me sternly and said, "Lilly, you need to change your ways. When you grow up, the man who marries you will want a rare pearl for a wife. Behaving like this will not happen to get you anywhere!" the nun advised.

All I could think of was losing my only friend and my only source of a regular meal. Still, I did not say a word. Years later, when hearing my story, someone asked why I had not told my mother the real reason behind my late return home. I replied, "One does not kick a dog already down in the gutter."

"She needs new uniforms, and I don't have the money to buy them," my mother added.

Asking us to wait at the reception, Reverend Mother headed down the corridor and returned with a bag containing some old school shirts and two blue pinafores. We took these home.

Farewell Cathy

"My mother is transferring me to another school, Cathy," I informed my friend dolefully.

"Why?" asked Cathy, mystified.

"Because she thinks I am playing truant with you," I confessed.

"Oh, Lilly, I am so sorry," said Cathy, though none was her fault.

"But it'll be just for a year because the two schools will be merging the year after... and we'll be together again in Secondary 3," I mused hopefully.

"I will miss you," she said.

"Me too," I agreed ungrammatically.

We hugged each other. There were still three weeks left until the end of the school year. We spent as much time together as possible. One morning in the school library, Cathy showed me a science book. It had pictures of a man and woman having sexual intercourse. There was a picture of a penis inserted into a vagina. It shocked me. I had never seen anything like that before.

"Is that what they do, Cathy?" I asked in astonishment.

"Yes, it is. That's me, Lilly!"

I looked at her, trying to understand what she was saying.

"Oh, you're such an innocent, Lilly," Cathy laughed. "One day, you'll know too!"

I laughed, and we left the library. I did not realise then that I had had my first lesson in human sexual reproduction! I did not know it then, but those were the last weeks I would spend with Cathy.

New School

"Lilly, you'll have to patch the pinafore where it's threadbare," my mother said. I was not looking forward to going to the new school. The two pinafores Reverend Mother had given us had certainly seen better days. "Look in the scrap bag. You might find something there," she urged. I found some pieces of matching fabric and began patching them to the worn seat of the uniforms. I used a close running stitch, making each stitch as small, neat and regular as possible. There was no avoiding it. Mum had signed the papers. I had to catch the first bus at 6.00 am to get to school on time.

School holidays would soon be over. My siblings showed me where to catch the bus and alight. I had to walk the rest of the way to school as that was all the bus fare Mum could afford. When I got there, I found that the school gates were still closed as I had arrived too early. I saw the nuns walking from the convent to the church to attend morning mass and followed them. Attending mass must have done something for me as I felt my spirit settle. After church service, I followed the nuns back to school because they left the gate open. I went to the back of the school out of reach of the aromas from the tuck shop that made my belly growl. I stayed there until the bell rang for the start of classes. It became my routine for the early part of the year.

"Hi Lilly", my classmate greeted me one morning as I sat at my place on the step at the back of the school.

"Hi," I replied.

"You want to be alone, do you?" She asked.

"Yes."

"I will leave you in peace then," she said as she smiled and walked away.

"Why, God, why is this happening to me? I am so hungry. Look at this uniform. I must wear it back to front so the patch won't fall apart. Some of my classmates come to school in chauffeur-driven Mercedes Benzes. They go to

Australia and have horse-riding lessons during the holidays. I don't even get a meal a day. I am still drinking water from the school garden tap. I fall asleep at my desk in hunger. Some girls look at me as if I'm some insect! Why, God, why?" I sat doubled over, hugging my water-filled belly. Closing my eyes, I tried to make my problems go away. Suddenly, I heard a voice say, *"If you want anything in your life, do it yourself. Don't expect anyone to do it for you!"*

The school bell rang to summon me to class. Walking to my classroom, I knew those words would never leave me for as long as I lived; they would remain in my heart. In later years as my faith grew, I knew, as all believers know, that it was the voice of God. God speaks to the faithful through the Holy Spirit at various times, especially when they reach out to Him from the depths of despair. It is reflected in the Bible;

> "But when he, the Spirit of truth, comes, he will guide you into all the truth. He will not speak on his own; He will speak only what He hears, and he will tell you what is yet to come." (John 16:13)

After much contemplation, I thought about those words and concluded that God was telling me I would have to exercise effort and initiative to make my life successful. I understood that he was responding to me because I had taken my woes to God. However, because he had spoken to me thus, He would show me the way. I was not to rely on other people to carve the path of my life, I was able to do it on my own, and I would be able to do it with Him and the Holy Spirit. This approach is very different to the standard train of thought for the average Indian woman whose life is often dictated first by her parents and close relatives and then by her husband and children. The message gave me the courage to stand on my own two feet because I knew God would be my guide. He would hold my hand through life's challenges; I need not be afraid.

Much later, I realised that the Bible abounds in scriptures, encouraging us to work earnestly for material and spiritual gains and live by faith and works. I also learnt that we only succeed when our efforts align with God's plans. The following scripture is an example of this:
> "By faith Abraham, when called to go to a place he would later receive as his inheritance, obeyed and went, even though he did not know where he was going." (Hebrews 11: 8.)

I did not know how I would be stretched to the limit. But throughout it all, I knew and felt God's guiding hand and loving, sustaining presence.

Live-in Maid
Soon after the term started, Mum took a job as a live-in maid or *amah,* to use the local word for women employed thus. It must have been hard for her to take on this role. She was raised and educated for higher aspirations for herself. Mum was effectively bilingual, able to read and write in English and Tamil. She was also a skilled and qualified seamstress.

However, all of the funds from our inheritance had been exhausted. There had been no help from any of the relatives. Mum's stepmother and step-siblings had turned her away when she'd asked them for help. Singapore has no social security payments; social welfare allowances were pittances. It was tough luck if you did not have an income. Mum had tried to sell beautiful children's wear she had made, but had had no takers. Becoming a servant must have broken her, but she did it for us. It was ironic: Mum left me alone to look after someone else's children to provide for me. She gave me keys to let me in and out of the flat. The following day while I was at school, she left to take up her employment. I came home to an empty flat. I was yet again a latchkey kid. It was the start of another era in my life.

"I may not come home sometimes, Lilly. The bosses have big parties on weekends; if I stayed and worked, I would earn more money. You must run the house and look after your brother, but you already know how. On the weekends, you must visit me," she said.

Though Mum could, in principle, return home on the weekends, she generally stayed at work for the extra income. She instructed me to bring all the household bills when I visited. She would go through each and then put enough money to settle each account in its respective envelope. At the end of each month, I would attend the different departments in the town centre to pay those bills. The clerk would stamp each bill with the date I made the payment. I would carefully file the statements in a folder Mum kept in her cupboard at home.

"Take care of the money. Don't lose it!" Mum would urge me every time I left her. She gave me $5 for pocket money every fortnight. With this, I paid my bus fares and was finally able to buy food in the tuck shop during recess.

New responsibilities

Life got better but also more complicated at the same time. With Mum no longer living at home, it fell to me to run the house. Although my sister and brother were older, it seemed to me that I bore the brunt of the housework. While my sister went to work, my brother attended senior school. With no friends at the new school, I headed home immediately after the final bell. My only companion was the little battery-operated transistor radio. I soon got hooked on a radio series called *The Sullivans*. It was a soap opera set in Melbourne during the Second World War. It was just a form of escapism. I was in another time and place every day for a short time.

Apart from studying, I had to shop for food, cook and wash all the family laundry. After soaking them in a large plastic basin overnight, I scrubbed the clothing on a wooden washboard. Then I threaded them onto long bamboo poles to dry. Heavy with wet clothing, the poles were lifted and slotted into cylindrical holders in the kitchen's exterior wall. The entire procedure demanded strength and skill, a challenge for a skinny teenager to master. Sometimes I lost my balance or could not manoeuvre the pole into its holder. The clean, wet laundry pole would plummet six floors down, activating Operation Retrieval. I would have to remove the clothing from the pole and walk back up to the flat with wet washing bundled under one arm and the bamboo pole in the other hand. Sometimes, the pole would get caught on the poles of the flats on the lower floors, and our laundry would become entangled with theirs. On those occasions, I would have to figure out which flat to go to and ask for the pole and clothing. It was something neighbours took in their stride. Thankfully our flat was on the top floor, and we did not have to worry about other people's bamboo poles falling on ours. Once in a while, a quarrel would break out because someone's nearly-dry laundry had become wet or stained by wet clothing hung out to dry on an upper floor.

    Regular visits to Mum on weekends as planned continued. She would scrutinise all the bills and place the cash to pay each one in its respective envelope. I would help her do the housework for her American employers. She never let me leave empty-handed. There was always a *tingkat* or tiffin carrier full of food to take home. I soon learnt how to run a house and cook for three. The various government departments that I visited to pay the bills became familiar. Mum would check my carefully filed paperwork on the odd occasion when she was home. Premature responsibility put an old head on my young shoulders. I grew up fast. Though I did not know it then, these skills would be my saving grace in another time and place in my future. My grades started improving with regular food in my belly, though they were far from spectacular. I did not feel sluggish and could stay awake throughout the school day.

Maths was still a big problem. I was not too fond of the subject and continued to freeze when confronted by numbers. Mum had taken her sewing machine to work and presented me with new uniforms one weekend. I was overjoyed. Mum used some new non-iron material from Japan called Tetron cotton, not the usual cotton fabric. The pleats were fixed permanently, the bodice had bust darts, and a plastic zipper was on the left-hand side. No one else had a uniform like it, and it fitted me like a glove. Wearing my new uniform to school filled me with pride. I felt unique and less like an outsider.

I was selected to perform in a Malay dance at the year-end school celebration. Plans to convert the school into a primary facility meant moving back to my previous premises. I could not wait to see Cathy again; we had not seen each other for a year. The class protested on masse. As we would make up the sixth and last Secondary 4 class, we were placed as Sec 4F. Each class was ranked according to the academic achievements of its students. We were better than an F, the grade given to students with the lowest exam marks. After some negotiation, I found myself in Secondary 4C. It gave me a real boost. I was not stupid after all. I had also unwittingly experienced my first taste of the power of democracy.

Final Year

"Hello, Lilly", one of my old classmates called out. It felt odd to walk back into the familiar old school grounds again.

"How is it that you're back with us?" She inquired.

"Didn't you hear? They've merged the two high schools into this campus, and the primary school will use our old campus," I explained.

"Are you going to join us in our class?" Asked another former classmate.

"No, I'm going to stay with my class from last year."

"Well, we'll still see you around then," they said, waving at me and walking on.

"Hey, wait a bit," I called. "Have you seen Cathy?" The two girls stopped and exchanged eloquent glances.

"Oh, hadn't you heard? Cathy doesn't come to school anymore. She stopped sometime last year," said one, her voice lowered.

"She had a baby!" The other one whispered.

Both were still scandalised. We all stood rooted to the spot for a long moment. Then the bell rang, breaking the spell and sending us in different directions. .I walked to my classroom in a state of shock. I recalled our last conversation in the school library a year ago. I finally understood what she had meant when she claimed to be the woman in the photographs of a couple having sexual intercourse. She had been hinting that she had a boyfriend and was sexually active. The penny finally dropped. It took me several weeks to get over this and the fact that Cathy had had a baby! The last year of school was a much happier one. I chose to study seven subjects—English, literature, history, geography, health science, art and Malay. I was thrilled to drop maths. English, literature, health science and art were my best subjects. Some of my still life and landscape paintings were exhibited around the school, and I read one of my essays at the school assembly. Though my grades had improved, they were not brilliant. I just scraped through the exams.

A home upgrade

The home situation remained largely the same. Mum still worked and came home whenever she could. I continued to visit her at work with the bills on the weekends, sometimes staying overnight to help her. After four years of living in the one-bedroom flat with the shared toilets, cockroaches and bed bugs, we heard that the government had finally condemned the building. We received notification of this and the offer of a new flat in another location. Although the new apartment featured only one bedroom, it was considerably more extensive, and we had an attached toilet and bathroom. We accepted this upgrade eagerly. My second brother, still in Boys Town, had already finished much of his carpentry course. He built a partition within the flat, dividing the single room into two, which gave us a living room and a bedroom, a welcome addition as it afforded us privacy. We still had no furniture and continued to sleep on mattresses on the floor. Despite this, living in the new flat was quite blissful.

Furniture

Over the next few months, Mum started to buy furniture. The first to arrive was a double bed, which I shared with her when she was home. The double-decker bunk beds were for my sister and brother. Eventually, a wardrobe and tallboy were purchased as well. The first level of the tallboy was my space. We shared the closet for our "good clothes" – the ones we wore on outings. My mother soon added a sofa set and a display cabinet. My sister, now working for a jeweller, bought a stereo system and some records. She enjoyed Motown recordings; I loved listening to Diana Ross and the Supremes.

Final Exams

Singapore held its high school-leaving exams at the end of the calendar year. The completed exam papers were sent to Cambridge, England, to be marked. Though the exams were over by mid-November, students only received their results in mid-January the following year. We continued to attend school for the two weeks following the exams before breaking up. Though it was sad to bid my schoolmates farewell, I was excited by the prospect of the next chapter of my life.

"What are you going to do, Lilly?" a classmate asked.

"I must repay my debt to society. Someone paid my school fees for many years. I will never know who. So, I'm thinking about training to be a nurse," I confided.

"Woah! You'll see a lot of blood and body parts!" She looked at me in horror. "You're brave."

We had photos taken, with good wishes and hugs were exchanged. Our autograph books were passed around to pen farewell messages as a memento of our school days.

"Do visit me over the weekend," called a friend.

"Yes, I'd love that. What's your address, Jackie?"

Jackie scribbled her address in my autograph book. She told me to call her on the phone to confirm a time, carolled a hasty goodbye and headed home. I waved at her, and several other girls gathered to say farewell at the school gate. As I walked out onto the street parallel to the tuck shop, I stopped for a moment and remembered how I'd walked furtively along the tables, looking for plates and bowls with uneaten food to wolf down at the end of recess. Though I had pocket money in my final year of school, thanks to my mother, I still felt a little sad to walk away.

As for Cathy, I visited her parent's home, and they gave me her new address in a nearby housing estate. When I visited, I witnessed a very different Cathy. She was no longer the carefree girl concerned only with looking her best. She was shabbily dressed and already had her second baby on her hips; the first was a toddler crawling around. We did not seem to have much in common, and our conversation was stilted, confined only to formalities. Gone was the girl I had gossiped and giggled with as I arranged her hair. It was the last time I saw her. Years later, I bumped into her younger sister, who had married and had a family. She told me that Cathy, her family, and her parents had moved to Australia and lived in Melbourne. When I asked for an address, her sister informed me that Cathy had taken up alcohol and cigarettes and was living the life of a hermit. She added that she was not at liberty to disclose Cathy's address. Perhaps my mother had been wise in separating me from her after all! I lost all contact with Cathy and her family after that.

Working life

"You're stupid. It would be a waste of money for you to continue schooling!" Mum declared.

"You are going to work. I've asked your sister to find you a job. I can't afford to feed and clothe you!" She said, looking at me balefully. "You start work Monday as a salesgirl in the store near your old school," she informed me.

"But Mum, it's Saturday. I finished school yesterday. Can't I have a break?" I pleaded.

"No, we have no money! You'll have to take on some of the bills, just like everybody else," she snapped.

"So, how's that Older Brother getting to repeat Secondary four while I go to work?" I demanded to know, outraged at being unfairly treated.

"He's my eldest son. He will look after me when I am old," she explained. "Paying for his education is like insurance for my retirement," she elaborated. "Thanks to me, you have completed secondary schooling and even have a full certificate to show for it. Most girls don't even get that. What more do you want from me?" She demanded.

I looked at her in disbelief. She had no means, but I knew that she was not being nasty, just realistic – she had to rule with an iron fist – she had no choice. I was on my own.

"My friend owns the store. He is expecting you at 8.00 am on Monday," said Second Sister as she gave me a piece of paper. "Here's the address."

And that was it. My working life was to begin on Monday; no rest for the wicked, as they say. Still, I had my last weekend to enjoy, and I would make the best of it!

The Shop

Monday morning, 8.00 am. I walk into the shop to be greeted by Mr Raj. He briefly explained my job and introduced me to his assistant Gabriel, who would help me if needed. The shop stocked *Hari Rama, Hari Krishna*, and hippy-style clothes, all the rage in the seventies.

"What are my wages to be, Mr Raj?" I asked.

"I'll pay you $60 a month," he replied. To someone like me, $60 was big bucks. It was 1972.

"What's expected of me?" I wondered aloud.

"Gabriel will teach all you need to know. Just ask him," said Mr Raj, busying himself with his ledger.

Gabriel showed me how to dust and stock shelves, replenish items, do the daily accounts and assist in sales. After a while, I started to dress the windows. I enjoyed this work part the most as it drew on my artistic talent. I looked forward to my monthly pay, my first taste of financial independence.

The call

"Hi Jackie, how are you? It's Lilly," I said into the telephone.

"Hi Lilly, I'm fine. How are you? What are you up to these days?" Jackie wanted to know.

"I have a job, Jackie. I'm working as a salesgirl in a shop near school," I told her.

"Oh, how wonderful! Do you enjoy it?" She asked.

"Yes, it's not bad …I get a wage. That's what matters most. I make $60 a month," I boasted.

"Wow!" said Jackie. "Lilly, we are having a party on Saturday night. It's my brother's 21st birthday. Please say you'll come," she invited.

"Sure, what time?" I replied eagerly.

"Come round six-ish?" Jackie suggested.

"OK, I'll see you then. Do you want me to bring anything?"

"No, no, thank you. We have it all in hand. I'll see you then?"

"Look forward to it," I sang and rang off.

The Party

When I arrived, Jackie introduced me to her brother Sam, the Birthday Boy. There were more boys than girls at the party. The dining room table was heaving with food: biryani rice, curry, vegetables and condiments, all cooked by Jackie's mother. Everything was delicious. We sang the birthday song, and Sam cut his cake. Then the lights were turned down, and the dance music up. Jackie's parents were not at home. I thought it unusual that they would allow a dance party in their traditional Indian home. Sam asked me if I'd like to dance with him. And so, we danced. At first, we boogied to the latest 1970s disco music. As the night deepened, the music slowed. I felt a bit heady. Never had I danced with a boy or been held so close in his embrace. Sam asked me what I was doing now that school was over. I told him I was waiting for my results to be released and wanted to train as a nurse. He said he had just finished senior high school and had commenced working in the airline industry as an office administrator. He wanted to apply for the flight attendant position, but would have to wait six months to be eligible.

"What is the meaning of this? Why are the lights off in the living room? What are you doing?" thundered a mature, male voice.

The figure of Jackie's father silhouetted in the doorway. We danced in the living room, and no one noticed her parents had returned. It was close to 11.00 pm. The lights came on, and everybody froze, blinking at the unexpected brightness. It seemed everyone stepped back from the dance partner in unison. Though we had not done anything wrong, we all felt guilty. The parents were home, and the party was over! Jackie's parents were from India. Traditional Indian culture did not allow a man and woman to be in close contact unless they were engaged or were already married. Dancing and kissing in low light were not permitted! As it was late, I said my goodbyes and exited quickly.

"Hey! Lilly, wait a minute. Can I have your telephone number?" Sam asked, catching up with me at the gate.

"I don't have a phone at home, but I can give you my number at work if you like," I offered. "Just remember that I won't be able to talk for long," I added.

"That's fine, I understand. Where do you work? Perhaps I could meet you for lunch one day," said Sam relatively smoothly.

"Yes, that would be nice," I agreed, trying to sound casual. My heart was thumping! It was the first time any boy had asked me for my telephone number.

I gave Sam the address and telephone number of my workplace, bid him goodnight and got into a passing taxi. We waved at each other as the cab drew away.

First Date

The phone at the desk rang, and I reached for it.

"Good morning, Kool Fashion," I said in my best professional manner.

"Hi Lilly, it's Sam. Shall we have lunch together today?"

"Hi Sam, yes, that'd be nice," I agreed. "I'm only working a half-day as its Saturday. I finish work at 1.00 pm. Meet me at the shop, and we'll walk to lunch together?"

My first date! My pulse was racing. I wore a simple floral dress cinched at the waist with a flared skirt. The skirt stopped about four inches above my knees, keeping the latest fashion. A pair of black-heeled sandals completed my outfit. I had at least two hours before Mr Raj, or Gabriel would come to take over, and the date would begin! As the clock inched towards 1.00 pm, I checked my hair and makeup in the fitting room. All good. I liked the image that looked at me in the mirror.

"Time to go, young lady!" Gabriel cheerfully called out as he walked into the shop.

"Thanks, Gabe. I'll see you next week," I chirruped, heading to the door.

"I won't be here on Monday, but you know what to do. You've learnt to run the shop quickly, and your weekly window dressing is excellent," enthused Gabriel.

"Thank you! I do appreciate the feedback. See you," I said as I stepped out of the shop to find Sam walking towards it.

"Great timing, Lilly," he grinned.

"Yes, it is, Sam. Good to see you," I gushed.

"Where shall we go for lunch?"

"How about the fish and chip restaurant? It's a bit more private than the food court," I suggested.

"Yes, I think so too," Sam nodded.

It became our regular Saturday lunch haunt. After lunch, Sam would often walk me home, a distance of almost 6 km. There was so much to talk about. I found myself falling in love with Sam. We shared our first kiss, stolen in the shop's fitting room. One afternoon Sam told me that he loved me too. I was over the moon. There was one major problem. Though we were both of Indian extraction, our families came from different parts of India. Sam's family came from Kerala, and mine was from Tamil Nadu. There would be opposition from his family to our relationship. We took care not to flaunt our meetings.

Exam Results
The results were out. The letter arrived at my home, instructing me to collect them personally at school. No other students came when I came, so I walked into the school office. With my heart in my mouth, I walked out of the office and, with trembling fingers, opened the envelope that the clerk had handed me.

"I passed! Oh, thank you, Jesus. I passed!" I murmured to myself, heaving sighs of relief and thanking God several times more.

I left walking on air even though my results were not spectacular. As I had not excelled at school, I had never thought I would achieve a grade. Not unexpectedly, my best marks were in English, literature and art.

Job applications

When the government released the yearly jobs available list for school leavers, I applied for the two job options permitted. My first choice was nursing, with librarianship as the second option. I was selected for nursing after a re-selection process. Preliminary nursing training school commenced just ten days short of my sixteenth birthday. In the meantime, Sam applied for the flight attendant position and was accepted. He began training and went on his first flight. With Sam now flying, we saw each other only when he was home. His family still did not know that we were dating. Although his sisters and Jackie suspected we saw each other, they didn't speak to anyone.

Heartbreak

"Sam, do you love me?" I asked.

"Of course, I do. Why do you ask?" came the quick reply.

"Because I want us to have a permanent relationship. We have been together now for more than six months. I want to know when are you going to tell your parents?"

Sam did not reply for a while. We were at the playground near my flat.

"Lilly, you are too young to be in a permanent relationship, and I have only just started work. I want to establish myself in my career first," Sam hedged.

"So, in other words, the answer is no," I summed up, hurt and disappointed.

"A permanent relationship is a big step. I'm not ready, and neither are you. You need to get qualified and maybe mature a bit. Then we can talk about a permanent relationship or marriage," Sam expanded.

I was quiet. My heart was breaking. We were both silent for a while.

"Lilly, I think it would be better if we separated," Sam said softly.

"OK, go then!" I ordered angrily. I refused to look at him. Instead, I looked at the sand beneath my feet as I swung harder.

"Bye, Lilly," he said. Still, I refused to look.

I felt him walk away; a while later, I saw his figure disappear around the block.

CHAPTER 3 – STUDENT NURSE

The first three months of preliminary training school (PTS) in nursing were precisely that. I found myself in the classroom learning the basics of the nursing profession: bed-making with those ever-important mitre corners, sterile procedures, anatomy and physiology, and setting up trolleys. It was an eye-opener, and I enjoyed it immensely because I was doing what I wanted. There were 400 students, mainly Chinese and the ethnic minorities -- Indians and Malays -- gravitated towards each other. We soon located the Indian restaurants near the school in true local fashion and often enjoyed eating together. I became good friends with Turvi.

"What is the matter, Lilly? You've been very quiet recently?" queried Turvi, her face full of concern.

"Oh, nothing, Turvi. Just life," I parried evasively.

"You can talk to me, you know," she said.

"Yes, I do know. Don't mind me. I am just in one of my moods," I sighed.

She must have sensed that something was wrong. but I was not going to tell her that I was pining for Sam. My heart was still heavy. I felt that I had put myself in a difficult position. I believed that because I had dated Sam, I could not now begin a relationship with another man. It was just how Indian culture worked. No man would want another man's trash, I thought.

A girl was cheap if she kept company with a man she was not engaged to be married to or was not her husband. Men were allowed to sow their wild oats, but girls had to be chaste and unsullied till they tied the knot. Just being in the company of a man sealed her fate. My mother had called me a "slut" for dating a couple of my brother's friends -- just one date each. I was going to have to learn to live with it.

An Indian male nursing student was beginning to show an interest in me, but I kept him at bay. I needed to concentrate on my course and qualify with good marks. I planned to travel after I gained my certificate. Besides, he was a devout Hindu, and I was Catholic. I would never marry outside of my faith, even though I believed at the time that the chances of finding someone was slim.

"He's come to get her!" Turvi whispered to me at break time.

"So, she is going to drop out?" I asked under my breath.

"Looks like it," Turvi murmured.

I was astonished but, oddly enough, not surprised. Arranged marriages are what happen in Indian culture. My fellow student would leave nursing school to get married and move to Canada with the husband her parents had picked for her. He had flown from Canada to meet, marry and take her back to Canada. It seemed so very romantic to me. My heart hurt just thinking about how Sam had rejected me. My classmate was happy to go on her way despite the tutors encouraging her to stay and finish her studies. We never heard from her again. She was just sixteen years old.

Fledgling

It was my first time on night duty. I had spent most of the afternoon trying to sleep with little success. I had already worked two weeks on the day shift. The night shift started at 9.00 pm and finished at 7.00 am. I didn't know how I was going to last through the night. I just prayed that it would not be busy.

"Sister, I can feel a pulse on the patient," I reported to the head nurse on the ward.

"Can't be; she's cold and blue," the head nurse intoned without even looking in my direction.

I went back to the patient. Yes, she was blue and cold, but I could feel a pulse. I was sure of it. So, I went back to the head nurse again. She placed her fingers on the patient's wrist, feeling for the pulse, and found it.

"I think you're right, Nurse Lilly. I'll inform the doctor on duty," she said, looking directly at me now.

The head nurse came back a little later with an electrocardiogram machine. I assisted her, attaching it to the patient. The patient's heartbeat registered on the screen.

"What happens now, Sister?" I asked.

"We must wait for the heart rate to die and for the machine to register a flat line. Then the doctor will pronounce her dead. What a sad case. She'd suffered an anaesthetic accident while in surgery. She's only thirty-five and not married," she mused.

I kept an eye on the monitor throughout the shift. It was 4.00 am when the patient's heart finally stopped beating. The doctor came to certify her death, and I helped prepare her for the mortuary. The mortuary porters came to collect the body; I was to accompany them. It was still dark as we left the ward and walked towards the mortuary, a stand-alone building at the far end of the hospital grounds. I walked behind the workers who pushed the gurney. They chatted with each other in Hokkien. As they did not speak any English, they addressed me in Malay. My heart was beating so hard I could feel it in my throat.

I had never seen the inside of a morgue before; another first on my first night shift. The ambient temperature in the morgue was low to keep the bodies from deteriorating. As we entered the premises, I shivered, and gooseflesh stippled my arms, not necessarily because of the cold. There were bodies everywhere, packed into the morgue. An odd smell permeated the place: a mix of antiseptic cleaning fluid, formalin and decay. The place was eerily quiet. The hairs on the back of my neck started to stand. I could not wait to get out. The porters deposited the stretcher with the body on the floor quite unceremoniously. They said there was no space in the cold chamber where temperatures are as low as 2^0 Celsius. They seemed desensitised to the dead and did not respect the bodies.

They pointed out a log book. I was required to fill in the patient's details and the time of placement in the morgue. Once completed, I could head back to the ward. Dawn was breaking, but the street lights were still on. I ran back to the ward, still stippled with gooseflesh. My stomach churned for the rest of the shift. I could not stop thinking about that woman: what a waste of a young life. All those bodies in the mortuary, each with a story to tell, are now silenced forever. There was never a dull moment! First-year of nursing was all bedpans, bed baths and bed-making. Then there were observation rounds for temperature, pulse, respiration and blood pressure monitoring. We also helped patients to eat and kept them comfortable as we followed instructions issued by second and third-year nurses and the ward sister.

"We are running out of beds!" I informed the sister-in-charge.

"Ring the porter and ask them to set up beds in the corridor," she instructed.

Soon beds poured over, first into the internal corridors of the ward and then into the main hospital corridors. It was admission day, and the ward had to take all the assigned cases. Privacy was a luxury for these patients in a Nightingale ward layout. This layout consisted of a large room with rows and rows of beds, without subdivisions for patients. We did our best for them. Nursing was hard work, and I went home exhausted most days.

Gastric Lavage

The smell of beery vomit made me want to throw up myself! But I had to carry out the procedure.

"*Buka mulut*", I said to the male patient in Malay, meaning "open your mouth".

The patient was swaying and intoxicated with alcohol. The police constable who brought him in was holding him down by the shoulders. My task was to put a sizeable tube down his throat and pump the alcohol out of him. Dressed in high plastic boots and a long heavy Mackintosh apron, this was a job I was not particularly eager to do. To make things worse, I was on night duty. The police brought in men they found wandering the streets at night, usually because they were intoxicated. The experience put me off beer completely. I promised myself I would never drink that awful stuff even if I lived to a hundred! I was glad when my posting to that unit was over. It reminded me of all my brothers-in-law who often stank of beer when visiting us. They all died young from excessive and chronic alcohol consumption, leaving my half-sisters to raise their children alone as widows. The inheritance they had sued my mother for, with no regard for the implications of forcing her to sell the family home, had all been drunk away. I swore that I would never find myself in that situation ever!

Men who smelt of alcohol, especially beer, were disgusting to me. As training progressed, we returned to school during the year for a four-week theory block followed by exams. We regarded this as a welcome break from the busy wards and some tyrannical nursing managers. If you were unfortunate enough to earn the ire of a nursing manager, your posting on their ward became a daily Hell. We all exchanged information in our group when our shifts coincided, usually during meal breaks. We were forewarned about the tyrants and knew to keep a low profile until the end of the posting. At that point, we had no choice but to see them for the performance evaluation, suffer their dressing down and quit their office as soon as possible. The first year of training flew by. It was hard work. Getting used to the Nightingale wards and night duty was hard. Often, I wanted to quit the course, finding everything daunting. Nevertheless, I persisted as I knew this was my passport to the world and that my qualifications would enable me to fly further. I was chuffed when I passed my exams and swapped my single-stripe epaulettes for double-stripe ones.

Home Front

It was one of those rare weekends when Mum was home from her live-in housekeeping job. She reviewed the bills I had paid over the last few months and checked the files I kept while she was away. I still went to her workplace to sort out the bills that came in the post when I had a day off. She was employed by a young American expatriate couple with three children, all under 10. The couple took an interest in me, encouraging me in my nursing studies.

"Lilly, now that you are working, you will take on a house bill as part of your contribution to the house's running." Mum told me firmly "I think you should pay the water bill."

"Alright, Mum, I'll take that on," I sighed as I assented.

I knew better than to argue. My wages as a student nurse were $90 a month. The water bill was about $20, more than 20 per cent of my wages. Besides, it was only fair as each of my siblings had taken on bills to pay. I knew that eventually; Mum would have to give up her job as she was getting on. She would soon find a job that began early in the morning and ended late in the evening, too demanding. Keeping up with three active children all day long, seeing to their every need and keeping them entertained as she kept house and prepared meals was beginning to show on her face. Mum still cried whenever there was a difficult situation at home. Usually, it was a misunderstanding with relatives who were still very cold towards us.

"What have I done to deserve this?" she would lament.

I knew her life had taken a complex and unfair trajectory, but there was no one else to turn to for help. All our relatives had turned their backs on us.

Second year

It felt great to help the first-year nurses when they asked questions; I knew something! The second-year nurse was mainly responsible for the nutrition of the patients. We ordered the meals for the day and cared for the patients with intravenous drips. Initially concerned about the intravenous drip calculations, I soon mastered the process and felt very comfortable. Ordering the different special diets for the patients was just as challenging. As Singapore is multicultural, the menus featured four cuisines: Chinese, Malay, Indian and European. Over and above, these were the therapeutic diets— Chinese, low salt, high protein, Indian vegetarian, diabetic, *halal* and low protein -- for the seventy-odd patients in one ward. I loved this part of nursing. Every day was different, demanding and exciting.

When posted to the paediatric ward, as feed nurses, we made the babies' milk feeds from Government-issued powdered milk. Full-strength, three-quarter-strength, half-strength, and one-quarter-strength milk feeds were made up according to doctors' orders. Weaker formulas were fed to babies with diarrhoea and vomiting. There were no alternatives to milk products in the 1970s. Some babies died of malnutrition from lactose intolerance when their mothers could not breastfeed them. It was unfortunate to see them become skin and bones with the classic malnutrition potbelly. They would bleed from the intestines and cry in pain when fed. Sometimes we resorted to providing boiled rice water to no avail. As lactose intolerance is high amongst Asians, many Asian babies die of a lack of an alternative source of nutrition. The Milton method of sterilising baby-feeding equipment using cold water and sterilisation tablets had not yet made its way to Singapore. Feed nurses packed glass milk bottles into cages lowered into large vats of boiling water for sterilisation.

Third-year Nursing

With a third stripe on each of my epaulettes, I was soon in the home stretch. Wound dressings, medication and injection rounds were the highlights of this year. We followed the doctors on the ward round, nursing sister in tow. She supervised us as we made the necessary changes to the care the doctors ordered. The maths tested me to the limit; I managed, thank God. Somehow, I mastered the formulas for medical calculations. On one occasion, I administered a penicillin injection to an asleep baby. I felt terrible about disturbing it but was unprepared for the milky white irises I saw when its eyes flew open. The baby screamed its pain as I pushed the antibiotic into its thigh, swollen from previous injections. On checking its notes, I learnt that the in-utero infection caused juvenile syphilis. Its mother was a sex worker or "prostitute", as they were referred to then. Trainees were posted to specialist facilities. At the Hospital for Infectious Diseases, we cared for patients with typhoid, diphtheria and leprosy. Polio was also rampant at the time.

The respirators so commonplace today had not yet been invented. Polio patients were nursed in large metal ventilators over 2 m long, known informally as iron lungs. Patients lay enclosed to their necks in the ventilator. They could see their faces in a mirror angled strategically over the machine that regulated their breathing with positive and negative pressure. We nursed them through portholes on either side of the lung, carrying out personal hygiene, dressings and injections through them. On the posting with the contact tracing nurse on the community health care team, we visited brothels to track down prostitutes who had defaulted on their hospital appointments. The women just ran away when they saw us coming.

A young boy's parents firmly declined to send their son for a follow-up appointment when a skin biopsy returned positive for leprosy. The nurse begged them to have him treated. She tried very hard for the boy's welfare, but to no avail. While posted to maternity services, I had a very confronting experience. The compulsory two-child government policy was introduced to control population growth. A woman who was expecting her third child or beyond came under tremendous pressure to have that pregnancy terminated. I saw live foetuses dying in kidney dishes in the sluice room. One particular case made me feel especially sad. The woman, paralysed from the waist down, had become pregnant due to rape. She was forced to have an abortion even though her pregnancy was advanced. Her baby would have been born alive and left to die in a kidney dish. My sisters were surgically sterilised after their second child was born to comply with government policy. They came under tremendous pressure to agree to the procedure, or they would not be able to enrol their children in schools of their choice eventually. All women discharged from the maternity unit after delivery were counselled by family planning nurses for re-admission ten weeks later for surgical sterilisation by tubal ligation. For my final two months of elective nursing, I chose the burns unit, shunting between the outpatient clinic and the ward. I was assigned to the wound dressing room in the clinic. Working completely unsupervised, I removed stitches from delicate skin grafts and dressed burn wounds with state-of-the-art dressing. I enjoyed the autonomy and working office hours.

In constant consultation with the medical team, we achieved excellent outcomes for many of our patients with granulation of skin tissue and managing keloids. In the ward, the patients were primarily children with injuries from burns and scalding. On the ward and back on shift work, one patient that I could never forget was a young man who had 90 per cent burns to his body from an explosion on the ship where he had been working. He looked like a mummy, covered from head to foot in dressings. Only the soles of his feet, the palms of his hands and his genitals escaped burns. I became his dedicated nurse to ensure continuity of care. Caring for him was both demanding and rewarding. When eventually able to walk, he would run away and hide under the tables to avoid having his dressings changed. Heavy doses of narcotics were used for pain relief. We became friends as I spent many hours with him. It was hard to say goodbye to him on my last training day. I had elected to be posted to another hospital closer to home.

Graduation

I had sat for my final exams before the elective posting. The day the results were released, all students gravitated to the nursing school to meet their fate. Together, my friends and I found we had all passed the exams. I had achieved what I had set out to achieve. I was now a State Registered Nurse. The British nursing council recognised the qualification as it had set the curriculum. I was thrilled; the world was at my feet. I could work anywhere in the United Kingdom if I so desired.

Two months later, I strode onto the stage at the graduation ceremony to receive my certificate. Mum was there to witness the event and celebrate with me. It was the happiest moment of my young life, the pinnacle of achievement. The hard work had been worth it. I would not be here had I not done the three-day walk for the primary school leaving exams. I promised myself that I would never be hungry again. This qualification was my passport to a better life. No one could take it away from me. I hugged Mum. She was smiling, happy for me. But she was still sad, tired and hurting from her life issues. In my mind, I could see my half-sisters' faces. All had lost their husbands to alcohol, leaving them struggling to raise children alone with hardship that could have been spared. When a woman puts her life into a man's hand in a marriage covenant, they commit to caring for each other. Wives should not be used as chattels for housekeeping and child-bearing to prove their husband's masculinity and ensure the continuity of their bloodline. What would it take for a man to understand his responsibilities as a husband and father? I made another promise: I would never put myself in that position.

First posting

For my first year of Graduate nursing, I choose a hospital close to home, within walking distance; no longer long, multiple-bus journeys to work. It was a year of skills consolidation. The ward I was assigned to was a female surgical ward, a Nightingale ward of about forty beds. Attached was a six-bed high-dependency cubical for patients returning to the ward post-surgery. Patients were admitted here before surgery for prep. We also took in accident victims, and I often walked to the mortuary accompanying the dead. It was a bustling ward, and I was exhausted after each shift. After I completed my first year here, I received my consolidation letter confirming that I had successfully transitioned from student to qualified nurse.

With it came a handsome pay rise. The well-earned reward meant I felt more confident at work and began enjoying my responsibilities. At home, I paid for the installation of our first telephone. In my second year, I was in charge of the ward on almost every shift I worked. Sometimes I worked in the intensive care unit (ICU) to help. On one such shift, I nursed a young woman drifting in and out of a coma due to a septic abortion. The doctors and her family asked her who the baby's father was and where she had had the abortion done. She steadfastly refused to divulge any information. She died a short while later after I had left work. Watching her life ebbing away slowly as I stood beside her bed was disturbing. She wanted to be loved and paid for it with her life. Where was the integrity of the father of the baby? Had he used her for pleasure and deserted her in her time of need? Or did she make a mistake and trust him? I was outraged by the unfairness of the situation. Women give so much of themselves and lose out as the emotional and physical turmoil of finding love takes its toll, often paying a high price.

Frying Pan

"What's the matter, May Ling? You look very upset," I asked my senior nurse. May Ling seemed very tense during the shift. We were enjoying a few minutes of quiet in the office.

"I am so mad at my mother-in-law!" She cried. "The woman drives me nuts. While I was at work yesterday, she took my brand-new non-stick frying pan and scrubbed the non-stick coating off. She then showed it to my husband and had the cheek to call me lazy!"

May Ling's face, furrowed with consternation, eased as she burst into loud peals of laughter. Soon we were laughing; so hard that she had tears streaming down her face.

"What did your husband say to her?" I asked eventually.

"Well, he explained to his mother that it was new technology and he had bought it for me as a present. The stupid woman did not even apologise; she just walked to her room mumbling," replied May Ling, in between deep breaths.

Two days later, May Ling came on shift and told me that her mother-in-law had returned to her own home and that her husband came home after work with another brand-new pan for her. As for the scrubbed-out one, it went with the mother-in-law!

Bread rolls

"Let's have lunch in a restaurant downtown," my brother suggested.

"Yes, why not? I can afford it now," I replied gleefully.

"You've studied and worked hard these last few years. It's time you lived a little," my brother agreed.

We went to a lovely open-air Western restaurant on High Street where the expensive hotels and high-end shops were. Once seated, we were handed the menus and ordered our meals. The waitress returned with a bread basket and asked if we wanted a bread roll. Unsure if that would take the bill over our budget, we both looked at each other.

"Do we have to pay extra for it?" My brother asked.

"No", the waitress replied with disgust on her face.

"Oh, yes, please," he replied.

"Well, what type do you want, white or brown?" She asked, raising her voice at us.

"White," I replied, "and you don't have to yell at us," I added sharply.

She dumped the rolls on our bread plates and huffed away. Another waiter served our meal. We did not leave a tip at the restaurant as we were both annoyed at the rude behaviour of the first waitress. That night I decided to do something about it. I realised that while I could not change what had happened at the restaurant, I could change myself. Perhaps we had looked like a pair of country bumpkins, I thought. I decided the only way to change it was to get an education in Western etiquette. My mother always said that education is never wasted. Growing up financially challenged meant we ate at hawker stalls and eating houses most of the time. There was very little Western table etiquette required in these places. At home, we ate with our fingers. If I wanted to travel overseas and live in another country, I would have to learn their manners.

Self-improvement

So, I scoured the newspapers and signed up with an agency for deportment and modelling. The training cost me $200! – a great deal of money. My monthly take-home wages were just $120. An English woman, Mrs Bay, ran the course at the prestigious Raffles Hotel, a quintessential English institution and a six-star hotel. Payment for the training was accepted in small instalments over six months, making the course affordable. I would have to ensure my shifts did not clash with the classes held in the evening. Mrs Bay covered a range of subjects: selecting clothes that flattered the complexion and made the most of the figure; accessorising the outfit; makeup and hairstyle to suit the face shape; table etiquette; and how to own the catwalk in a fashion show. I was the only young woman of Indian extraction amongst the participants. The rest were Chinese, primarily daughters of wealthy parents seeking to marry them to rich men. The training in style, deportment, good manners and Western etiquette was necessary for securing a high-quality husband. It was a confidence booster for me. I learnt how to sit and carry myself like a lady and pose for photographs. I learnt how to conduct myself in a high-end Western restaurant. Even though I did not own a lot of clothes, I learnt how to dress well and make the most of my physical assets. Graduation day soon came, and I happily chalked up yet another milestone. My second brother had taken up photography, and I modelled for him.

Modelling

"Hello," I said, picking up the telephone.

"Could I speak to Lilly, please?" said the female voice at the end of the line.

"This is Lilly speaking," I replied.

"Mrs Bay's secretary here. Could you come to the Raffles for a viewing? We're looking for models for a fashion show. You will have to be in a bikini."

"Oh!" I said in surprise. Having never considered modelling a career option, I had not expected catwalk work. It was work I did not want to do, mainly if it meant parading in front of people in a bikini I did not own.

"Hello," the secretary said. "Are you there?" I had gone quiet on the phone, thinking about what to do.

"I am sorry, I don't have a bikini, and I would not wear one for a viewing," I said.

"OK, that's fine," the secretary said and hung up. I never heard from them again. I was not interested in modelling. It was enough for me that I had learned many things that would hold me in good stead for my future.

Love your bride
"What do I do? Do I get her another bed or put her into another room?" the elderly gentleman asked, concerned and worried. He was taking his wife home. She had undergone primary bowel resection for cancer treatment and now had a permanent colostomy opening in her abdomen where her bowels ended. For the rest of her life, she would have a bag attached to the surgically created opening in her belly for faecal matter and urine. The frail 70-year-old woman also faced further chemotherapy treatments.

"No, that is the last thing you do. Your wife is the mother of your children and the bride you took home to spend the rest of your life with. You treat her the same as that day you married her," I replied.

"Thank you, Sister," he said, accepting her discharge papers.

I watched him walk her out of the ward with a smile that reached his eyes. I wondered how long they would have before cancer took her. They stopped at the office where I was seated, again saying goodbye and thanking me for their care. I wished them well with a pang in my heart.

Sam again
"Lilly, phone call for you," called a nurse from the office.

"Thank you," I replied, walking to the phone in the nurses' room adjacent to the manager's office. We were discouraged from making or taking personal phone calls unless they were urgent. The manager was sitting at her desk.

"Hello", I said.

"Lilly, my name is Shanti. You don't know me, but I know your ex-boyfriend Sam. Have you got someone already?" she asked. "He is missing you and wants to see you again," she added.

"No, I don't have anyone," I informed her.

"If I gave you my number, would you please give me a call after work so we can talk?" she asked.

I quickly took the number down and rang off, conscious that the manager was within earshot. We met about a week later. Shanti told me Sam was still talking about me and drinking heavily to drown his sorrows. As I still felt for him, I agreed to a meeting a few weeks later when he would be home between flights. We recommenced our courtship when Sam told me he had never forgotten and missed me. He also observed that I was more mature than the teenager he had walked away from five years earlier. It did not take me long to fall in love with Sam again. There was still the issue of our differing ethnolinguistic family backgrounds. His parents would never agree to a marriage between him and a girl from outside his clan like myself.

Moving up

The five of us had lived in cramped accommodations for almost nine years. Then my second sister married and moved in with her in-laws while my second brother left to share a private rental with his mates. Suddenly, it was just Mum, my first brother and me in the flat. First Brother, who now had a steady job in the national armed forces, decided to buy a flat. The government had been building and establishing what it called satellite towns. These were clusters of high-rise apartment blocks built around amenities such as schools, playgrounds, shopping centres, clinics, etc. To engender commitment to a young nation, inspire everyday nationalism and promote community cohesion, people were encouraged to buy homes in these towns. The move was part of Singapore's nation-building exercise to facilitate a largely migrant or migrant-descended population to put down roots in a new post-colonial state. Mortgage rates were desirable, with other incentives and conditions potential buyers had to meet. These homes were to be owned and occupied by families, not single individuals.

However, young singles could co-own their flat with a parent. A common practice was for this parent to be named head of household while their co-owner child serviced the mortgage. It was how my brother came to own a flat. Indeed, my mother, second brother, and I formed a family unit for First Brother's application. We were delighted to learn that his application had been successful. Soon after, we moved into a three-bedroom flat in a new housing estate. Moving into a home purchased by her son must have made Mum feel like she had finally arrived; no more fretting over rent and fearing eviction. She must also have felt vindicated. Over the years, Mum had weathered heavy criticism from my siblings and me for the privileges accorded her elder son. She was also relieved to stop working and be looked after by him. She was tired, and it showed on her face. Life had not been kind to her. In return, she kept house and managed the household, budgeting, shopping and preparing meals. Our home was always clean and well-maintained, and there was now always something to eat. An unexpected and welcome consequence of all these changes was that I finally got my first room at 21! Even though Mum did not attend church, she instilled in us our faith, so we were all observant, practising Catholics. Mum was chagrined to discover that the senior priest in the local parish was he-who-had-denied-us-rations all those years ago. Seeing him reminded her of the humiliations she had endured during the difficult years in the past and hardened her resolve not to attend mass. However, this did not stop my brothers and me from attending church in the thriving parish with its large congregation.

Well played

"Right, shall we do this?" Sam asked as we stood outside the office of the public housing authority. We had been dating for about a year. Sam's parents had got wind of our relationship. He had had a showdown with his parents about "that Tamil girl", as they referred me. They continued to withhold their blessings. Mum made it clear that no help would be forthcoming from her quarter.

"You get into trouble; you sort yourself out. I can't help you. The education I have given should teach you to use your brain. That's what I sent you to school for," Mum said. She was just being realistic because she did not have the means to help.

Mum's position on the matter suited me. She considered Sam a good catch as he came from a Catholic family and had a steady job with good prospects. Everyone wanted to work in the aviation industry as Singapore began making a name for itself as a tourist destination and a regional flight hub. My siblings did not have any objections. Indeed, my brothers remembered Sam from attending the same Christian Brothers school. We lived a stone's way away from each other when we resided in the family home that was sold due to a court order.

"You realise that once you sign this, you will have to produce your wedding certificate within three months of being allocated your flat," the clerk reminded us.

"Yes, we know that," Sam replied. We signed the documents and walked out of the building with a sense of accomplishment.

"Sam, we've done it!" I said, grasping his arm with both hands.

"Yes, Lilly, we have. Now to tackle my family!" Sam replied, hugging and kissing me.

We had taken the bull by the horns! All Hell broke loose when Sam formally introduced me to his parents and informed them, he was marrying me. They were not pleased to learn that we had outplayed them by applying to buy a flat as a couple. Everyone knew the government stipulation that engaged couples had only three months after they received the keys to formalise their union and produce their marriage certificate. Young singles could only purchase homes in the private real estate market, where prices were exorbitant and well out of the reach of 85 per cent of the population.

"My parents want to meet your mother," Sam informed me.

A date was fixed for my mother and me. We were surrounded by a herd of Sam's relatives when we arrived. There was a babble of voices as they all spoke simultaneously, demanding answers. The main thrust of their queries seemed to be why my mother allowed her daughter to carry on so, suggesting that I was a young woman of questionable character and easy virtue.

"I have educated my daughter. She can think for herself, and clearly, so can he," Mum shot back, referring to Sam, so his relatives were reminded that he was just as keen to marry me. They were taken aback by Mum's refusal to play the shamed parent. After a while, the elders had a productive discussion about how best to go about the wedding.

"I am a widow. I can't afford to pay for wedding expenses. Lilly will pay for everything herself," was Mum's contribution when the talk turned to finances.

After much discussion, Sam's parents agreed to hold the wedding as soon as possible. They accepted that their hands were tied by the paperwork we had signed for a government flat. There was no easy way out of that, so they finally capitulated. We agreed on a date and began planning our wedding. Sam and I met openly now at his home. Initially,

I felt uncomfortable, but Sam was always by my side to support me.

Wedding bells

Because we were getting married at short notice, no wedding venues were available for hire. We decided to hold the wedding feast on Sam's family home grounds. Over their front yard, a marquee was erected, and the living room turned into a pop-up dining room for the wedding feast for some 80 guests. Most of the guests were Sam's relatives. My guests consisted of immediate family and two colleagues, about twenty. I walked into the church on my brother's arm, the same church to which my school was attached. I had attended many a mass here with my classmates and teachers. I wore a white silk saree, lace gloves, and a bouquet of orchid sprays. My two little nieces were flower girls. Sam stood waiting at the altar with his brother as his best man. We had seen the officiating priest agreeing on the wedding vows and the Bible reading for the traditional wedding mass.

Sam read the first reading at the altar:

"…walk in the way of love, just as Christ loved us and gave himself up for us as a fragrant offering and sacrifice to God." (Ephesians 5:2).

This scripture urged us to be subject to one another out of reverence for Jesus Christ. It stipulated how husbands and wives are to treat each other.

"Wives, submit yourselves to your own husbands as you do to the Lord. For the husband is the head of the wife as Christ is the head of the church, his body, of which he is the Saviour. Now as the church submits to Christ, so also wives should submit to their husbands in everything. Husbands, love your wives, just as Christ loved the church and gave himself up for her to make her holy, cleansing her by the washing with water through the word, and to present her to himself as a radiant church, without stain or wrinkle or any other blemish, but holy and blameless. In this same way, husband's ought to love their wives as their own bodies. He who loves his wife loves himself. After all, no one ever hated their own body, but they feed and care for their body, just as Christ does the church -- for we are members of his body." (Ephesians 5: 21-30)

I read the scripture below for the second reading, taken from the first letter of St John. It highlights how we become one with God when we love. I was to reflect on this passage many times in the following years.

"Dear friends, let us love one another, for love comes from God. Everyone who loves has been born of God and knows God. Whoever does not love does not know God, because God is love. This is how God showed his love among us: He sent his one and only son into the world that we might live through him. This is love: not that we loved God, but that he loved us and sent his son as an atoning sacrifice for our sins. Dear friends, since God so loved us, we also ought to love one another. No one has ever seen God; but if we love one another, God lives in us and his love is made complete in us." (John 4: 7-12)

The priest's reading from the gospel of Mark highlighted the sanctity of marriage as a lasting covenant.

"But at the beginning of creation, God 'made them male and female. For this reason, a man will leave his father and mother and be united to his wife, and the two will become one flesh. So, they are no longer two but one flesh. Therefore, what God has joined together, let no one separate." (Mark 10: 6-9)

We chose the standard version quoted below for our wedding vows. Did Sam fully appreciate the meaning of his words on the day? I know I did and meant them with all my heart:

I take you, for my lawful wife/husband, to have and to hold from this day forward, for better, for worse, for richer, for poorer, in sickness and in health, until death does us part. I will love and honour you all the days of my life. With this ring, I thee wed.

I walked out of the church, the happiest girl on Earth. I was walking on air with my dream man by my side. I am married; the thought filled me with delight. As the night progressed, we walked around the reception, thanking our guests for the pleasure and honour of their presence at our celebration. We stopped at a table of Sam's friends. One of them, a Hindu, made disparaging comments about the scriptures from our wedding ceremony. I was disappointed Sam did not say anything to counter his disrespect, which clouded our special day for me. I moved into Sam's home the following day. Sam's elder brother gifted us a bedroom for our wedding night at a hotel downtown. We shared a tiny bedroom, but I did not mind. I thought it was cosy and was happy to be with the man I loved. Besides, our three-bedroom flat would be ready in a couple of months. In the meantime, I was busy with work, shopping, and planning for our new home. Over the next few months, word came back to us that Sam's parents and guests had loved the wedding as it reminded them of weddings back in India, where receptions are held on the home or village grounds.

Quickly disillusioned

We did not have a honeymoon. I had only four days off work though Sam had two weeks of marital leave. He could have taken me somewhere, even for those four days. Instead, he left me alone while participating in a daily card game marathon with his friends. I was very hurt and disappointed. What have I done? I thought. What had happened to the wedding vows he had taken at the altar? Have I made a mistake marrying Sam? Has love made me blind? I had witnessed these gambling marathons before, but had naively thought he would change after the wedding.

Not long later, I realised Sam was dirty and untidy, which went against my grain. No matter how poor we were, my mother instilled cleanliness and tidiness in us.

"That's your job," Sam said and walked off when I raised the issue with him.

I set about cleaning our room and the common areas of the house. It did not take long before my parents-in-law began to respect me. I made it a point to carry my weight in the running of the home, helping in the kitchen on my days off. My one difficulty was the journey to and from work. There was no direct bus service, and I did not know how to drive. Before the wedding, I left government employment to work in a private hospital. The journey required changing three buses, with a long walk to and from the bus stop and the house. I had to leave much earlier to get to work on time. When Sam was home between flights, he would give me a lift to and from work in his father's car. It was not without problems as I would have to prise him away from his card game.

"In five minutes," he would promise when I reminded him that we should leave to get me to work on time. It was followed by another five and a further five after that. Eventually, bringing me to work on time would take a mad rush. After work, he would sometimes take an hour or more to pick me up, leaving me waiting on the side of the main road in the blazing afternoon sun or alone at night after a hard day's work. The quick-shift change was the worst. This shift finished at 9.00 pm and started again at 7.00 am. The work was exhausting, and I needed as much rest as possible to stay sharp and alert.

As Sam was always late picking me up, I got less sleep. Worse, getting him out of bed to take me to work the following morning was a battle. Sam's uncaring and callous attitude towards me -- and his disregard for my commitment to my career -- hurt and disconcerted me. Going on the buses would have been less stressful, but I was naive and forgiving. Tomorrow will be better, I told myself. But that tomorrow just never came. It was worse when Sam was drunk. I would worry that the traffic police might stop us, do a random breath test and suspend his licence on a drunken driving charge.

Private Hospital

I soon realised that there was a great deal of difference in nursing care between the government and private sectors. Only the very wealthy could afford these services. I was assigned to paediatrics and adult suites. The suites were more like hotel rooms than anything else. Each bedroom with its sitting room was priced at $250 a day. Over and above this amount was the cost of nursing, medication and doctors' fees. Patients often had private nurses working round the clock in addition to everything else. The mother and baby rooms in the paediatric wing were opulently appointed. The children and babies were my first love. I dreamed of the day I would hold my baby in my arms. It was babies galore every morning as I dallied in the corridor to my unit. The maternity unit was just next door. Under the watchful eye of a senior nurse, babies with neonatal jaundice were stripped and placed in the sun to help treat the condition so common among Asians. When sunning proved insufficient, admission to my ward in the paediatrics wing for phototherapy was necessary. The severe cases had to have exchange transfusions. The process involved removing some of the baby's blood and replacing it with donor blood to remove jaundice toxins and antibodies while ensuring enough blood was circulating in their system. It happened pretty often. There were many foreigners admitted to the hospital. One wealthy businessman admitted himself to the suites for a month each year to have a break and undisturbed peace from his business partners. He would have private nurses look after him around the clock. Upon discharge, he would give the entire ward staff a gift each. Every Christmas, he would fund a ten-course Chinese dinner for the whole hospital staff in the dining room. Whilst still new to the private hospital routine, I put a patient's pyjamas in the bag that headed for the laundry. I received a dressing down from the manager for the mistake. All patients sent their clothes home for washing. The pyjamas were expensive, and the manager had to go to the laundry department and look for them.

Another big difference in private hospital nursing was the pre-packed commercial dressing equipment. We were spared the tedious job of cutting gauze and cotton wool rolls to make swabs and gauze squares. In government nursing practice, these would be packed into autoclave drums and sent to the sterilising department daily by the nurses. Overlooking this task would mean that the dressing nurse of the next day would struggle with a shortage of supplies, obliged to beg and borrow from other wards. Best of all was the use of plastic disposable syringes and disposable needles. No more washing of used glass syringes and steel needles was needed. In a government facility, these had to be cleaned and boiled in small sterilisers on the ward.

The needles had to be dragged over a cotton wool ball to test if they were blunt and then sharpened on a whetting stone. If someone forgot to do this, the patient suffered an injection with a dull needle! As I gained more experience, I decided to specialise in midwifery. Several of my colleagues had gone to England to upgrade their skills and further their careers. I sought them out, asking about their training and life in England. I heard many stories and was eager to go there myself. No matter how often I re-configured my options, the stumbling block was always the same: how would I get Sam to agree? Some days, it seemed like a pie-in-the-sky notion, yet I held on to my dream.

On our own

I moved out of Sam's parent's home and into our flat as soon as it was ready. There were three bedrooms, one with an ensuite, a dining room, a living room and a kitchen. Our only furniture was the bedroom set we had commissioned from a local carpenter. We sat on cushions on the living room floor, and there was no dining set. I did not care. I wanted out of Sam's parents' home. Our combined wages meant we were allocated the largest flat in the public housing entitlement under government regulations. We would not have qualified for public housing if our salaries had increased. Instead, we would have to buy a house with a garden or a unit in a private condominium.

"Lilly, I have something to tell you," Sam said one afternoon. It was one of that once-in-a-blue-moon occasions when we had a day off together, and he was not playing cards. I attributed it to the fact that it was a weekday, and his friends were all at work.

"What is it?" I asked.

"I gambled in the casino in Las Vegas and lost $35,000," he announced. He was smiling as if it was an accomplishment. Confused and discombobulated, I searched his face for some sign of remorse. I could find no trace of it. I stared at him in disbelief. The flat we were living in cost $37,000. We were only four months into our marriage, and I was still a new bride. My breath caught in my throat, my mouth went dry, and my stomach turned.

"What? What did you do that for?" I could barely speak the words as I struggled to catch my breath. I could hear my heart thumping in my ears.

He did not give me a reply. He knew that I was upset. My world had just come crashing down around me. I did not speak to him until the following morning, spending the night in a state of restless unease, worrying and wondering how we would deal with this crisis. When the day dawned, I gave up. I got out of bed and got ready for work.

"Sam, you created that problem; you deal with it!" I snapped as I left.

We found ourselves in the office of one of Sam's uncles two weeks later. Sam was in tears as he told his uncle what had happened. His uncle offered to loan him the money to pay off the loan shark operating amongst his colleagues. The interest rates were exorbitant; there was no chance we could have paid this money off without getting into further trouble.

"Don't tell anyone about this!" Sam instructed me sternly as we were driving home. He was back to his usual arrogant self. I was foolish enough to believe him. Sometime later, I discovered that his uncle had told Sam's mother about the gambling debt and the loan. Sam's mother returned the money to her brother, demanding that Sam not be told she had sorted it out. Otherwise, she said, Sam would not honour the monthly repayments.

Regret

As time passed, I realised Sam was not the person I had believed him to be. He was the life of the party, the comedian quick with a joke and the smooth-talking charmer. Everybody loved Sam. But Sam had changed. Marriage and moving out of his family home seemed to allow him to live without accountability. He continued gambling, borrowing money from family, friends or anyone who would lend it to him. Ring! Ring! Ring! the phone rang while I was in the shower. Grabbing the towel, I stepped out of the bathroom onto the mat, which slid from under me. I landed heavily on my back -- on the concrete floor. I picked myself up hurriedly and made for the phone. It was Sam's sister. His mother wanted him to drop by the next day to run errands. I told her that I would inform him and hung up. Sam was returning home that evening. I started to dry myself and found that I was bleeding vaginally. I suspected that I was pregnant. I ought to have taken a quick trip to the hospital immediately. Instead, I stayed home and told Sam when he came home -- a dreadful miscalculation on my part.

"You did that on purpose!" He accused and walked away. He had just two days off. In tears and with a heavy heart, I washed and ironed his uniforms as a dutiful wife would. He left. A positive diagnosis was made of a miscarriage the next day at the outpatient clinic where I worked. The gynaecologist's referral accompanied it for a dilation and curettage. Sam's father took me to the private clinic for the procedure and drove me home to our flat. I was filled with regret and felt utterly alone and unloved. Apart from Sam's parents, I did not tell anyone about the miscarriage. I did not reveal to my family what was happening with Sam. My marriage was a farce. We looked like a happy couple outside, but we were not. I felt neglected and abused.

Why?

"Why God, why?" I asked. The waves were rolling in. Crystal blue water reflected the sunlight as it rose from the sea and crashed onto the coral-white sand. The beautiful bright day with a cloudless sky and brilliant sunshine was wasted on me. My thoughts consumed me. What had gone wrong with my marriage? All I wanted was to be a happy wife and mother with a doting husband by my side, loving our children and me. I stared at the sand at my feet. Sitting on a large rock, I was bent over, chest on thighs feeling the sand run through my toes. Suddenly conscious that I was not alone when I looked up, I saw a Caucasian man walking towards me. He seemed out of place on a beach, dressed in black trousers, a white business shirt and a tie. He was also carrying a black briefcase. He walked up to me and said, "Don't worry, I will look after you."

My eyelids flew open, and I sat bolt upright. It's a dream! I was covered in a cold sweat. Sam was away, and I felt guilty. My Catholic faith and scripture, Matt 5:28 specifically, had taught me that the very thought of another man was a sin! I will have to repent and do penance for it! But I soon pushed the dream aside and carried on with my life.

Lonely holidays

Even though Sam benefited from special rates for flights as a flight crew, he did not initiate any plans for trips with me. Instead, I would hound him asking to get me a seat on his flights so we could go on holiday. There were repeated trips to London and Hong Kong. Once, I accompanied him to Hawaii. I had hoped for a romantic re-set of my marriage. Instead, Sam drank and smoked heavily, taking advantage of cheap, duty-free whisky and Marlboro cigarettes. He often came home so drunk that I would find him sleeping in a drunken stupor in his underwear on the living room floor. His clothes trailed from the front door. It was a miracle that he had driven himself home without mishap. On these occasions, I would recall the promise I had made to myself never to be in the same situation as my half-sisters, who had all married alcoholics. At the time, I had been somewhat scathing of my sisters. I realised they had been naïve and perhaps blinded by their love of a particular version of the man and had failed to see his flaws. Or maybe, some men change after marriage.

Decisions

"Oh God, I can't bear this any longer!" I prayed. As Sam continued to behave the way he did, I decided not to have children. I felt it would be wrong to continue trying to get pregnant while hoping he might change and commence contraceptive treatment. I had suffered enough in my childhood and could not bear to subject my children to a father like Sam. Children do not deserve that.

I longed for Sam to love me, lead our marriage and live the way God intended for faithful men. God had given Sam the shoulders and ordained him as the head of the household. He had failed to show himself worthy of my trust in his headship despite his vows on our wedding day in the name of Jesus.

"Sam, I want to go to England and study Midwifery," I said to him one day.

"No!" came the firm reply.

My disappointment in our marriage escalated to the point that I was happy to see Sam leave for his flight. Once, he brought friends home when I was working a week of night shifts. All nurses were rotated through the dreaded, interminable week. The shifts were each 10 hours long and the bane of my professional life. I did not sleep well in the hot, humid heat of the tropical day and its blinding brightness. Our flat had no air conditioning, and the fan gave little respite even at full speed. Sleep came only out of sheer exhaustion. I woke up abruptly one afternoon to hear loud voices coming from the living room. I waited a while, hoping the commotion would end, but the unrest became louder and rowdier. I dragged myself out of bed and went to the living room. Sam and some eight of his friends were gathered around the coffee table with cards in their hands, enjoying their game.

"Sam, might I speak to you?" I asked. Receiving no reply, I repeated my request. Sam finally got up and followed me to our bedroom.

"What are you doing? I'm on the night shift. I can't sleep with all the noise you guys are making!"

"OK!" He snapped and turned to go back to his friends.

"Go back to sleep!" He threw it over his shoulder.

But the noise did not stop. While I was dressing for work, Sam came into the bedroom and said, "One of my friends said you're lazy, not getting up to make afternoon tea!"

The comment came from one of his Hindu friends, and it was no surprise to me. The wife in some Hindu households was subject not just to her husband, but also to her in-laws, regarded as little more than a servant expected to be subservient to everyone at home, bear children and turn over their wages from their job. In the meantime, the men came and went as they pleased. I stared at him in disbelief. We had had words about this friend's comments on a previous occasion.

"You're lucky I don't beat you up!" He threatened

My immediate and spontaneous reply surprised him and shocked me.

"Touch me! I know my rights and will use them," I cried. I spat the words at him. His jaw dropped, and I walked away. Things only got worse. Sam did not appear to have any consideration for my needs. Once I asked him to do something useful with his time at home, not just watch television all day. I had hoped he would prepare dinner for us as I was on the night shift. Instead, he started knocking nails into the wall and woke me up. One afternoon, I was in deep sleep between working the night shifts and was awakened by a shooting pain in my foot. I jerked upright to find Sam at the bottom of the bed with a smile of glee on his face. He had driven his finger deep into the sole of my foot. He showed no remorse for the pain he had caused me or for disrupting my much-needed rest. Sleep deprivation became a significant concern for me. I worried about making work mistakes with drug calculations, already being compromised in mathematics. I worried about causing damage or killing a patient and the repercussion of legal pursuits with being disbarred—the loss of my career, which I had worked so hard to achieve. I worried about being found asleep on the job. At quiet times during the night shift, I found it hard to stay awake, sometimes falling asleep standing up or at the nurse's desk. I took my one-hour meal break to catch up on sleep. That sleep was never quality respite. Working seven nights of ten-hour shifts with a lack of sleep, coping with Sam's nonsense was just sheer mental and physical torture. I can only say that my guardian angel and Jesus watched over me.

After that, I proposed moving to England three more times. He gave in on my fourth attempt. By this time, I was determined to go. I knew he would drag me down with him and destroy my life if I stayed in Singapore. I had to save myself. I knew this from witnessing bad marriages first-hand. Mum was always in tears, asking, "What have I done to deserve this?" All my sisters had experienced beatings from their husbands and had to suffer the consequences of their husband's love of the bottle. I was not going to end up the same as them. I still remember the time I sat at the back of my school, hungry and asking God why I was so poor, and the words that I had heard in my mind: *"If you want something, don't expect someone to do it for you. Do it yourself!"*

I knew now, as I had known then, that that had been the voice of God speaking to me. From that day on, I was a woman on a mission. No one was going to destroy my life, I resolved. I prayed harder and searched the Bible for strength and wisdom. I found both in the Books of Proverbs and Ecclesiastes. They brought great comfort to me whenever I felt alone. I could not talk to anyone about what was happening to me. However, even on my darkest days, I knew God the Father was talking to me, giving me strength and direction. My family did not know what was happening. I could not tell them; I was embarrassed and ashamed. Mum thought Sam the bee's knees.

On your marks

There was not a moment to spare. I had to be registered as a nurse to study in England. A colleague gave me a list of midwifery schools. I sent out four applications once the application to the General Nursing Council of England and Wales registration confirmation arrived. One school would accept me only after an in-person interview. Sam had started to inform friends and relatives about my plans. He seemed to have had a change of heart. He looked forward to carrying on like a bachelor once I was out of the way. His mother, unusually, said nothing. Ordinarily, a dutiful newly-minted daughter-in-law like myself would devote her time and energies to home-making and having babies, not going overseas for studies to further her career. I suspect she knew I was trying to save my marriage by doing what I was doing. Some older women openly criticised me. They said I should have babies hanging on my skirts, not packing bags to go overseas to study.

Interview
Having made several trips to London for the holidays, I did not find it daunting to go there for the interview. Another colleague had already started midwifery studies and invited me to stay with her at the nurses 'campus. I accepted her offer gratefully.

"Oh Jenny, it's so cold!" I told my colleague when she met me at the local train station where she lived. It was mid-February, and snow had started to fall a week earlier.

"It's just winter, Lilly. You'll get used to it," she said, smiling kindly. I stayed with her for a week.

"Lilly?" The tall English woman called out.

"Yes," I replied. I was sitting in the waiting room.

"Good morning. I am Miss Tattle, director of the midwifery school," she said.

"Good morning," I replied, holding my hand for a handshake.

"If you would like to follow me to my office, we can chat there," she said, gesturing towards a door.

I followed her past the door down a short corridor until we arrived at her office. When we were seated, she asked how I was coping with visiting England and seemed pleased that it was not my first visit.

"And your husband is happy for you to be here? It seems rather unusual for you to leave home to study on your own when you are married," she observed.

"Yes, we've talked about it, and Sam is happy for me to embark on this course," I said, thinking of Sam and all that was happening at home. "Moreover, there are no further education opportunities for nurses in Singapore. We all have to come to England for it."

We continued talking for at least half an hour. Miss Tattle outlined the curriculum and the school's policy that students stay on for a year to consolidate their education after graduation. The agreement was for eighteen months of training and one year of consolidation. I would live on the nurses' campus for the duration. I accepted without hesitation; glad my work life for the next two years was mapped out. There were forms to sign, and then Miss Tattle took me on a short tour of the school and the maternity unit before bidding me goodbye.

"Well, Lilly, I'll send you a formal offer of a place amongst the next batch of students in August this year. Congratulations, I look forward to seeing you then. Please keep in touch so I know that you are committed and should reserve a place for you," she said.

"Thank you, Miss Tattle. I hope to see you again in August," I replied warmly. We shook hands and parted.

England, here I come! School of Midwifery makes way for me! I walked out into the snowy winter's day feeling ten feet tall. Jenny took me to the usual tourist places on her day off; Piccadilly Circus, the Tower of London and Buckingham Palace to see the changing of the guard. I cooked meals for her when she was at work as a gesture of thanks. On the last night of my stay with her, she wrote letters for me to post to her family in Singapore when I got home

"Bye, Lilly," Jenny called and waved as the train started to pull away from the platform. She had accompanied me to the train station in her town. From there, I would go to Heathrow Airport for the flight home.

"Bye, Jenny, keep in touch," I responded, waving out the window. I watched her figure get smaller until she turned to walk back into the station. It was freezing and snowing.

Farewell Singapore

"Lilly, we won't be able to come to the airport to see you off. We'll be at the registry of marriages. Your brother and his fiancée will be filing the legal documents for their marriage that day," Mum sighed, dismayed at the clash in our schedules.

"That's OK, Mum," I reassured her.

"Why don't you and Sam come to the registry to meet his fiancée and her family?" She suggested.

"That's a great idea. Let's do that," I concurred.

I continued working at the private hospital till the end of July. They did not want to lose me and offered to double my wages earlier than the five-year promotion period as an inducement to stay. I declined. Sam booked flights for us and decided to come with me to help me settle in. I was looking forward to the peace that distance from him would bring as he had become verbally abusive. He seemed very encouraging and happy that I was on my way. On the morning of my departure to England, we witnessed my brother and his fiancée sign their certificate of intent to marry at the Registry of Marriages. His fiancée seemed somewhat aloof. Other than saying hello during introductions, she did not say anything else. With the formalities over and the photographs taken, I said goodbye to my mother and brother. We went home to finish packing.

I packed as much as possible, taking advantage of Sam's allocated baggage allowance with the overflow. At the airport, we met some of Sam's family, my two sisters and their children. There were many good wishes, hugs, kisses and instructions to study hard and come back victorious. Sam reassured them I could return home whenever possible due to his staff discount benefit. Sam and I went through checkout and immigration when the boarding call came. I stopped and turned to take one last look and wave goodbye to all the faces on the other side of the glass partition. Although I was smiling and seemed happy, my heart was breaking. I knew that this would be a permanent break. I would never return to live in Singapore again. As we headed towards the departure gate, the family was soon out of sight. When the flight took off, I looked out the window for as long as I could, watching till the bright lights of the Lion City faded into the night sky. I thought of my family making their way home, seeing the familiar streets in my mind's eye. Blinking tears away from my eyes, I settled down for the long overnight flight to London.

CHAPTER 4: BACK TO SCHOOL

"Lilly, time to go," Lee called out to me.

"Coming, Lee," I replied.

A month had passed since I had arrived in England with Sam. My accommodation with three other student midwives was an apartment in a building with four flats, each with three rooms. I was pleased to meet Lee, who was from Malaysia. She had been in England much longer than me and had earlier trained in general nursing in another hospital. Lee proved to be a massive help in adjusting to the move, both on campus and in England. Sam stayed with me for a week before he left to go back to Singapore. We shared my little room. Although I had already worked for ten years in Singapore, my wages were only first-year RN or registered nurse wages, which were meagre. I had to pay rent for the flat and feed myself. Thankfully, the rental covered all amenities as well.

"Have you got any money to tide me over till I get my wages?" I asked Sam. He produced a plastic bag of English one and two copper pennies. I did not know what to say to him. In a sense, I was happy to see him leave so I could get on with my life. I had the pleasure of meeting another ten midwifery students. We were all living on campus in similar digs.

The first training block had commenced, and I was back in the swing of things, studying the anatomy and physiology of the human female reproductive system. There were weekly written exams. I attended my uniform fitting session: a blue checked buttoned-down dress with a purple belt and buckle. Some of my colleagues wore buckles from their previous hospitals bought after successfully qualifying, so they were symbols of distinction worn with pride. A long thick, grey coat, a navy-blue cloak lined in red for winter, and a pillbox hat topped it all off. These were all provided. We had only to purchase our shoes and stockings. I joined Lee at the apartment door. Smartly turned out in uniforms we made for the unit.

"Have you got your workbooks with you?" Lee asked.

"Yes," I replied. "I'm in the antenatal clinic, so I should get a few abdominal palpations in."

"Postnatal ward for me, so I should get some postnatal and baby checks under my belt," Lee chirruped back. We went separate ways upon entering the main door to the maternity unit, promising to exchange our days' experiences with each other when we got back home. Debriefing and comparing notes was helpful after a long, hard day.

The training was demanding, and the instructors were strict and thorough. Stringent training standards required us to record several tasks to prove that we were competent in a midwife's necessary skills. During the eighteen months of training, we had to perform one hundred baby checks, one hundred postnatal checks and forty normal deliveries managed solely by a midwife without a doctor attending. We also had to assist with forty abnormal deliveries in which a doctor performed the baby's delivery. Forty vaginal examinations and one hundred antenatal abdominal checks followed. These did not include theory exams. Students staffed the wards on all the shifts around the clock.

Antenatal Clinic

The hospital's maternity patient catchment numbers were three and a half thousand a year, with adjustments to changing area borders.

Clinics, which ran from 8.00 am to 4.00 pm Monday to Friday, were busy. Several hundred women attended it every week. Three consultant gynaecologists, each with their team of registrars and trainee doctors, shared the workload with a weekly midwife-led clinic. Midwives prepared patients' notes before each clinic, with the relevant forms for blood tests, scans and referral letters ready for the doctors to sign and hand to the patient.

"Lilly, you're in Room 3 with Midwife Jane. Dr Stewart will be working there. He is very thorough and loves teaching new staff. You'll enjoy your morning with him and Jane," the antenatal midwifery sister-in-charge said.

Pregnant women were swiftly guided in and out of each of the eight consultation rooms. Over 60 women came through that morning and another 60 or so in the afternoon. Dr Stewart was an excellent teacher. He taught me how to perform antenatal abdominal palpations. Although I had studied diagrams of the procedure in textbooks and practised on a dummy in school just a week ago, putting my hand on a live mother's abdomen for the first time was mind-blowing.

Dr Stewart slowly guided my hands over the mother's abdomen, steadying it on one side and feeling it with the other. Finding the baby's back, limbs, and firm round head was exhilarating. Best of all was listening to the heartbeat through a Pinard horn, a funnel-shaped instrument used like a stethoscope. I was so pleased with myself. By the end of the day, I was allowed to use an electronic heartbeat monitor called a Sonicade. Seeing the mother's face light up and listening to her baby's heartbeat was a pleasure. The doctors at the hospitals attended all the high-risk and first-time pregnancies -- called primigravida --. Only women with a previous normal delivery participated in the midwife's clinic. Doctors were called when an abnormality was found. Lee and I always had much to exchange at each day's end.

Shopping

Food shopping proved to be a challenge. Britain in the 1980s was not very cosmopolitan where food was concerned. There were very few Asian groceries on the shelves of the local supermarket. The Malaysian midwives took me under their wing and showed me where to shop for Asian groceries in

Soho, Chinatown. The cafeteria in the hospital served stodgy meat and three vegetables. I was not too fond of overcooked grey Brussels sprouts and cabbage, but I loved the English desserts: Spotted Dick and Apple Pie were favourites, extra lashings of custard, please! A weekly open market in the town centre became my favourite shopping venue. My shopping sprees were on sightseeing days. Once again, I toured the tourist staples: Piccadilly Circus, Buckingham Palace, and the Tower of London.

There were so many other places and shops to discover. It was fun to go in a group. We laughed and exclaimed over price tags, sought cheap places to eat and despaired of finding clothing in the correct size. Oxford Street boasted the posh Selfridges and John Lewis. Then there was Harrod's and Fortnum and Mason's. I fell in love with Liberty of London with its exquisite British fabric. In London, I never failed to stop for dress fabric and always left with a bag full of materials. Laura Ashley's, a beautiful British dress and housewares store, where I bought clothes that fit, but I only ever could afford to shop there during a sale. We often looked at things that only the wealthy would buy. Sometimes we returned home with something small that fitted our budget, such as the house brand of speciality food items. Selfridges Salt Beef Sandwich was a favourite of mine. The cafeteria on the top floor of John Lewis had a beautifully presented delicious spread for a meal.

Everyone knew I was on shift when they caught the scent of White Lily by Bronnley. I bought my signature perfume from John Lewis. I could not go past Marks and Spencer, though I primarily frequented the outlet in my local shopping centre. To satiate my Asian appetite, I ended my foray in Chinatown, feasting on *yum cha* or roast duck. I kept a sharp eye on my pennies until my wages were adjusted. Upon noting that I had ten years of nursing experience, the director of midwifery arranged for salaries and back pay adjustments. My bank balance now looked very respectable, and life was much easier after that pay rise.

Postnatal Experience

"Oh, will these babies ever stop!" My colleague groaned.

"I think they are in cahoots with each other. As soon as one finished wailing, the other started," I replied.

It was 3.00 am in the middle of a night shift. Mothers stayed in the hospital for ten days after delivery. For the first three or four nights, their babies were sent to the nursery overnight to be looked after by the staff, giving them a break after labour. Some nights, the nursery had over ten newborns. There were two postnatal wards in the hospital. Each ward had their nurseries with Nightingale-style rooms of either four or six beds for the uncomplicated cases. On the other side were single rooms for complex cases. Staff who were having their babies would also recover here. It was a small privilege to be part of the unit. During the day, mothers who recovered from a Caesarean section or complicated delivery were moved to the Nightingale wards. Beds in the postnatal wards are constantly changed to cope with patient load. The day was full of helping mothers to breastfeed. We also taught them baby care: how to bathe, change the nappies and dress their precious little bundles of joy. Students in the postnatal ward did most of the baby and postnatal checks. My books were slowly filling up, and my skills were improving.

Christmas

"The Christmas cot will have to be decorated. So will the dining room," announced Sister.

"Can I help?" I asked.

"Yes, just follow nursing aide Mrs Jones; she'll tell you what to do," said Sister, glad to have a volunteer.

Almost six months into my training, I began to feel homesick. It was my first Christmas away from my family.

There was no communication from Sam and my family. I had visited him in London at the hotel he stayed in whenever he came in on a flight, but we had no contact otherwise. My exam grades had suffered a little, and my tutors wondered why. When I told them I was homesick, as this was the first time I was separated from my family, I received tactful counselling. Ten years of previous working experience did make a difference. My strength was in practical procedures, which came very naturally to me. The theory took more effort, but I hit the books hard, and my grades soon improved.

Mrs Jones and I decorated the Christmas cot, a wicker basket placed on a stand with a lace skirt and canopy. We then decorated the dining room, and tables were set up for Christmas lunch. I was on an evening shift and returned to work the following morning on Christmas Day. I had offered to work the morning shift to fight the blues of being away from home during the festive season. I could imagine the family homes being scrubbed clean and decorated, everyone gathering to go to midnight mass and the parties after. When we finally could afford it, Mum would pour a shot of sherry and cut the Christmas cake when we returned from midnight mass. That was the only time everybody, no matter how young, had a small glass of alcohol. Christmas morning was busy. Mothers who could go home were always anxious to be out the door and return to their families with their bundle of joy. Their discharge was expedited. All the postnatal and baby checks had to be completed before lunch. Then the beds were made, and the ward was cleaned up. Visiting hours would be longer on this one day of the year, from lunch till 8.00 pm, to make the day as happy as possible for the mothers staying behind. A special Christmas meal was served at lunchtime. A consultant obstetrician and his family would serve the mothers and staff lunch. It was the only time we saw him in a non-surgical apron, carving knife and fork in hand. His wife and children served the meal. The guest of honour was the mother with her Christmas baby in the Christmas bassinet.

I remember Christmas Eve; my mother took me to visit my Grandmother, Aunt and Uncle. Aunt was stuffing a huge turkey. I was about seven years old and stood no higher than the kitchen benches my aunt was working on. Grandmother and Uncle were in the living room. Young though I was, I could sense the tension in the air. They spoke in Tamil, and I understood enough of the language to know that Mother was asking them for money to buy food. They refused her. My mother cried all the way home. That Christmas, we had nothing to eat. The hard times had already begun for us.

After my shift, I returned to the nurses' campus and had a lovely evening with the rest of my Malaysian friends. Those who had not worked that day had prepared the evening meal. As I climbed into bed that night, I wondered what my family would be doing. Christmas Day would already be over for them. I almost smelled the delicious fragrance of chicken biryani and all the trimmings.

New life
"Jane, take a deep breath, hold it and use it to push as hard as you can and as long as you can when your next contraction comes," Senior Midwife Dot instructed.

The atmosphere in the birthing suite was charged with emotion and expectation. I had been with Jane since her labour started some four hours ago. First-time mother-to-be Jane had been working hard to bring her baby into the world. Supported by her doting spouse, Ron and Dot, I was about to perform my first delivery. Dot stood next to me and guided my hands, controlling the birth of the baby's head.

"Push, push, push, that's great, Jane. Let it go. Now take another breath and push. You're doing so well. We can see the baby's head. It shouldn't be long now," Dot instructed.

Dot was now covering my hands with hers, and I was astonished by the pressure she placed on the baby's head to control it. With two more pushes, the head was born. The body soon followed, and the baby cried its first cry. Jane was smiling and in tears simultaneously, so happy to meet her new baby. Also in tears was Ron, who was kissing Jane's forehead.

"It's a girl! Congratulations, Jane and Ron," Dot said and placed Baby in Jane's arms to keep her warm. Jane kissed her baby's head and smiled, not realising she now had blood on her nose and cheeks! "Now, here comes the placenta," Dot announced. The placenta plopped loudly into the kidney dish. With all the necessary checks done, we made Jane comfortable and left her to clean our trolley and complete our notes. It also gave Jane and Ron some precious moments with their newborn.

"And you did well, too, Lilly," Dot said.

"Thank you, Dot. My heart was in my throat during the birth. I almost forgot to breathe myself!" I replied.

"Lilly, those feelings are all normal. By the time you get to your twentieth, you'll sail right through," Dot reassured me.

After the shift, Lee and I talked about our day's experiences. Lee was assigned to the postnatal ward and had completed her birthing posting. As a fellow student, Lee was a great source of support to me.

Birthing Suite

Working on the birthing suite was an eye-opening experience. The unit was midwife-led. Whilst there was a full complement of obstetric specialists consisting of consultants, registrars, and senior house officers, the midwife cared for all normal pregnancies, labours, births and postnatal mothers. The obstetric team was called upon only when birth became complicated. Doctors did not enter a labouring mother's room unless asked to. I observed my seniors running in response to a bell activated in a patient's room. The combined effort of multiple midwives working together like a well-oiled machine to get the mother to the operating theatre as quickly as possible was a sight to behold.

Colour codes were used to determine the urgency of cases. Green for a planned Caesarean section or one that could wait, yellow for one that could wait till the patient in the operating room was done, and red for immediate attention usually meant that the next general case was pushed back. All complicated labours and births needed extra staff, and a doctor and nurse from the special care baby unit attended the birth. The heavy scent of amniotic fluid permeated the entire ward. Was I to be led blindfolded into the unit, I would know exactly where I was. When a bell rang from a room summoning another midwife to attend a birth, all ears were pricked for a baby's cry. We knew then that all was well. There were also occasions marked with grief as we did lose babies. Staff would be restrained in how we spoke or behaved, conscious of the events unfolding in a room and helping to move the parents into a particular set of rooms away from crying babies. These mothers were discharged into the care of community midwives as soon as possible.

There was the constant cleaning of rooms and replenishing of equipment. We cleaned as soon as possible because the next labouring woman would be waiting for a bed. I got used to drinking cold tea; drinks left on desks were never cleared away as we knew the midwife would return to their cuppa. We cleared our cups at the end of our shifts. There were also quiet times when we could debrief and socialise. While working in the birthing suite, I realised how much power a midwife had in autonomous practice in England. I had never experienced that level of autonomy in Singapore. The feeling was a confidence booster for me. The Royal College of Obstetrics and Gynaecology worked closely with the Royal College of Midwives, setting strict standards in the framework of care by midwives.

Special Care Baby Unit

The special care baby unit was an extraordinary place. Premature or sick babies were nursed here, sometimes for months. They were discharged only when they passed their predicted full-term date of birth and had met all the stringent criteria to go home and be cared for by their mother. They would have spent some time in the mother-and-baby room, where the mother would care for her baby with limited or no support from the staff.

"She's listening to you. Every time you say something, she turns her head towards you, Lilly," a mother said as she watched me tend to her baby in the incubator.

I nursed her baby every day for over a week. This process was known as the continuity of care. It allowed student midwives to witness the progress of a baby's health and learn from it. But it was more than that for me. More than anywhere in the unit, the special care baby unit was where I was constantly reminded of the loss of my baby. Mulling over it often made me depressed. I had to come to terms with the loss and attendant heartache. I trained myself to concentrate on the job and care for the babies I was assigned as if they were my own. In the intensive care room, tiny newborns, small enough to hold in an adult's hand, fought for their lives. The room was a hive of activity, alive with the constant beep of multiple tubes and monitors attached to these tiny patients. One midwife to one infant never left a baby's cot without another midwife to keep an eye on them. As the babies progressed in health and weight, they would be transferred to the growing rooms and then the mother-and-baby room before discharge. Parents could visit as long as they pleased because these babies stayed in the unit for long periods, sometimes months. Though mothers were discharged and parents went back to work, they came in to feed their babies, attend to their baths and love and cuddle them. Parents were asked to step outside when medical procedures were carried out. Medical staff had to work fast to save a little life. There was always the knowledge that if their baby took a step backwards, they could deteriorate rapidly. I was sorry to leave the unit for my next posting: I missed those gutsy little human beings.

Antenatal Ward

"Morning, Jody. May I do your daily monitoring?" I asked the young mother-to-be in the antenatal ward.

With her consent, I placed the external electrodes on her abdomen after palpating her baby's position. Observations of blood pressure, pulse and temperature completed the morning routine. Then it was on to the next mother-to-be. What a difference from the special care baby unit! Pregnant women with early labour, antenatal bleeding, premature labour and raised blood pressure came here. The only monitor here was the cardiotocograph machine (CTG). The noise it emitted often made the mothers sit up with wide eyes the first time they heard it. It is because the foetal heart beats 110 to 160 times per minute and sounds like a horse galloping wildly! Monitoring the foetal heart and maternal observations was the bulk of the day's work. Often done twice a day or more, and sometimes continuously if there were foetal or maternal well-being concerns or suspected commencement of early labour. The CTG also picked up a mother's contractions. Induction of labour – when labour was artificially started – also occurred in the antenatal ward. The night shift was almost a pleasure working, as most mothers slept, and there were no babies to nurse. Visitors were restricted to regular visiting hours unless a mother was unwell. Then, only the baby's father could visit and stay with her. She would be moved to a single room attached to the Nightingale ward to facilitate this. Sometimes a mother with early ruptured membranes or bleeding stayed in the ward for weeks or months. I talked to them when the ward was not busy to keep them company. It was an excellent opportunity to get to know them.

Community Placement

On Community placement, I was housed in another hospital close to the turf of the community midwife to whom I was assigned. Pat was a big, burly woman with a voice to match. When she spoke, she thundered. Pat picked me up daily from the front of the nurse's accommodation at the start of our shift. We visited mothers and babies in their homes, checking their progress postnatally. We also monitored women at their GP's surgery and followed up on reports of raised blood pressure in their homes. Once a week, we conducted midwife-led antenatal clinics and parent education classes at the local health clinic. Regular on-call shifts for the birthing unit at the main hospital kept the necessary hours for continuing practice current and in line with registration standards.

The phone at the end of the corridor rang out. I could hear someone run to pick it up. I was in the shower. I was on call and rather unwisely decided to wash my thick, long, waist-length hair. I imagined I could dry it in time for the call-out if needed. Boy, was I wrong?

"Lilly, your midwife is coming for you in ten minutes. You've been called to birthing. One of your ladies is in labour," my colleague called through the bathroom door.

Bother! I still had shampoo in my hair. Quickly washing off the lather, I finished my shower and returned to my room. I towel-dried my hair, arranged it whilst still wet into a bun, and stuck my hat on. Half an hour had passed since CM Pat dropped me off after work. I guess that's what it means to be "on-call".

"You took long enough, Lilly." Pat scolded me when I ran to her car and jumped in. "Any longer, and we might miss the birth."

"Sorry, Pat. I was in the shower when you rang," I replied, feeling a trickle of water run down the back of my neck. It was going to be one damp hair night, I thought to myself. But I was well rewarded for my discomfort. That night, I had my first community hospital delivery with the help of Pat. She was the only midwife to conduct her deliveries, with the mother lying on her left side, the left lateral delivery. The experience with Pat gave me the material I needed for a case study for my course: a critique of women's positions in labour. My hair was partially dried when I got home in the wee hours of the morning. I had forgotten how uncomfortable I had felt under my hat. I was so tired that I did not bother using the hairdryer and went to bed with damp hair. My experience with Pat had a significant impact on my practice. I also became one of the few midwives practising the left lateral birth position.

Being in a different area allowed me to see another part of the hospital's catchment. With no driver's license, I relied on my two feet and public transport to get about. This hospital was closer to the London Underground line, making getting into London relatively easy. Whenever I had a day off, I would visit London to discover marketplaces, museums and other places of interest. My favourite was the Victoria and Albert Museum and Covent Garden markets. I was transferred back to the main hospital after completing my community posting.

Growing into myself

Campus living proved to be an enjoyable experience. Lee and I were the only Asian students in our batch; the eight other students were mainly Irish or English. I had a great time with all of them. The mixture made life easier for me. I felt at peace though I missed my family and Sam. I became surer of myself and more confident about my identity. My self-worth and self-regard grew. I was now not just my mother's daughter or Sam's wife. I had a separate identity, independent of the two most important people and their influence over my life. I did not depend on Sam or anyone else. Sam did not support me financially. I met him at his hotel whenever he flew into London. If I could not meet him due to work, he would come to the campus bringing groceries I could not get in England, things I needed from home and family news.

Final Exams

Eighteen months quickly flew by; final exams loomed on the horizon. We were in a frenzy to get our practical books filled. We had to hand them to the tutors prior, or we would not be allowed to sit for the exams. There was a written and an oral exam or *viva*. The *viva* was held at the Royal College of Midwifery in London. We all travelled to London for the *viva* after the written exams. It was a sad journey into London. We were preoccupied with our thoughts about what the examiners would ask us. One known fact was that we would have to demonstrate the birth process with a doll and pelvis model. When I entered the examination room, my mind turned to another set of exams from when I was twelve years old: the walk to and from school with Peng and the English language oral exam. Here I was taking another oral exam, this time in another country. The examiner's questions ranged from anatomy and physiology to care of the pregnant mother. I had to demonstrate the process for normal birth. My heart was thumping madly when I finally finished and left the room. We waited for everyone to complete their turn before heading back together.

"Let's celebrate tonight. How would you like an Indian meal in our town?" An Irish accent called out. The suggestion met with resounding approval. As it was just getting to half past five by the time we reached our town, we went straight to the restaurant.

"Lee, the wine and food taste bad," I whispered into her ear.

"I should have warned you the Irish girls always have cheap red wine with their food," Lee whispered.

It became clear that cheap red wine did not marry well with Indian food. The wine tasted terrible, and it made the food taste awful. But the Irish girls enjoyed their meal, but Lee and I declined further top-ups! A lively group walked back to the nurses' campus that night.

"Why don't you go to the home office and speak to them about your work permit?" One of the Malaysian midwives advised. It had been two months since I received my results. I passed my exams. I had to fulfil my contract obligation to work at the same hospital for a year as a qualified midwife before returning to Singapore. I could have returned to Singapore to wait it out, but I was afraid I might not be granted re-entry into England. Taking heed of the advice, I left early to join the extended lines of people waiting at the home office. But the wait paid off when my passport was stamped with a work permit. I was relieved and gratified.

New job

With a deep sense of pride and accomplishment, I walked to work wearing my new uniform and hat; my midwife badge from the Royal College of Midwives was pinned proudly to my lapel. Posting was to all the different areas of the unit on a six-monthly rotation. Shift work continued. As the contract year ended, I was surprised to receive a letter from the home office stating that I would be granted permanent residence if I continued to stay and worked for another three years.

"Take the opportunity, Lilly," Sam said when I told him on the phone. "I'll come and join you in England."

I had become used to being independent in England and did not think I could return to living in Singapore again. I continued to live on campus. When I was due for annual leave, I asked Sam to send me an air ticket to return home. He agreed.

As the spouse of an airline employee, I was entitled to staff fare rates: of S$100 for a return ticket.

Home

Back in Singapore, I walked into the flat Sam and I had bought to find that he had turned it into a gambling den. Now, he and his friends could play cards all hours of the day without disturbing anyone. The flat was unoccupied. Sam had moved back in with his mother, enjoying the convenience of the family maid to launder his clothes and a mother to cook his meals. He was living in the same room he had occupied as a boy. Our flat was dusty, and countless beer bottles lined the dining table! I cleaned up the flat and wondered what I was doing there. It just did not feel like home anymore. Sam was still on a flight, and I was yet to meet him.

"We had to do it. We couldn't live with Mum anymore!" My eldest brother said. We've been waiting for you to return, Lilly, to discuss this."

My mother, brothers and sisters had gathered at my eldest brother's house. His wife was also present. Trouble was brewing between my mother and my brother's wife. They complained that my mother was difficult to live with and had kicked her out by changing the front door lock when my mother had gone to spend a few days with Grandma. She came home to find that she could not enter the flat. The flat the family had been allocated less than a decade ago, where the application forms state that she is the head of the household. It was the only way my then-single brother could have purchased the flat. She had done it to enable him to do so, secure in the belief that he would care for her as she aged. Now that he was married, elder brother wanted it for himself and his wife. There had been no negotiating.

"What did you do, Mum?" I asked her in the presence of everyone.

Mum just looked at me and wept. But I had my suspicions. For as long as I remember, Mum, like a typical, traditional Indian mother, had declared, "My eldest son will look after me till I die." To that end, he had received preferential care. When it was his birthday, he had his favourite meal at the expense of the rest of us. Mum would steam an entire pomfret, an expensive, delicate white fish, just for him. I would watch, yearning for a morsel as he ate it with tomato sauce. The rest of the family had something simple. When he did not do well in his Year 10 exams, she sent him back to school to repeat the year and the exams, somehow finding the money to finance it all. In contrast, I had to go to work the Monday after I had sat for my last exam paper because she said "too stupid" for further schooling.

When my brother wanted a flat, we all rallied around him to form his application-required family unit. When he wanted a wife, she found him one by contracting the services of a matchmaker. Throughout his life, Eldest Brother had had the best she could give, often at a high cost to the rest of us, despite Mum's minimal resources. And now he had thrown her out of her home, the ungrateful wretch. The whole thing was so outrageously wrong and unjust it took my breath away. It made me seethe with such rage that I could barely find the words to articulate my thoughts. I also felt helpless. Mum should be living a life of ease after all these years of hardship. She had done everything she could to raise us to live productive lives and succeeded. We were all gainfully employed, earning more than decent wages. Having lived with my in-laws, I was not unsympathetic to my sister-in-law. I could see that Mum could be hard to live with. However, I could not take Mum in as coming home to Singapore was not something I had planned.

"Come live with me, Mum," my eldest sister invited.

That settled the issue. Before leaving to return to England, I visited my mother. She was heartbroken by what she regarded as her son's betrayal. She was pretty depressed. Having to move in with her daughter and son-in-law added insult to injury. It was like salt in her wounds as it flew in the face of tradition. Mum would likely have imagined the scathing disdain of the rest of the family and her further loss of face as the story made the rounds. "Come back to Singapore. I want to live with you. Things are not good here either. Your brother-in-law beats your sister," she wept, "and he tells me daily to find somewhere else to live."

"What have I done to deserve this." She said between sobs, gasping for breath. She looked at me with eyes full of hurt and despair. I was wracked with guilt at having to leave her like that. I could only hug her hard.

Couple Time

Sam had come home for a few days between flights, and we spent time together. "You hypocrite!" he called me when I told him casually that some Irish girls and I would meet for Bible study on campus. I was shocked at his reaction. Coming from a devout Catholic family had done nothing for his attitude toward me. Later, at a party, he pointed out the wife of one of his friends to me and said, "Look at her, she looks beautiful, and she's a lawyer. You, you're ugly!"

His words cut me to the quick. All I had ever wanted was to be his wife. I had done my best to support him, standing by him loyally even though he was both an alcoholic and a gambler. He seemed to think he had a right to demand everything of me and not give anything in return.

"Come with me to town. I need to go to the money changers to get some currency for the next flight," Sam commanded, so we headed downtown.

Prior arrangements had been made for when we arrived as his colleagues were waiting for him. The service was frequented by most of the cabin crew. I noticed two Chinese women, presumably fellow flight attendants, hanging onto Sam and talking too familiarly with him. One, in particular, was just about plastered to him even though I, his wife, was right there with him and in full view. Women in Singapore did not generally conduct themselves in this brazen manner – indeed, no decent, self-respecting woman I knew did. Her effortless proprietary style spoke volumes of something much more intimate than collegial camaraderie. Sam lapped it all up, not attempting to pull himself away from either of the women. I felt excluded, disrespected and angry. However, I held my peace. "Let him sow his wild oats; perhaps it might make him more of a man," I told myself. I noticed that Sam's attitude towards me had changed. He had become distant and, at times, was aggressive, insulting and obnoxious.

"Ha! You'll never get it," he scoffed at me when I informed him that I was taking driving lessons as I wanted to work as a community midwife. "My younger sister will pass her driving test before you!"

I left Singapore to return to England and work, feeling gutted.

Holidays alone

Now fully qualified, I could return to Singapore or move anywhere I pleased. The world was my oyster! Disappointed with my marriage, I decided to treat myself to holidays just in case the time I had left in England ended. I booked bus tours to see parts of England during the long breaks, travelling to Edinburgh in Scotland. There I experienced a Scottish evening of traditional song and dance with a meal that included their famed Haggis. At Windermere, I roamed over parts of some 4,000 acres of the Lake District that Beatrix Potter had purchased and donated to the National Trust as an act of conservation. A visit to her home was the highlight of the trip. From there, I took a boat trip across Lake Windermere to tour William Wordsworth's home. I heard one of his poems read in front of his fireplace. I visited Bronte country in the southwest of England, Torquay and Torbay, and the Isle of White. I could not pass up a visit to Shakespeare's home in Stratford-on-Avon. It was beautiful to see where the man had lived after studying and staging his plays at school. Then I took a tour of Europe. It was my biggie, my gift to myself to celebrate all that I had achieved by myself.

I visited Paris and viewed Leonardo da Vinci's *Mona Lisa* at the Louvre. In Switzerland, I rode the cable car to the top of Mount Titlis, where I could only afford a glass of milk for lunch! Then it was on to Lucerne to view the Kapellbrücke, a covered heritage wooden footbridge spanning the River Reuss, before going to Liechtenstein. The next stop was Monaco, the playground of the rich and famous. Here, I was self-conscious due to my poor choice of clothing: a tracksuit. I was travelling with a small borrowed backpack. In Italy, I visited Venice and rode in a gondola. Rome's highlight was visiting the Vatican City and the Sistine Chapel. Like a good Catholic, I waited with thousands of people to see the Pope on his balcony and receive the Papal Blessing. Florence and Pisa were on the list as well. The leaning tower of Pisa was an enjoyable outing with walks up and down the tower.

King Richard

"Why are you cooking for him? I would have given him a cup of coffee and a biscuit and sent him on his way!" My Irish flatmate scolded me.

"It is done in my culture to offer a meal when friends or relatives visit," I explained.

Richard was Sam's cousin, who had come to England to study for a degree. Sam had told him to visit me, and he had accepted his offer, and I had not been consulted. Like a good Indian wife, I entertained him with a home-cooked curry that took me a while to produce, considering the lack of ingredients and implements needed. Richard enjoyed his meal. I felt uncomfortable being alone with him for the first time. When he visited Singapore, there were always other family members at home.

"I'll bring my friends the next time I visit you," he presumed. I felt rage rise in me.

"I'm sorry, but you can't. These are female nurses' quarters. I have flatmates who could put in a complaint against me for entertaining men in our flat. We are not permitted to entertain groups of men," I replied frostily.

The man's audacity, to presume that he could turn up with his mates in tow for me to feed and wash up after them. He must have been offended by my brush-off, for I never heard from him again. I had not come to England to skivvy for the likes of him.

Death

Mum wrote letters to me after I returned to England. She informed me of her continued difficulties and always ended her letters imploring me to return to Singapore. I sent her money and gifts to try and soothe her, putting off telling her the truth about my plans for myself. As the end of my contractual obligation to work in England drew close, the Home Office offered me permanent residence. I had no choice, but to inform Mum I did not plan to return. Two months later, my sister rang me and said Mum had passed away. I had known that her health was deteriorating due to diabetes which she had been diagnosed with nearly 20 years prior. As a medical professional, I had seen the signs of the advanced disease progressing. I knew I would lose her in due course, probably sooner rather than later, but this was too soon, far too soon. I went home for her funeral. During the funeral service, one of my sisters nudged me. "Look who's at the back of the Church!" she whispered.

I had leaned into her in my grief and wondered what had brought this on. I turned to look and was shocked when I saw who it was. The priest was hunched in the very last pew of the church. He looked broken and sad, a far cry from the self-assured, confident man I remembered. He was the priest who had summarily dismissed Mum's request for additional food rations when she'd asked for help all those years ago. In the days that followed, my family filled me in. He had been named as a witness in a murder trial. The prosecution alleged that the accused had confessed to the crime to the priest in the confessional. In the witness box, he had steadfastly refused to break the sacramental seal of the confession and did not disclose anything the accused had told him. Rumours had it that the authorities had continued to pressure him and his archdiocese superiors to divulge the fateful exchange's contents. His mental health began to suffer, and he eventually suffered a breakdown leading to his removal from the position of a parish priest. The accused and his accomplices were eventually sentenced and sent to the gallows. I wondered if he remembered what he had said and done to my mother all those years ago. Perhaps God had played his hand here! I felt vindicated for my mother and family. Mum's cremation was followed by going through her personal effects, deciding what we would keep and how to distribute it fairly amongst the family. This task fell to Elder Sister and me.

"A lot of her drugs are missing, Lilly!" Elder Sister said, "There should be a lot more here. I used to give them to her!"

We both looked at each other and wondered the same thing. Did Mum take an overdose of drugs? It seemed too much of a coincidence that she would die so close to our father's death anniversary though it was in keeping with her sentimental character. Mum was hurt by a life that had cheated her of the better times that she should have had. She was only fifty and had begun monthly contributions to a funeral fund years before. Mum often said that we would not have to worry about the cost of her funeral and that she felt a burden to us. Has she been trying to tell us that she was disappointed with us for our lack of care for her when she had given us her whole life?

My thoughts tightened into a knot of guilt in my stomach. So much for the Indian tradition of caring for their elders. The much-vaunted filial piety of our political leaders always reminded us of the hallmark of Asian culture. Let's not forget the Christian injunction to look after the widows and their orphans by extension.

"She looked like her last hope had gone, Lilly. Mum cried and was very quiet after I read your letter to her. It was as if the life had suddenly been drained out of her," said Elder Sister.

She was referring to the letter in which I had finally told Mum I was not returning to Singapore. Her eyesight was failing due to her diabetic condition, and she struggled to read anything, especially if it was handwritten. Elder Sister noticed that Mum had become withdrawn after that letter and even stopped engaging with her two little granddaughters. The family's live-in maid had found her in her bed on the morning of her death. The death certificate stated "Advanced Diabetes" as the cause of death, adding "No autopsy necessary." Given her diagnosis and the advanced stage of the disease, the Doctor did not find her passing suspicious.

Praise

"You will have to be in charge today and over the next few days, Lilly. Sister has called in sick for the rest of the week," the nurse on the previous shift told me as she did her hand-over briefing that morning. I was nervous but refused to be daunted. It was the first time I would be in charge of a ward. As a junior midwife, I had never been in charge of a postnatal ward though I had done so many times in a decade of general nursing in Singapore. With no time to spare and a ward full of patients to care for, I got on with it, delegated the tasks for the day, and accompanied the doctors on ward rounds. Then I informed the staff of changes in the care of patients, scheduled meal breaks and managed the discharges, along with anything else that came up. It was exhausting yet rewarding, and I was happy to hand over the ward to the next shift. I was in charge for the rest of the week and delighted when my days off arrived but pleased with my achievement.

"Hello, Lilly," The director of midwifery greeted me as I walked along a unit corridor sometime later.

"Hello, Mrs Stevenson," I replied.

"Lilly, it had not gone unnoticed that you managed the postnatal ward at a drop of a hat when the in-charge had been taken ill for a week. You did very well. I do appreciate your efforts."

"Thank you, Mrs Stevenson, it was a good experience for me, and I enjoyed the challenge," I replied, gratified by the compliments.

"You have a good day, Lilly. I will look forward to hearing more about you in the future," she said, continuing down the corridor. I felt on top of the world. It was good to be noticed and appreciated!

Homeowner
"I'll have the flat packed up and our things shipped to you in a container," Sam explained over the phone.

With the Home Office's offer of permanent residence, my spouse could also live and work in England. We sold our flat in Singapore and moved our home to England. I bought a little three-bedroom house within walking distance of the hospital. When the container arrived with our shipment, fitting everything into our home was challenging as the flat had been more extensive.

Thus began a new chapter for me, ending a four-year stay at the nurses' campus. Soon after I passed my driving test and got my licence, my interest in community midwifery grew, and I approached management for a posting. I was awarded a trial period of three months under the supervision of two very senior community midwives to see if I was suitable for the position.

Community Midwifery

As a community midwife (CM), I was allocated mothers to visit their homes on my own and manage their care independently. In addition to all the GP surgeries in our assigned area, CMs worked out of community health centres, conducting midwife-led antenatal clinics and parent education classes. I ran some of these on my own. My ability to manage time and decision-making skills were crucial to being awarded a permanent position.

Initially nervous, I soon settled into the job. We held antenatal clinics with the GPs; newly confirmed pregnant women were referred to consultants at the hospital. I learnt to book non-high-risk mothers at the local community health centre. Soon, I was asked to attend antenatal clinics at the GP's surgery independently. I was very proud of my job. While I was aware of the increased accountability and my ethical and legal responsibilities, I found the autonomy exhilarating. Seeing mothers progress in their environment differed vastly from caring in the hospital. Home visits were my pride and joy. A first-time mother stayed in the hospital for at least four days. For following births, she could return home within four hours of delivery if all was normal. We visited them daily for the first ten days, with ad hoc days off when they progressed well. After this, we saw them twice or thrice until twenty-eight days after the birth. At this point, they were handed over to their GP. The number of visits increased in the event of abnormal development in the mother or baby. Sometimes they would have to be re-admitted to the hospital. CMs could refer the mother or baby to the hospital for care independently of her GP, who would be informed.

Homebirth

One morning I was asked to attend a home birth and was given the mother's address and advised to check that my homebirth kit was in good order before setting out. I started with anxiety as I had only witnessed one home birth before. One of the senior midwives would join me as the birth was imminent. When I arrived at Ann's home, her husband, Kevin, greeted me at the door and led me to their birthing room. I found Ann sitting on a large exercise ball, moving her hips to and fro as she breathed through a contraction. It was Ann's first birth. I waited till the contraction was over before I introduced myself and performed observations of blood pressure, pulse, temperature and foetal heart rate, followed by a vaginal examination. I was satisfied that Ann was in active labour, dilated at 4 cm. All was well.

"Have you got your case notes, Ann?" I asked, and Kevin pointed to a side table where everything was placed.

I reviewed the notes and found that all was well with her pregnancy. She had been put through a vigorous check by the consultant and midwifery team to ensure her case would be low risk. I checked all the equipment delivered to her home and then settled down to wait for the labour to progress. Looking around the room, I found all the furniture removed, leaving only a thick single-size mattress covered with soft plastic, as was the carpet. Kevin brought us each a cup of tea and some biscuits. We all sat on the floor, making small talk and coaching and encouraging Ann as her contractions continued. Kevin often applied hot packs to her back as he had been taught in parent education classes. Ann moved about the room, sometimes sitting on the ball, then walking, squatting, taking a couple of showers, and bathing to help with the pain. Kevin supported her, and I tried not to be intrusive as this was a special time for them. I felt like I was watching a very private dance. Finally, after five hours, I performed another vaginal examination to find that she had dilated to 8 cm, and the baby was lying relatively low in the birth canal. It was time to get reinforcements in. I rang my senior midwife and informed her of Ann's progress. She assured me and said she would come over as soon as the clinic was over at the end of the day.

"Don't forget to alert birthing in case we need the flying squad, Lilly," she reminded me.

I made the phone calls and hoped we would not need emergency services, especially the flying squad. The obstetric flying squad comprises an obstetric register, a paediatrician and a nurse from the special bare baby unit. They would come out in the ambulance with the paramedics to transfer the mother and baby to the hospital for continued care. My senior midwife arrived with a sandwich for me. I was grateful for this as I was famished. Ann had progressed and was now fully dilated. She delivered her seven-pound baby in a textbook birth just a few minutes past six o'clock. When all the necessary checks were done, we left Ann breastfeeding her baby, whom she called Annette. Mother and baby were sitting on the mattress with Kevin. Both were chuffed with their new addition and how their home birth had gone. I returned to the hospital with the used equipment and entered Ann's delivery into the birth register. I was happy that things had gone so well for her. Home births would be cancelled any time an abnormality set in during pregnancy, during labour or if she was a week or more overdue. I got home at eight in the evening and enjoyed a restful evening. I would be seeing Ann and Annette again the following morning.

After my three-month trial as a community midwife, I returned to hospital work to await my evaluation. It was highly positive, and it made my day. I took on additional skills to ensure that I could work independently. About a year later, I successfully applied for a promotion to midwifery sister, clinical nurse specialist position. This was another promotion which would have been unachievable had I stayed in Singapore.

My next career move was applying for a community midwife post. I had the qualifications and necessary skills for this position with parent education and preceptor certificates. I was given a relief position to fill in when another CM went on maternity leave. I was issued a hospital car and took over her patient load. I worked in this position for a year, enjoying the autonomy. I was so sorry to leave that I was reluctant to attend the farewell lunch the staff held for me on my last day. The following week, I returned to the hospital but only for a short time. A permanent community position became available, and I gladly accepted the offer.

A very special cake

"Can you make one for her farewell lunch?" My Malaysian colleague asked me.

I have been baking cakes and decorating them for some years as a hobby. I made a few cakes for my friends, who received them well. This one would be for a senior community midwife who was retiring.

"All right, I'll do it," I agreed.

The slab Madeira cake was iced in the colours of the Royal College of Midwives: royal blue and yellow. I had piped the college's logo, her name and the dates of service on it and delivered it to my colleague early in the morning before starting my rounds. The room was crowded by the time I got there at noon for lunch

"This cake is beautiful, Lilly. Thank you. You've put so much effort into it. I must ensure I have a photo of it before we cut it. Almost a shame to destroy it. You're an artist!" Sally, the retiring CM, said.

"Sally, a cake is designed to be eaten," I laughed, pleased with her delight in my efforts. "I hope it tastes as good as it looks!"

"Have you spoken to Betty yet?" Sally asked. "She is envious of your uniform," she said, laughing. Sally was referring to the uniform which came with my promotion to midwifery sister.

"Yes, I've had a brief word with her," I replied. Betty and I had trained together. She had married one of Sally's sons. Sally had introduced them to each other while we were all living on campus. As I mingled with other staff, I felt the uncomfortable sensation of someone staring at my back. Turning around, I met the eyes of another of Sally's sons. He was over six feet tall and had dark hair, thinning on top. He sported a close-cropped beard and stark black-rimmed spectacles that made him look like a scholar. He smiled at me. I smiled back at him and then turned again, admonishing myself, "Watch where you put your eyes; you are still a married woman!" I left the party to return to work early as I had some distance to travel and a midwife clinic to conduct. Some weeks later, I received a heartfelt thank you letter from Sally.

Discord
The house Sam and I bought was old and needed much work. After the first winter, I replaced the glass in the old wooden windows with new double-glazed ones. The musty, busy old carpet, rotting wood panelling and outdated kitchen cabinets went out. The kitchen cabinets, which had traversed oceans from Singapore, were installed in their stead. Our fresh new carpets in a solid colour did not compete with the furniture for attention. The tiny old wooden extension at the back of the house made way for a more considerable pine extension that became our entertainment area. These additional costs were added to the mortgage. I paid all the contractors and supplies bills.

"Fuck OFF! Give me the $100 I paid for your flight," Sam raged.

"Don't you speak to me like that!" I spat back at him.

It was almost a year since we bought the house in England. I had asked him about his promise to send me the mortgage payments. I knew he had money because I had seen his credit card statements on his bedroom table in Singapore when I visited a few months earlier. The bills listed exorbitant payments to expensive entertainment establishments worldwide, like the Playboy Club in London and the Golden Nugget casino in Las Vegas, USA.

"I sent it to you. I don't know what you did with it." He claimed.

"You're lying! I am tired of this nonsense. Perhaps we should call it quits. Get a divorce!" I shouted, speaking the dreaded D-word. No one in either of our families had divorced.

"That's fine by me. You can keep the house. I don't want it." He threw it over his shoulder and walked out of the London hotel room, slamming the door. I had gone to visit him at his stopover. Earlier in the day, he had asked me to come to the toilet to look at something. As a nurse, I was immediately concerned and unsuspecting.

"What?" I asked, becoming aware of the smell of a bowel movement.

"Look at my shit!" he said. I looked, thinking there was something wrong with it.

"There's nothing wrong with it," I said.

"Ha, ha, ha. That's all you're good for, looking at my shit!" He hooted.

I felt my blood rush to my head. I flushed the toilet and walked out. The sight of him repulsed me. What had he become? When had he changed? He was still chuckling, thrilled with his little 'accomplishment'. His pilot colleague had told him he'd played the same trick on his wife, who was undoubtedly another long-suffering woman. This man did not have any self-respect, let alone integrity! I should have left him then. But I stayed and stood his abuse many more times. Despite my many professional accolades, I was still naïve, timid and unsophisticated in my personal life. I clung to my marital vows, hoping for the "better" to come after the "worse." Sam's shameless financial irresponsibility, lack of accountability, and remorse left me footing all the bills. I should have been outraged that I was always the one forking out. Instead, I was grateful that my wages were sufficient to cover the costs. They did so by a whisker, leaving me little leftover for luxuries.

Clinical Nurse Specialist

My promotion to midwifery sister and grading as a clinical nurse specialist meant working autonomously in the area where I had been appointed. Eighty women were on my books at various stages of pregnancy and postnatally. I worked with GPs in their surgeries at antenatal clinics. There were two other surgeries in the area that CM did not attend. I negotiated with the practice managers and secured midwife-led clinics for both surgeries, a service that GPs and patients appreciated. At the community health centre, parent education classes were in the hands of health visitors instead of the midwife. I intervened and re-claimed the service. I was mystified that my predecessor had not seen fit to address these service shortfalls. "You girls always bring back your home birth packs with items missing!" the sterilisation department manager growled. After each home birth, the pack used by the midwife was routinely returned to the sterilisation department, where the items would be sanitised and then placed in birth packs again.

"I'm sorry, this is the first I have heard of it, so please don't take it out on me! Rather, let's look for a solution to the problem!" I replied.

The matter was resolved only after an extended series of consultations involving the community midwifery manager and the sterilisation department manager, who doubled as the pharmacy manager. Thus far, almost fifty birthing packs have been lost, costing the service a fortune.

Our first goal was to lose no more packs. Together we nutted out a plan. On being approved for a home birth, the midwife who managed the case filled out a form and sent it to the sterilisation department. She would be issued a birthing pack of instruments and drug packs. The latter contained the drugs required to manage the baby's delivery. The pack would be handed to the birth mother to keep safely at home till her due date or when she went into labour. All CMs were instructed to inform their GPs that they were to use these packs should they get to the home birth before the midwives. After use, the packages were returned to the sterilisation department for reprocessing. While I was no longer harangued when I returned my used packs to the sterilisation department, my efforts were not recognised! The plan did not cost the three departments any more money and, once implemented, ran smoothly.

Rose

"Morning, Mr and Mrs Bates. My name is Lilly. I am your midwife for your delivery today. I'll support you through your preparation till your baby is born," I said by way of introduction.

Elective Caesarean sections were scheduled weekly; a midwife was assigned to handle these cases. I was the midwife assigned for the day.

"Please, call us Jack and Carol," Carol encouraged.

I explained the process to the couple and did the pre-operative surgical preparation required. When the call came for us to proceed to the theatre, I stayed beside her as she lay on her bed. Handing her over to the theatre staff, I asked an orderly to assist Jack in getting gowned for the sterile protocol of operating theatres. When Jack joined me in the theatre corridor, he was dressed in the same green outfit and a cap as all the theatre staff. He had the widest smile, and his eyes sparkled in excitement and anticipation.

"We've waited so long for a baby. Carol lost three other pregnancies before this one. We are calling her Rose as all the scans and tests show that baby is a girl," he told me. Before meeting them, I had read their case notes and noticed the antenatal documentation in the theatre. Rose was indeed a precious baby. Carol was already in a position for the anaesthetist to insert the epidural for pain relief. When completed, she lay on the operating table, and the obstetric team got to work. Jack was seated beside Carol at her head. A barrier was placed between Carol and Jack, and the team. The characteristic hum of an operating theatre ensued. Soft music played in the background to diffuse tension for the patient. I checked the resuscitator and was joined by the paediatrician per protocol for Caesarean birth. Accepting the sterile blanket from the scrub nurse, I waited for my cue: the sound of the suction machine.

"Baby coming!" called the obstetrician as he pulled the baby out.

Everyone at the table went quiet. The obstetrician looked at me while the scrub nurse made room for me to come closer. Baby Rose had gross abnormalities. Her face was perfect, but her arms and legs were like spindles. They were fused to her torso. Thankfully, she cried. I quickly wrapped her up and took her to the paediatrician waiting at the resuscitator. He promptly looked Rose over and instructed me to take her to Carol and Jack because she was crying robustly. I wrapped her up well, exposing only her face, and gave Rose to Carol for a cuddle. I instructed them not to unwrap her so she would stay warm to buy us some time before we broke the news to them. After a few minutes, I asked for Rose and told Jack to head to the special care baby unit for observation -- a normal progression. Here, the paediatrician gently broke the news to Jack. He looked at his precious baby and burst into tears. I could not stay with him as I was required to go to the theatre for the next Caesarean section. A few days later, I met

Carol in the postnatal ward. Baby Rose was behaving like any normal baby, but her abnormalities were so profound that the medical team did not know if she would survive at any given time.

"I'll still love her, Lilly. She is my child," Carol said, epitomising a mother's love for her child.

I could only wish her all the best. If I have but one regret today, it is that I did not continue to keep in touch with Carol and Jack and follow up on the progress of Baby Rose. I perused their notes and found the questions about consanguinity in a box on the booking page. The answer was yes: Carol and Jack were first cousins. Medical knowledge informs us that first-cousin marriages have an increased risk of genetic disorders.

The Bible tells us we should not marry our close relatives because abnormalities are likely. The book of Leviticus states:

> "None of you shall approach any one of his close relatives to uncover nakedness. I am the LORD. You shall not uncover the nakedness of your father, which is the nakedness of your mother; she is your mother. You shall not uncover her nakedness. You shall not uncover the nakedness of your father's wife; it is your father's nakedness. You shall not uncover the nakedness of your sister, your father's daughter or your mother's daughter, whether brought up in the family or in another home. You shall not uncover the nakedness of your son's daughter or of your daughter's daughter, for their nakedness is your own nakedness ..."(Leviticus 18:6-16)

Perhaps that is why Carol had so many miscarriages. The obstetrician had given Carol standard pregnancy drugs to prolong the pregnancy. Had that been a wise intervention? I wondered. Thousands of healthy babies are born in the maternity unit, and some grow into healthy children despite a difficult start. Others don't make it. They are the unforeseen casualties of the maternity unit, especially the birthing unit.

"Why are you not in tears, Lilly?" the sister-in-charge of birthing asked. "Everybody is shaken up by what has happened. Have you not got a heart?" Sister added.

I looked at her, astonished at what she said to me.

"Are you not a Catholic, Sister? Do you not believe God wanted this baby more than its parents? Do you not know that baby is now in heaven where Jesus will look after it for eternity!" I replied to her. She looked at me with wonderment before spinning on her heel and walking away.

Parting

"Lilly, we're all going to Australia!" One of the Malaysian midwives announced.

"Really, how come?' I asked.

"The Australian government is recruiting nurses and midwives to work for them. We have assisted transport, accommodation and a job when we get there," she informed me.

Over the next few years, I waved goodbye to my Malaysian friends as they gradually left England. I was losing the best circle of friends I had ever had. I had come to love them as an extended family. When the last one left, I almost felt abandoned! But life goes on. I hoped Sam was coming over. Perhaps things would improve between us. I settled into a quiet life. Gone were the raucous Asian dinner parties, group trips to London and short holidays. Although two Malaysian midwives were still in town, they were married and had their husbands and children. I still saw them periodically. No matter how hard I tried, I did not have good friends among my Caucasian colleagues. It was just not the same. Outside of work, I was very much on my own. I was used to it, and the years of being a latchkey kid taught me to cope with being alone.

The dress

"You certainly knew what you were doing. You look smashing!" My colleague exclaimed.

She had come over to have tea and seen the dress I had made for Sam's sister's wedding. I had bought the fabric from my favourite fabric store, Liberty of London and sewed it following a paper pattern for a formal mid-length dress. The peach colour complimented my tan skin. I was pleased with the way it had turned out. My skill in sewing had grown by leaps and bounds since I had moved to England. It became my saving grace. Clothing was expensive and rarely fitted well, as I had a petite frame. During an office function, a colleague who saw me in something I'd sewn had exclaimed: "And you made that? Oh, I do hate you!" I often felt my Mum's spirit when I worked sewing. I thought she was guiding me; usually, techniques I had never done before fell into place! Mum had been an exquisite dressmaker.

The wedding

Once again, I found myself on a plane bound for Singapore. This time though, I would not be returning alone. Sam's youngest sister was getting married. Sam would be moving to England as a permanent resident. Sam's mother and youngest sister lived in a new triple-story terrace house built on the land that used to be occupied by the family home. Because the plot of land was large, the developer built four residences. Two of these had been handed to the construction firm as payment for their work. The third was for sale, and the proceeds would be split among family members. I was not informed of this at the time. The development was part of a government campaign to advance the country and raise living standards.

Sam's family gathered for an important meeting days after the wedding. Several hundred guests attended the traditional church wedding and lavish hotel reception, not uncommon by Singapore standards. I wore my dress and was grateful for air conditioning in the humid tropical weather.

"Mother is now technically homeless with the development of the property. We need to give Mother a home and ensure that she is listed as the owner on the deed of this property," Sam's eldest brother said. I spoke about what had happened to my family, explaining how when my father died without a Will, it allowed the sons-in-law to force the sale of the property, causing my family to spiral into poverty.

"I don't want that to happen to Mum, so I strongly recommend that her name be recorded on the deed for this house," I said. A vote was taken, and most of the family agreed. Mother-in-law was soon legally listed as the owner of the home where she currently lived.

There were several farewell parties for Sam and me. When friends and relatives asked what Sam would do in England, he retorted that his wife would keep him! He sold his car, an Alfa Romeo, and I found him sitting at the dinner table, separating the money into little piles.

"What's this?" I asked him.

"Repayments for all the money I owe!" Sam answered.

I watched every dollar disappear till there was none left.

"So, what are you taking to England?" I inquired.

"Nothing Lilly; you will have to support me!" He replied, smiling at me quite arrogantly and expectantly.

Sam had quit his job and had been on annual leave since his sister's wedding. My heart plummeted. I was almost down to the last few pounds every month with no support from him. Now I would have to keep him too.

"Well, you will get a job as soon as you hit the ground in England. It should be no problem as you have permanent resident status because of me, and your airline experience will come in handy!" I declared.

Migration dramas

Immigration officers questioned us separately about our entry into the United Kingdom. Sam became agitated, and I was concerned. I had to prove that he was indeed my legal spouse, that we owned our home in England and that my local health authority had employed me for several years. I spent the flight to London mostly in prayer that things would go more smoothly for us this time.

"I'll take the next flight home and get my job back. I still have two days annual leave left till termination is complete if they don't let me in," he threatened.

Our flight landed just before 7.00 am. Immigration officials at the airport had us wait till the administration office of the maternity unit I worked in opened so verification of my status could be obtained. Once that was done, we were allowed in. I heaved a sigh of relief as they let us through the barriers.

Settling In

"What's for dinner?" Sam asked.

It was six in the evening, a month after we arrived in England. I had just returned home from work. He was still in his pyjamas and dressing gown. He had not bothered to shower and change since waking up! He was spread like a lord, reclining on the sofa, a smouldering cigarette in his fingers. The ashtray on the coffee table was overflowing with butts, and the acrid smoke of Marlboro cigarettes clouded the air. The television was blaring, and the living room was strewn with several things. The place looked like a tip. Exhausted after a full day's work, his presumption, entitled attitude, and the mess he had made of our home that I had looked after so well rankled me.

"Fried farts and onions!" I replied, standing in front of the television.

"Have you no self-respect or common sense? I have been at work all day. You could have at least cleaned this house up and made dinner. For two months you have been disappearing to London supposedly to look for work. Did you? Or was it an excuse to stay at the hotel and party with your ex-colleagues? All those phone calls from them whenever they're in London. I have had enough! You will clean up the mess you have made of the home I've cared for, and you will cook for yourself," I yelled at him.

"Moreover, from tomorrow, you will find a job. I don't care what, but you will work to pay your share of the cost of running this household. You will also service the loan of the car you wanted. I am not paying for it!" I flung at him before I stormed off.

A few weeks later, Sam got a job in a restaurant in a neighbouring town. He was a head waiter. He worked from the late afternoon to the early morning hours. Things settled down a little between us. He frequented London less often. We visited two of his friends who were living in England. Life seemed normal. For a short spell, I was happy, but the peace was not to last.

Soon, I noticed a familiar pattern emerging with phone calls. A male voice would ask for Sam, and when I replied that he was not in, he would politely thank me and hang up. But the calls became frequent, with the caller hanging up when I answered. When I questioned Sam, he shrugged it off. A while later, Sam started asking me for money.

"Give me some money!" He demanded.

"I pay for just about everything here? You're working; what are you doing with your wages?" I wanted to know.

"I owe someone," he replied.

"You've barely been living here and already started gambling again?" I asked, incredulous.

"Don't worry about it. I'll sort it out," Sam replied.

After a while, Sam said that he was quitting his job. He was unhappy there and applied for another with a large fast-food chain. His application was successful; he secured a managerial position there.

A lifetime of holidays

"Look at this advertisement for a lifetime of holidays. There's a presentation to attend and a gift for attending it. How about we go and see what it's all about?" Sam said.

"Let me think about it," I replied, but Sam continued to bug me. I finally capitulated for a bit of peace.

The presentation in London was a flashy, hard-sell event. It would cost us £10,000 to secure a two-week stay in many holiday residences and European hotels. There was no way I could take it on in addition to the mortgage, the bills and the additional loan for the conservatory. It all looked excellent, but we had no cash to spare. I made Sam promise that he would take on the payments for more household bills. Between Sam's enthusiasm and the sales team's hard sell, I finally agreed to pay £50 monthly, which would stretch our household budget to the limit. As for the gift, it was just a useless trinket.

Fertility treatments

I knew that if we did not try again for a baby, I would soon be too old to have children safely. We discussed it, and I made an appointment at the gynaecology clinic. I was sent for a series of tests and told that there would be no difficulty getting pregnant with the commencement of infertility drugs to hasten the process.

"But I can't treat just you, Lilly," the obstetrics and gynaecology consultant politely said.

"We do need to test your husband as well," The clinic provided some sterile plastic containers for Sam's semen samples.

"I am NOT doing that!" Sam insisted loudly and emphatically.

"Well, nothing will happen if you don't provide the sample, and I might as well call it quits," I replied. Sam thought about it for a while and then agreed to provide the samples that I hot-footed to the hospital lab.

Sterility

"I am sorry, Lilly, your husband's sperm sample has returned as sterile. There is nothing I can do to help you unless you want to try donor sperm," the gynaecology consultant suggested sympathetically.

"I must talk this over with my husband first, of course. I appreciate everything you've done, Doctor. Thank you," I said and walked home with a copy of the result.

"Well, whose baby was it then that you miscarried before if I am sterile!" Sam yelled at me.

As usual, it was my fault. Sam had abused his body for many years. His frequent bouts of alcohol intoxication and chain smoking must have taken a toll. I could not tell how many women he had been with in all his travels or what he might have caught from them. Two years had passed since he'd moved to England. I was gutted and spent the rest of the week wondering where all this would leave us. After that, Sam did not speak to me, giving me the cold shoulder. I knew I had to make a decision.

CHAPTER 5 -- STRIPPED

"Davis and Warren, can I help you?" said the female voice at the end of the line. Sam and I purchased our home using this firm for conveyancing.

"Yes, I'd like to see a lawyer about commencing divorce proceedings, please," I replied. The receptionist secured an appointment time for me.

Sam was still giving me the cold shoulder. Sometimes he did not even come home. It did not bother me. Indeed, I was relieved that I did not have to share my bed with him. Thoughts of divorce weighed heavily on my mind. When Sam finally came home, I did not speak to him either. The air was so thick with hostility that one could cut it with a knife! My faith was taking a beating. I knew now that I had been misguided in thinking that because Sam and I shared the same faith, we also shared the same values. We attended church together whenever possible, but it was all a farce. The disappointment and pain were almost unbearable. I thought that being alone for the rest of my life would be better than this.

"Hello. A large hand stretched out towards me. Lilly, is it?"

"Yes," I replied to the man standing before me. He was over six feet tall and had a kind smile. He was dressed formally in a business shirt, tie, slacks and black-framed glasses that made him look studious and severe. His dark hair was thinning at the top of his head, and he sported a beard. I put my hand into his to acknowledge the shake and found the firmness of his grasp reassuring.

"My name is David. Do come into my office," he said, leading the way.

I had been in this office with Sam when we bought our home. He sat behind a large desk; two chairs were on the other side of the desk facing him. It was a typical lawyer's office:

piles of folders on a table and thick law books lined one wall on a bookshelf.

"Please take a seat. How can I help you?"

"I've come to see about a divorce," I replied.

"On what grounds do you want me to file this case against your husband?" David asked.

"Gambling, lack of financial support, high living and running up debts," I listed.

"I need more information. Can you give me more details?" he asked.

I went on to tell him about Sam's gambling habits, how he gambled in the casinos of Las Vegas, the massive credit card bills that Sam ran up and his lack of responsibility with the finances. I also described how Sam accused me of mismanaging the household finances and some of the troubles he had encountered over the years. David took some notes and then asked me if I was sure I wanted to do this.

"I have had enough of the man. I can't take anymore!" I declared.

"Alright. What I want you to do when you get home is this. Don't cook him meals or do his laundry. Don't do anything at all for your husband," David instructed.

"With great pleasure! What do I do about sleeping arrangements? I don't want to share my bed with him anymore," I added firmly.

"Move him into a spare room. Do you have one?" David asked.

"Yes, I do. I'll organise that as soon as I get home. I have one problem: my wages are swallowed up by all the household expenses. I don't know how I'll pay you!" I confessed. The thorny issue of lawyer's fees had kept me up at night. It was one of the reasons I had taken so long to initiate divorce proceedings. David assured me he could work out an arrangement that would suit us. Thanking him, I left the office for my next appointment, the doctor's surgery. At the surgery,

I asked my GP to help me lose the weight I had put on with infertility treatment. I moved all of Sam's things into the spare bedroom at home. He did not been home for a few days. It gave me time to rehearse what I would say to him. Fortunately, I was in the house when he eventually returned home. I felt this gave me an advantage. I watched how he would react when I told him the news.

"Sam, I've started divorce proceeding against you. That's why I've moved you into the spare room. You'll be hearing from my solicitor any day now," I announced as he stood in the living room.

"What did you do that for?" he yelled at me.

"I can't stand your nonsense anymore. I've had enough!" I threw back at him.

"You have been mistreating me since I came here," he shouted.

"Me mistreating you? Go to hell!" I retorted, retreating to my bedroom. My bedroom had become my refuge now that I had moved Sam to the guest bedroom.

"You are so ugly." He said

Yes, I had put on some weight with the infertility drugs I had taken because I wanted to have his baby!

"No one will want you!" he taunted as I walked away.

I had started on the medicines my GP had given me, throwing away the infertility medication with a knot in my stomach. The weight soon fell off. I gladly ditched the oversized baggy clothes I had been wearing and slipped into my old form-fighting outfits and uniform. I regained my figure quickly and was as trim as I had been the year before. My battered self-esteem recovered somewhat when my friends and colleagues noticed and complimented me for it.

Informing family

"What about the $10,000 I lent him ... and his share of the inheritance, Lilly?" Sam's brother asked.

"I have no idea what you are referring to!" I replied. I had rung Sam's brother out of courtesy to inform him of the divorce. He had been dismayed and wanted to know why. I filled him in on all that had happened since Sam moved in with me in England. It was a short, sharp conversation, the last one I would ever have with him. He informed the rest of his family.

Waiting

I was regularly in and out of Davis and Warren over the next few years. The most challenging appointment was formally advising the courts that I wanted the divorce. When David placed the documents before me, I regretted that I had wasted the best years of my life trying to make a life with someone who just wanted to use me for his convenience. It was some weeks before Sam received formal notification of my intention to divorce him. David took it to the restaurant to serve Sam. Though I no longer shared a bedroom with Sam, he made my life at home hard. One night he and his workmates created such a commotion partying in our house during the wee hours that I had to call the police. His mates left when the police arrived to investigate. He racked up an enormous phone bill, forcing me to block all incoming and outgoing calls. I had to key in a code to make or receive calls. One night at about three in the morning, the phone rang. I picked up my bedside handset, fearing bad news from home. The operator wanted to know if I would accept a call from America for Sam. The caller was his Black girlfriend! I refused payment and hung up.

"Please get him out of the house!" I begged David. Sam had left photos of himself in the embrace of his Black girlfriend on the dining table. David looked at the photos as I handed them to him.

"You will not get any additional points for this," David informed me. It disappointed me to hear it.

"Leave it with me. I'll try and get Sam out of the house for you," he said.

David arranged for Sam to move out, and I had some peace. He left behind a mess that had to be cleaned up. His bedroom was no different: the duvet was stained brown with nicotine. I had to scrub the thick coat of nicotine off the walls.

Repossession

Letters had come through the slot in the door for the car and the holiday timeshare. I was naive enough to trust Sam and sign as the guarantor for the car loan and the holiday timeshare. It did not take long for the bailiff to come to the house with the car yard owners and repossess the car. Then came the court order summon for the timeshare company; I did not attend the hearing as I was already coming apart at the seams. Sam had promised to reimburse me when he received his share of the inheritance. I had been a fool to trust him. Then, the inevitable happened: I was served with a repossession order for the house. Yet again, I was going to lose the roof over my head. I would have to move out. Soon after Sam moved out, the *Decree Absolute* was issued. I felt a heavy weight roll off my shoulders. But I was not out of the woods yet. With the contents of the house to sort out and the move to a smaller, more affordable rental flat, I had my hands full. Shamelessly, Sam claimed half of the proceeds from the house sale. So once again, I found myself entangled in court fighting a legal battle over the property. The entire excruciating process was to take six years! The wheels of the English legal system turned very slowly indeed.

Decisions

I often heard from my Malaysian friends in Australia. The rounds of group holidays, weekly lunches and dinner parties we had established here continued in Melbourne. I missed them.

"Well, Lord, if you want this to happen for me, you will open the door for me!" I prayed. A friend once told me that

God does not drive parked cars. By this, she had meant that we had to do more than pray; we had to take action too. I remembered the voice I had heard as a child that had instructed me not to depend on others, but to do for myself. After praying hard and researching, I decided to take decisive action.

"You will have no problem with your application," the officer behind the glass barrier informed me. "You will hear from us periodically as we process your forms," he added.

I left the Australian Embassy in London feeling reassured I was doing the right thing. The decision to make the application was based on several considerations. Thanks to Sam, I was on the financial deny-list in England. I needed a fresh start. I felt that it would be better for me to move to Australia than Singapore so soon after the divorce. However, I would be close enough to Singapore to be able to visit my family and my friends as frequently as I wished.

Advice

I continued practising my Catholic faith, observing every day of obligation and attending Sunday mass whenever work permitted. I had a good relationship with the local parish priest. He met regularly with the Catholic nurses on campus for pastoral care. I arranged a meeting with him to inform him of my divorce from Sam.

"You have lived a strange life, separated from Sam for so long. I am sad to see you break up, but I can understand why," he said when he heard my reasons for the divorce.

"Why don't you apply for an annulment of the marriage?" He suggested.

I decided to take his advice and put in an application with the information he provided. The interview took place in the Catholic Church's headquarters in London by priests who were also lawyers. The interview was long, and their questions were probing and personal. I was informed that the process would be extensive, and I left mentally and emotionally drained. Local Catholic Church officials also interviewed our families in Singapore, and the application was then forwarded to the Vatican for approval. I submitted to the process because I knew that without an annulment, I would not be able to marry again in church. I wanted to prove to Sam and his family that ours was not a valid marriage.

Sleepless

It is said that our fears and worries are at their worst in the dark of night. Many a night, I found myself awake and in tears. My mind was always uneasy, and even when I did fall asleep, I would jerk awake to worry and fret. After a while, I realised I could not return to Singapore. I believed I would never be able to have a relationship with a local Singaporean man. I would be treated with contempt, as divorcees were regarded as cast-offs. Really, what did I have to worry about? I did not have the same burdens as my mother, who had been widowed with ten children to care for with no means. I had just myself to look after. I had an education I had secured with great determination and a sterling professional reputation. I would always have a job and so would be able to keep myself. All my years of running a household singlehandedly proved that I did not need help to put a roof over my head. Yet here I was, crying Mummy's tears as if history was repeating itself. How had the man of my dreams deceived me? How had I not seen through the façade of his lies and falsehoods? These questions swirled round and round in my head as I berated myself. Where was I to go from here? Thus, sleep eluded me many a night.

Term of endearment

"Why did you choose to use this firm?" David asked at one of the appointments.

"Why? Because I had used this business when Sam and I bought our home. The lawyer who handled the conveyancing sat in the chair you're now sitting in," I said. I could not understand why he asked the question. "Besides, your office is in town, just walking distance from my home," I replied.

"You know my mother and sister-in-law," David said. I looked at him blankly, trying to process the information he had given me.

"My mother is Sally, and my sister-in-law is Betty, whom you trained with," he expanded.

I looked at him for a few moments, processing this information. Then the penny dropped: David was the man I had felt staring at me and with whom I had locked eyes at his mother's farewell party! That information was to change things between us. I floundered, not knowing how to deal with the change and the feelings that came with it. Sometime later, David started addressing me as "Sweetie". Such open expressions of sentiment floored me. I battled for a long while, liking the man, but not knowing how to tell him. He would often volunteer personal information about himself when I attended his offices. Once, he said he was a Speleologist. I just looked at him and smiled. My face must have registered my ignorance as to the meaning of the word.

"Someone who studies caves or climbs in them for sport," he explained.

I nodded, wondering why he wanted me to know this about him. Did he expect me to share something personal about myself in return? As I became increasingly fond of him, I started baking cakes for the firm. It became my signature. I ensured I dropped off a traditional fruit cake at Christmas and gave him a personal gift. As my feelings grew for him, I found it more and more challenging to attend appointments. I was aware of a conflict of interest. Was David just being kind? Or was there more to it? The years were rolling one into another, and I was still awaiting the dates for the court hearing. Sometimes I attended appointments with David after work, but still, in uniform, he would look at me and smile. I had become very comfortable with him, trusting him unquestioningly to do the right thing as my lawyer. Being on such warm terms with him made me feel more at ease with the legal matters I faced. But still, I could not find a way to tell him that I cared for him. I do not even know if he was already spoken for. Would I have an egg on my face if I told him how I felt for him? It was as if my lips were sealed! He continued to call me "Sweetie" throughout. I battled with my Asian notions of courtship, where a man did the pursuing, not the woman. Sometimes I felt so conflicted that I could not wait to leave his office. I would ask rather brusquely if he was done and if I could go! I looked awful because he'd asked me if I was OK. I would nod, as that was all I could manage and flee. I was running away from him as my feelings were running away from me.

The blue ledger
"How are you going to prove it?" David asked.
"Oh, that I can. I have the evidence!" I assured him.
We were discussing the finances of my household. I had kept a blue ledger of all financial transactions to do with the home ever since Sam sent me the deposit of £10,000. Every entry was backed up with a printout from the automated teller machine (ATM) or an official bank statement. As a teenager, I habitually kept detailed records of disbursement when I paid the bills and filed the paperwork for my mother while she was at work. The court case for settlement was approaching. There was more to it this time around. With Sam accusing me of mismanaging the funds he claimed to have given me, I decided to document everything to do with running the home. I purchased a blue accounting ledger and recorded every last penny spent. When all the bills for the household were paid, I was left with just £20 to get by! I baked and sold cakes to colleagues to afford the bare necessities of living. Even then, I had to eat just one meal daily. It had not been hard to do this due to my experience of poverty as a child. I

still did not eat breakfast. Plus, I enjoyed the compliments about my new trim figure and the appreciative glances I knew I drew. These were like a salve after Sam's repeated put-downs about my appearance. I took the blue ledger to David's office as soon as possible after updating the entries to make them current. David's receptionist called me in for another appointment soon after that.

"Why did you do this?" David asked, looking at me in disbelief.

I had to think hard to put years of scrimping and penny-pinching to get by in just a few short sentences. David waited patiently for my answer. Eventually, I said.

"To cut a long story short, this is how my mother taught me to run a household. I know down to my last penny what I can afford when shopping. Moreover, Sam is a habitual bare-faced liar! He accused me of mismanaging the housekeeping money when he rarely gave me any. I started keeping records soon after we bought the house to have proof on hand should he ever demand it."

"And what are these entries – money to live on?" David asked.

"That is all I have to live on after settling all the bills!"

David continued to look at me in astonishment and disbelief.

"Go through the ledger. It's all there!" I assured him.

Negotiations

"How much lower can I go?" I asked the bank officer.

"What can you afford?" He countered.

We were in a private office at the bank that handled the mortgage. I had made an appointment to inform the bank of the repossession order on the house.

"Would you accept £50 per month? You will get your money back when the house is sold anyway," I reassured him.

"Yes, that will be fine. You will have to inform us of any revisions in the future," the bank officer instructed.

That re-arrangement of my finances made a big difference in my life. I now had 80 per cent of the mortgage for living expenses! I saved up, went on cheap short breaks around England, and returned from these refreshed and renewed.

Support

My elder Sister began calling me regularly from Singapore when I told her I had started divorce proceedings against Sam. She chastised me for not talking to her about my problems with him earlier. During this time, I grew closer to her, and our chats and her loving support were like a lifeline. No one else in my family asked how I was faring, even though they knew I was going through a divorce.

"Remember, Lilly, you have been starved of love for a long time. Don't mistake friendship for love!" She advised. Two days later, I received another phone call.

Gone

"Mummy's gone!" my niece, elder Sister's daughter, who was my goddaughter, said to me from the other end of the line.

"What do you mean 'gone'?" I asked, feeling dread creep through my veins.

"Mummy died in a road traffic accident last night. A lorry hit her while she was riding her bicycle," Goddaughter said mechanically. After speaking to her for a few more minutes, I told her I would return to Singapore as soon as possible. The following day I handed my cases to the on-call Community Midwife, informing her that I would see the manager about compassionate leave until the beginning of the New Year. It was mid-November. I wanted to be with the family during their first Christmas and New Year without my elder Sister. I rang Davis and Warren to inform David of the circumstances of my return to Singapore, just in case they were looking for me. At lunchtime, I was still waiting for a flight ticket in an alley when David walked out of the shopping mall. He noticed me and stopped, mouthing, "Are you OK?" I nodded, and he continued on his way towards his office. I raced home, packed a bag and caught the train to Heathrow Airport. The ticket was issued mid-afternoon.

Gift

My elder Sister lay in her casket in her living room, in the same position as my mother's casket was a few years ago. At 43, she was too young to be in it and too beautiful to be reduced to ashes. She was the only family member who cared enough to keep in touch through my years abroad. I had lost a best friend. My elder Sister died three years into my divorce proceedings. I lost the only pillar of support I had had. I could only hope she was resting peacefully in the care of Jesus, finally free of an abusive husband, though she had left two young daughters behind. After the funeral, her husband and my goddaughter handed me the money she had saved to visit me in England. I knew I had to make good use of such a precious gift. My successful application for entry to Australia had come through. I needed to visit or move to Australia within the first year. I then had four years' grace to take up permanent residence there. I used her gift to visit my Malaysian friends in Melbourne. The family observed a quiet Christmas and New Year in Singapore to signify our loss.

Though we attended Christmas midnight mass and had meals together throughout the season, there was neither a tree nor decorations. There were no rowdy parties or lavish presents. Instead, we gave each other the gift of time and solace, sharing memories and telling old family stories to the younger generation. The break was like a tonic after the last few years of struggle and strife. I flew out of Singapore the day after New Year's Day. I was taken around Melbourne and shown all the sights. In Melbourne, I was petted and spoilt by my circle of old chums. It was lovely to see them again after so long.

Professional overhaul

While waiting for the court hearing, I decided the best thing to do was throw myself into my work. The midwifery sector was undergoing massive change. The government surveyed maternity patients, and hospitals were charged with enforcing changes patients demanded. A failure to do so would see government-appointed officials effecting said changes on their behalf.

Staff meetings discussed "women-centred care", a new term that entered the service vocabulary. Pregnant women had the right to choose how they had their babies as long as no abnormalities developed. Water birth was introduced following a movement by a prominent French obstetrics and gynaecology consultant. Two water birth units were added to the birthing unit. To reduce waiting for post-delivery procedures, customarily attended by Doctors, all midwives learnt to suture simple perineal tears and straightforward episiotomies. An episiotomy is an incision made into the perineum to enlarge the vaginal opening to deliver the baby's head. It is a pre-emptive procedure to prevent uncontrolled tearing of the birthing mother's perineum. Two high-dependency rooms for birthing were converted into operating theatres. Midwives were trained as scrub nurses and runners to ensure quality and continuity of care. Under the old regime, CMs handed over their cases to a hospital midwife in the event of an abnormality. The changes dictated that CMs continue with the patients. These new procedures were so swiftly implemented that some senior midwives opted for early retirement rather than re-train. As I had not long transitioned to CM, my skills were current. I was grateful for this overhaul as it took time and concentration, leaving me little time and energy to fret over my impending divorce.

Hay fever

Government subsidies encouraged farmers to grow canola as a cash crop in parts of England, including the area I lived. Field after field dedicated to the crop would ripen to gold as the crop burst into bloom at the height of summer. I felt the cold English winter and looked forward to summer. However, I developed a severe allergy to canola pollen. My face would swell, my eyes would tear constantly, and I would sneeze hard and suffer nosebleeds. My nose and nasal passages burned as if I had inhaled chilli powder. I wheezed when I breathed through my nostrils clogged with blood clots. At night, the wheezing worsened, and there were times when I feared that I would not make it through the night despite being on high doses of drugs. One summer, I took a trip to Spain. I was symptomless within 24 hours of leaving England. It was so good to be able to breathe normally. Returning to England, I was already sick when I arrived home on public transport. It dawned on me then that if I stayed in England for much longer, I would likely develop chronic obstructive lung disease and shorten my lifespan.

In court

I was standing in the foyer of the courts using the public telephone. "What do I do?" I asked the receptionist of David's office. "There is no one here!"

"Don't worry, I'll tell David to go over," she promised.

David soon arrived, and we trooped into the courtroom, where my barrister met us. I noticed Sam and his mother. With them were two Indian men whom I assumed were his legal team. They sat right in front of the courtroom. We sat at the back on the opposite side, far behind Sam and his team.

"All rise," the court attendant called, and we stood up as the magistrate entered. I was pleased that the magistrate was a woman. Perhaps she would be more compassionate with me. After the formalities, she declared the case open. There was much discussion and many questions directed at Sam's lawyers. At one point, something untrue was said.

"That's a lie!" I called out loud, looking at David for defence. David immediately put his finger to his lips, gesturing for me to be quiet. I was annoyed and sat squirming next to him. The magistrate called Sam to the stand. He was sworn in, and she began to question him. His ambiguous answers appeared to annoy her.

"Stop beating around the bush!" She had questioned him about the inconsistent financial statements from selling our flat in Singapore and his share of the inheritance from his parent's property development project. She scolded him. After some discussion, the hearing was adjourned to the following day. The next day the magistrate delivered her decision. She could not comprehend why we were in court, as no residual finances were available after the house's repossession order was settled. Before her lay my blue ledger, evidence that David had submitted for her deliberations. She complimented me on my prudent financial management and detailed bookkeeping. Perhaps as a woman, the magistrate could see things from my perspective. She eventually ruled in my favour. There was little to celebrate as the divorce did not improve my financial situation. I was still losing the roof over my head for a second time. I never saw Sam again.

Over

"The magistrate had a lot of good things to say about you!" David said at the post-hearing appointment in his office.

"Took a judge in a courtroom to show him my value!" I replied.

"I want you to buy my house!" David said.

His comment threw me off completely! I was so unprepared for his suggestion that my quick reply must have bruised him.

"I might as well rebuy my own house!" I spat out, sounding unappreciative of all the help, kindness and support he had offered me over the years.

David looked hurt at my reaction and buried himself in the papers before him. From then on, he communicated with me only through formal letters. The first was instructions to put the house on the market. It sold in the last week of the first contract with the real estate agent.

Moving

I rented a one-bedroom apartment a hundred metres from my house. There were multiple trips to the op shops and car booth sales. I gave away anything anyone wanted, only packing what meant most to me and engaging a shipping company to supply removal boxes for storage and removal to Australia. The bulk of the furniture went to the Salvation Army. There were just 18 months left of the four-year window for me to move to Australia as a permanent resident. I realised I had little money and a £400 credit card debt to pay off. I had to find a way to earn much money quickly to facilitate my move to Australia. After tossing some ideas with friends, I applied to work in Saudi Arabia. A colleague who had worked there shared her insights on what living and working in the largest country in the Arabian Peninsula would entail.

Christmas present

"Lilly, please leave the door open, so I can see the Nativity crib," Mandy, a labouring mother, requested. It was Christmas Eve, close to midnight. I had looked after Mandy for several hours as the on-call CM. Mandy was one of my cases. I had cared for her since she had tested positive for pregnancy. It was a joy to be caring for her at the birth of her baby. We had become quite friendly with each other over the months. I visited her in her home as part of her antenatal care. Positioned on a linen cupboard just outside her room was a Nativity crib. The atmosphere in the maternity unit was quite festive. Another midwife brought a cassette player, and Christmas carols played softly in the background. There were several other women in labour. It was anybody's guess who would have the Christmas baby.

"Will I make it?" She gasped in between contractions.

"I think you just might. You're fully dilated, so it's all up to you!" I encouraged her along.

And she did. At just eight minutes past midnight, Mandy pushed out a whopping four-and-a-half kg baby to meet the world. Her doting husband by her side was in tears. I was happy for them. Hers was my first and only Christmas birth. I continued with Mandy's care postnatally at her home. She proudly handed me the local newspaper on my last visit. The front page carried a photograph of her holding her baby with her husband's arms around them both. In the accompanying article, she mentions me as her midwife, thanking me for the care I had given her throughout her pregnancy, birth and postnatal care. I was both flattered and touched by the public acknowledgement. It is a gift I will never forget.

Resolution

Most homes I visited during my postnatal rounds during Christmas were decorated for the season. Several of my wealthier patients had homes that were Christmas card perfect. One such house was my undoing. It took all my self-control to keep my composure till I exited the beautiful house with its young mother, her baby, and her doting husband.

I burst into tears when I got into my car and wept as I completed my paperwork. While I was happy for them, their domestic bliss only deepened my sorrow at losing my dreams of a happy family. In contrast to my professional achievements, my personal life was in shreds. I had nothing to show after thirteen years of marriage. I had no children, no husband, or even my own home. How had this happened? How had I let this happen? After a while, I drew a few deep breaths to calm myself. I decided that life was too short to keep dreaming after the unlikely. Instead, I resolved to make the most of whatever opportunities came my way in my next life phase.

Saudi

"I can only accept this agreement if you arrange for me to have all my annual leave at the end of the contract," I informed the recruiting agent for Saudi Arabia. The request was acceded to, and I signed the contract. I would work in Saudi Arabia for eleven months and move to Australia in the twelfth month before my visa expires. It was a calculated risk. I was cutting it fine, but it was the only way to escape this mess. The wages earned in Saudi Arabia were tax-free, as was accommodation. My salary would be the same, but I would not pay taxes, and the free housing equalled savings. It would give me a small nest egg to draw on while moving around Australia to find a suitable position.

Departure

I resigned in the last few weeks of my life in England. I sold the furniture in my flat to my colleague's son, who was setting up a home for the first time. I rang Davis and Warren to ensure that nothing was outstanding. I did not speak to David. My last shift as a midwife in England was an evening parent education class. I farewelled my pregnant mothers. I locked the community health centre and drove away with a heavy heart. I was saying goodbye to the best midwifery position I would ever have. In my heart, I knew that these were the best years of my career.

One of my colleagues organised a farewell dinner where I was presented with a nurse's fob watch. The last trip to Heathrow was just as heartbreaking, and I savoured every sight, knowing it would be the last time I saw it. All my possessions were in boxes in a removal depot. As the plane pulled away, I watched England disappear from view, silently saying goodbye to all the people I had met over the 13 years it had been my home. Goodbye, David. I hope you have a great life!

I recalled the girl I had been all those years ago when I was interviewed for admission into midwifery school. I had been full of hopes and dreams. Admittedly, I had many wonderful and enriching experiences here. But as a young wife, I would never have imagined that my marriage and all I had striven for materially would go up in smoke. I was moving on to better things, God willing. I was confident that my God would see me through as He always did. Indeed, while reading my bible during those difficult last few days, I came across the following verse: "For God did not give us a spirit of timidity but a spirit of power, love and self-discipline." (2 Timothy 1:7)

It was to sustain me through the following year, even though my faith was still in its infancy.

CHAPTER 6 – A WHOLE NEW WORLD

"Help, help!" I called, waving to catch the attention of anyone in the car park below. I was ten floors up on my apartment's large box window sill in a high-rise block. Saudi men and women came and went from the shopping centre on the ground floor of my building to the car park below. After a while, a man looked up and waved. He ran into the building and returned, signalling that help was coming. A few long minutes lapsed before a nurse opened the window; she occupied the neighbouring unit in the same block.

"What on earth are you doing there?" She cried. "The manager said, 'in trouble already? She has only been here two days!' and asked me to rescue you," she laughed.

"I was trying to clean this filthy window when it locked me out," I replied, pulling the chair into the flat that I had lowered onto the window sill to help me reach the top.

"Get the Filipino cleaners to do it for you. They are dirt cheap. You can afford them," my rescue nurse advised. She turned over the spare key to my apartment, which she had used to get in. "Hand it back to the office," she instructed.

"Thank you," I called out as she walked out.

A few days later, the window was just as dirty as I had found it when I moved in! It was impossible to keep it clean due to the heat, desert dust and air pollution. I never cleaned it again.

As instructed by the London office, I arrived mid-week to give myself time to settle in before orientation began the following Monday. A Saudi official met me at the airport. He held a board with my name on it. He did not speak English and gestured that I follow him to the car. He drove me to the apartment block in which I was to reside. An Englishman managed the apartments. He welcomed me to the country and issued the keys to my tenth-floor flat and a set of uniforms.

"You are coming in when the money is running out of this country," he said.

He told me where the nearest supermarket was across the street and handed me a folder of instructions to read about the rules and regulations of the females-only accommodation. Also in the folder were instructions for my preparations for work on Monday. In the mid-1990s, Saudi Arabia, also known as the Kingdom, was the seat of Islam and was not open to the outside world. I knew from growing up in multi-cultural Singapore what the Muslim religion required in life. The London office had briefed me on what clothes to wear while living in Saudi. All apparel had to be fashioned loosely from opaque material with only the head, upper neck, hands and feet exposed. I had already sewn some mid-thigh-length loose blouses, long sleeves in breathable fabric, and pyjama-type trousers to match. I knew I would have to buy a black *abaya*—a long-sleeved, loose-fitting, floor-length outer cloak which went over my street attire. A mentor would be assigned to me to show me the ropes. All Saudi women wore an *abaya and sometimes a niqab or face covering.* The colour was always black. The men sported white *thobe*, a floor-length, long-sleeved shirt. Saudi men wore a *keffiyeh,* a headdress consisting of a square cotton scarf with a traditional pattern held in place with a thick cord known as the *agal*. The *keffiyeh* was cheekily dubbed "the tea towel" by expatriates. My uniform was a baggy knee-length, long-sleeved top with loose pyjama-like trousers. Made of white cotton, it shrouded the figure.

Settling in

If ever there was a dull place to live, it was my apartment. Compared to all the places I had lived in, it was huge, almost twice the size of my old home in England. The two-bedroom unit had a sizeable sitting-cum-dining room, a large kitchen and a bathroom with a shower and toilet. But a shade of dark grey paint surrounded me. I found some cheap plastic tablecloths that had pictures of a sunny seaside and another of a pretty garden at the nearest shopping mall. I bought these and stuck them to the living room and bedroom wall to break the monotony of the dull grey, reassuring myself it would be for just a year. I was delighted to find that Saudi food was similar to Indian food and cheap. It only cost me a couple of British pounds in Saudi Riyals to buy a quarter of a chicken and heaps of rice cooked into a biryani with a wedge of lemon and some gravy. I was not going to miss Indian food here. All things Indian and Filipino graced the supermarket shelves. Unsurprising as the city was crawling with Indian and Filipino workers. There were many Indian men in the malls and on the streets. They tended to stare at women in public spaces. Colleagues warned me not to wander around late at night. Men kidnapped unsuspecting women; some of these men would not have been with a woman in years! I was unsure how much truth there was in this claim, but decided not to tempt fate.

Just as well. On my first day of walking around the mall, I dressed in my usual style: make-up and long, waist-length hair worn loose over my shoulder. Big mistake! The Indian men in the mall stared unblinkingly at me. It was unnerving. Worse, one followed me. Breaking into a run, I ducked into the grocery store closest to my apartment block. The man followed me into the shop, strolling among the shelves of sundries, looking at me through the gaps on the shelves. I dashed out of the shop when he turned around the corner of a stand out of sight. I made a beeline for the lobby of my accommodation block. It was a close shave, but I managed to lose him. After that, I never wore make-up and always had my hair up in a bun which I hoped would do the trick. Things significantly improved after I bought myself an *abaya* with the help of my mentor. I never ventured out after dark. The streets reminded me of colonial Singapore, littered with domestic rubbish and building rubble. Buildings were painted mainly the same drab grey as my apartment. The road divider featured some palm trees at regular intervals. Saudis appeared to favour large, expensive American sedans or four-wheel drive vehicles. One morning, I walked to the beach about 200 m from my block and stood at the water's edge. The ambient temperature was about 40° Celsius, and the breeze was scorching even by the water. Desert breeze from the middle of the Arabian Peninsula, I was informed. There was no relief from the heat except for air conditioning. Roll on, winter!

Orientation

Monday morning, my first day at work. Several of us waited together in the block's lobby and eventually boarded a large bus from the air base. The local military airbase hospital provided a door-to-door transport service for their employees. There was no need to wear the *abaya* to get to and from work. No one could get in without a permit. A couple of English nurses introduced themselves to me. They had arrived a few months earlier. I settled into a seat and watched the desert and the buildings go past, wondering if I had done the right thing coming to work here. I found myself in tears. The bus went through a checkpoint at the airbase entrance; an official bordered the bus and checked all our passes. When we reached the hospital entrance, a manager escorted me to the orientation room, where I met other new arrivals. These were largely Filipinas.

Maricel, a Filipino nurse, introduced herself to me, and we chatted briefly before orientation commenced. Orientation took two days. We spent the first hours filling out more forms and getting a briefing on the hospital's protocols. There was a language class to learn essential Arabic words and converse with patients. On the second day, Maricel asked how much I was earning. When I told her, she walked away and never spoke to me again. I later learned that the Filipinos were on a lower salary. She must have assumed because I was of Indian extraction, my employment as an Indian national would be of similar terms to hers. All expatriate nurses from England, Australia or America were employed as managers or high-dependency area nurses. The Indians and Filipinos were primary care nurses. Wages were paid in Saudi Riyals, and we were informed which banks in the city would transfer our money to our home bank accounts. I was assigned to work in the birthing unit. The shifts were 12 hours long, four days a week. There were no enhancements for after-hours, and the night shifts were worked four nights in a row. We could only work one extra day a week if we wanted to work overtime. Friday was the Kingdom's Sunday.

Birthing

"Welcome to the Kingdom and birthing." Anna greeted me and enveloped me in a big hug. Anna was a sight that made my heart jump for joy. We had worked together in England, and she had proved to be a good friend. Anna had been a senior midwife in England. Her husband had worked in Saudi for many years, and Anna eventually decided to join him, concerned that she would lose him to another woman. Anna was the birthing manager. I was glad for this as I knew I was in good hands. She introduced me to the other midwives on duty -- American, Australian and English-trained midwives. They seemed a happy bunch. The unit was lavishly appointed. There were two labour rooms with two beds in each room and two birthing rooms with special electronic birthing beds. Every bed had its own set of equipment. I was thrilled that midwives did not have to chase gear. The unit was state-of-the-art and in a modern building. There were four midwives per shift to provide one-on-one care. The operating theatres were just next door, accessible by a connecting door. No expense had been spared to ensure that the wives and babies of the airbase personnel received the best care. It was also the first time I learned to use a computer for patient data entry.

The screen was black with green letters, and we used a touch pen for entries.

A mixed model
The model of care here was a curious marriage of Western medical standards and the Kingdom's cultural needs. Once girls reach puberty, they are married off. In the Muslim culture, men were permitted to have more than one wife, sometimes up to four! It wasn't extraordinary for a teenage girl to be brought into birthing for her first baby by her much older husband. She would, after that, be pregnant every year till she reached menopause. She was only separated from her husband for four months in the postnatal period. Therefore, having as many as thirteen babies was not unusual for a woman! Midwives working in birthing did not look after the women during the antenatal period. What care they received was fragmented. The women travelled with their air force husbands around the Kingdom and did not receive continuous care from one provider. They came to the unit to give birth to their babies. If we were lucky, we had some notes to work with for her.

"Sister, Sister, *wilada, wilada!*" means "baby's coming" in Arabic, heard daily as the swing doors opened with a crash. Guards would come flying in with a woman in a wheelchair, usually in an advanced stage of labour. There would be barely enough time to get her into bed before her baby was born. One such case happened during a night shift. Unfortunately, two midwives rostered to work with me were not on talking terms then.

"This is going to be a long 12 hours!" I said to the third midwife. She laughed as the other two went in different directions to find something to do to take them out of each other's way. When the doors crashed open to their usual accompaniment of "...*wilada, wilada!*" one of the two said she would take on the case. As she declined our help, we left her to get on with things.

"Help!" the call out rang from the labour room a minute later. The third midwife and I dropped what we were doing and raced into the room just in time to hear a loud grunt. The mother had just made it onto the bed and pushed her baby down one leg of her ankle-length bloomers -- some women wore these as underpants. We could see the baby kicking and crying down one bloomer's leg. It was a mad rush to get the bloomers off the mother and free the baby from them. With the umbilical cord cut and the baby placed in the arms of the mother, we were summarily dismissed by the attending midwife. It was just as well as neither of us could contain our giggles and chortles. We made for the staff room, where we burst into laughter. We laughed so hard that tears ran down our faces. The rest of the night paled into insignificance. Once labour commenced, the protocol made it mandatory for all women to have a set of blood samples taken.

A cannula would be inserted into the woman's hand to administer saline intravenously or for blood transfusion if patients bled or needed medication. The procedure was necessary because of the high rate of drop-in patients with no records. Teenage and young mothers often suffer extensive birthing trauma and bleeding from vaginal trauma. A timely incision (episiotomy) in the tissue between the vaginal opening and the anus during childbirth when the vaginal opening does not stretch enough for the baby's head to be delivered will aid in preventing vaginal tears and further damage to surrounding external areas. The midwifery team decided to take pre-emptive action and entered into discussions with the obstetric team to encourage elective episiotomies for young mothers to prevent trauma. We were also concerned that the possibility of a haemorrhage was very high. Negotiations were successful. Active management of all births with drugs was introduced. I noted that while the younger mothers cuddled their babies, the older ones motioned for them to be taken away. Most babies were separated from their mothers soon after they were born.

Doctors did not attend any normal births or assist in suturing a normal episiotomy. It was the midwife's responsibility to care for all standard deliveries. Like Britain, doctors were summoned to participate in a case only if an abnormality occurred.

The Saudi father

I was taken aback by how expectant mothers in Saudi Arabia were treated. In England, husbands treated their labouring wives with loving concern and care. They hovered about and assisted with respect, at once distressed by the birthing process, but also eager and excited to meet their new son or daughter. The Saudi husband dropped off his labouring wife at the birthing unit and returned home to his other wives. The men had to be carefully watched if they stayed, as they sometimes got up to no good. One midwife, who had just inserted a cannula into her patient's hand, left her briefly with her husband to fetch some supplies. The husband came running out to the nurses' station in distress. When the midwife had stepped out, he had pulled the cannula out, causing his wife to bleed profusely from the gaping hole in her vein. He received a telling-off from a Saudi doctor on duty when the incident was reported

"Watch them, Lilly. You'll find some of them fondling themselves while staring at you working! Make sure your jacket is buttoned up to the neck so they can't see your cleavage," I was warned.

Saudi men reputedly had a herbal remedy that they consumed as an aphrodisiac. The formula was a closely guarded secret, believed to increase their stamina and sexual prowess. Many expatriate men have tried to discover the secret remedy but failed. We had to make sure privacy curtains were tightly drawn in the two-bedded labour room just in case a man spotted a woman -- or some part of her anatomy and fell in love with her, causing problems. The men were instructed to stay with their wives behind the curtain and not wander around. They could only walk out of the birthing unit and straight for the exit.

Emergency

During after-hours emergency surgery, the surgical and midwifery team experienced tremendous stress and anxiety waiting for operating theatre nurses to arrive half an hour from their accommodation in an emergency as they feared maternal or infant mortality. Saudi law enforcement meant a jail sentence or a beheading if a practitioner was found guilty of medical neglect. This problem provided an excellent opportunity to urge management to adopt English protocol: train midwives to be scrub nurses so they could start the operation with the obstetric and anaesthetic teams -- both specialists lived on-site at the airbase and would arrive within minutes. In the plan approved by management, midwives were duly upskilled to take on the scrub nurse role when necessary. The theatre nurses could take over from the midwife when they arrived.

Domestic help

"Don't do the cleaning, Lilly."

"Why?" I inquired.

"Because if management comes to know that we have the time to do the cleaning, they will do away with the domestic staff. They'll lose their jobs, and we'll have to clean!"

For twenty-three years in Singapore and England, I cleaned and made-up beds in the wards and birthing rooms because the domestic staff were not allowed to handle blood products. Initially, I regarded domestic help as a luxury. However, I soon learnt to appreciate it and accepted it as an essential service, especially when we had as many as ten births in one shift. It often felt like I was working on a mass production line, with women coming in hard and fast. I welcomed a hot shower and bed by the end of these shifts. The rest was essential for recharging batteries before the next twelve hours hit. I had never worked twelve-hour shifts before. The days rolled one into another, and time began to fly by. My yearning for England and Western civilisation slowly evaporated.

Social life

"Come on, let me take you to the American supermarket," my mentor said.

She took me to a supermarket a few hundred metres from our apartment block, about five hundred meters from the Indian and Filipino shops I had been going to. It was not much different from many English supermarkets, except for the preponderance of American products, many of which I had never seen before.

"Gee, these people must drink an awful lot of apple juice!" I remarked, looking at the large vats, some as big as 20 litres. Also noteworthy were big boxes of yeast. Lots of baking? My mentor laughed and said she would explain when we were outside. Once outside, she told me, the Americans purchased giant vats of apple juice and packets of yeast to make moonshine! We bought what we needed and headed back to our flats.

"I thought alcohol was not permitted in the kingdom!" It would warrant instant dismissal, I said, astonished as I was given strict instructions by the recruitment agency never to be caught with alcohol.

"Not if you live on an American compound, Lilly." She replied. "I will have to take you to one. I know someone who works with the American oil company."

True to her promise, I soon found myself at a party inside an American compound. We arrived in a taxi and had to register at a compound gate checkpoint. The Saudi guard had a gun slung over his shoulder. He looked at our Saudi identity cards and recorded our names before handing them back to us and waving the taxi into the compound. I noticed the high concrete wall surrounding the buildings, about 5 m tall. Razor wire, reminiscent of a prison, rimmed the top of the wall to deter locals from climbing in. It was still daylight when we arrived for the party. As the taxi continued into the compound, I was amazed at what I saw. It was equivalent to Club Med! Large American-style homes lined the street with manicured lawns and gardens. There was a sports complex with a swimming pool, tennis courts, a football field and a stadium. My colleague informed me that a large restaurant served meals all day, so no one ever had to cook. The same restaurant also catered for parties when commissioned.

We were ushered into the luxury home of our host, who invited us in warmly and directed us to the backyard, where there must have been a hundred people. They seemed to be in their twenties and thirties and were mainly African American. I had never seen so many of them before. Music boomed from loudspeakers. A bar was in free flow. The backyard led to a private beach that joined a row of similar houses. I was amazed. My mentor explained that the American and British agencies had an understanding with the Saudi government: whatever happened within their compounds was their business. The compounds were mini-America, where American law ruled. The people living in the estates were senior American personnel. There were quite a few of these compounds dotted all around Saudi Arabia. I was introduced to several people and made small talk. A drink was put into my hands at the bar without my asking. When I enquired what it was, the bartender replied:

"It's the Saudi version of a G&T," he said, referring to gin and tonic.

"No, thank you, I don't drink. May I have a lemonade, please?" I asked.

"Sure thing," he replied, looking at me oddly.

I was warned to be careful with drinks at parties. I watched the bartender pour the lemonade from a can into a glass he handed me. The homebrew was as good as straight meth! I have, over the years, been around intoxicated male family members and developed a dislike of alcohol and its effect on the behaviour of people who over-indulge. It was easy for me to stick to non-alcoholic beverages at social events. Admittedly, I indulged in the occasional Irish Coffee or fruity cocktail. As the night wore on, my mentor told me she would spend the night with her gentleman friend. She left me in the care of a group of soldiers, instructing them to take me home safely. When I went to claim my lift home, I was confronted with a car full of them.

"Where shall I sit?" I asked, noticing that there was no space in the car.

"On my lap," one of them replied.

"Oh no, I don't think so," I said, taken aback.

"Well, if you wait, Gary will take you home. Talk to him; he's in the kitchen," one of the soldiers advised.

Gary took me home. I later learnt that it was common practice in the Kingdom for expatriates to have casual relationships when they worked there. People moved quickly to the next liaison when one or the other had their *masalama* or farewell party. No one batted an eyelid.

Swimming pool

The glossy brochures for the nurses' accommodation in Saudi showed pretty, inviting dwelling places. They had accompanied the recruitment papers I was given in England when I had decided to apply for a job there. I was disappointed upon arrival to find my flat dull and poorly cared for; the whole building needed an upgrade.

"Let me show you the swimming pool on the rooftop." my mentor suggested.

We took the lift to the top floor and walked to the pool to find several other staff members swimming and sunbathing in bikinis. The pool was tired and needed upgrading. There were missing tiles and broken deck chairs.

"It's no use." I was informed. "Management knows we are here only for the money and are a transient population. So, they'll do things at their own pace, if any at all!" my mentor added.

"Oh! I have to go shopping for dinner," one of the girls in the pool called out. She threw her *abaya* over her bikini and sailed out the door.

"Make sure you don't meet with an accident on the road. You've nothing but that bikini on under your *abaya*. The Saudis will have a good time with you if they find you dressed like that!" her friend warned as she disappeared.

Finding my way

After two months, I began to feel like I had found my feet in the Kingdom. My circle of friends widened with introductions, and I attended various homes within the American and British compounds for swims, lunches and dinners. What caught my fancy were the ballroom dancing classes held on the British compound. I attended these classes every week and found that I liked dancing. It was also a time to meet with other people and enjoy drinks at a bar in the hall of the dance class. There were almost 50 people there each week. At the time, Islamic Saudi Arabia was closed to the rest of the world and intolerant of all other faiths. I was introduced to a Bible study group that met through word of mouth every Friday. The Americans brought Bibles in on their military aircraft alongside an ample supply of pork products! I had taken a risk and packed my most miniature Bible in my bags when I entered the Kingdom. I need not have bothered as there was a good supply at the home where the group met. Still, it was comforting to have my own, and I was careful not to take it out of my room for fear of being caught.

Disappointment

"Please call the firm as soon as possible regarding matters relating to the divorce settlement." the letter read. I had left my forwarding address with David's firm before leaving for the Kingdom.

"Hello, Davies and Warren," said the familiar voice of the firm's receptionist. I explained that I was asked to call, and she told me to hold on. Then David's voice came on.

"Hello, Sweetie, umm, Lilly, I'm married! "He announced as soon as he came on the line. My heart sank.

"Congratulations, it's about time," I replied, trying to sound happy despite my disappointment and confusion. The rest of the conversation went right over my head. The only knowledge I took away from it was that David was now married.

Debt-free

In just two months, I paid off all my credit card debts. I also saved almost all of my wages. Whenever possible, I worked an extra shift. It was with great satisfaction that I watched my bank balance grow slowly and steadily to over £10,000 by the time I was six months into my employment. It was a sizeable sum in the mid-1990s, worth about £18,000 today. I was often tempted to go on a spending spree, but I held on to the fact that I would need every penny when I got to Australia. Some of my colleagues who had lived in the Kingdom for a long while boasted that they only travelled business class with an entire matching set of Louis Vuitton/Pierre Cardin luggage! A friend convinced me to pamper myself after six months with beauty therapy. Naively, I fell in with her plans.

A door opened when our taxi stopped in front of the private home. We were greeted by a couple of Filipino women who ushered us into the beautifully decorated premises and assisted us into thick towelling dressing gowns. They instructed us to lie on massage tables. I had opted for a full body massage, facial, feet, and hand therapy. When asked if I wanted my nails painted, I declined. Three hours later, we both left the premises refreshed but 500 riyals -- almost £400 -- poorer. That was the only time I had beauty therapy. I learnt that some of my colleagues used the house nearly every week before attending a party. They had their nails and make-up done in colours that matched their outfits for the event. All professionally done! Working in the Kingdom for more than ten years, this had become their way of life. I could not bear the thought of wasting my hard-earned money this way.

Family matters

"Where are you going?" a colleague asked, noticing that I was soon due to go on annual leave.

"Singapore to see my family and Darwin in Australia to see about a job," I told her.

When I got to Singapore, I stayed with my eldest brother, his wife and their daughter. I managed to spend some time with my sister-in-law alone. We talked about her family and her marriage to my brother. It was great to be back home and see the family again.

"My Daddy spoilt me, so I had these conditions for my marriage. I will do no housework or babysitting. All I want to do is study. He agreed to it!" she said confidently and with authority. She was, of course, referring to my brother.

The penny dropped for me. I realised this must have been why they threw my mother out of the home! My brother had accepted the conditions of his marriage but had neglected to inform the family about it. My mother was a typical, house-proud Indian woman. To have a daughter-in-law who did no housework would have gone against her grain. I remembered my second brother telling me that my sister-in-law had not cleaned up after doing some cooking, leaving a pile of dirty pots and pans in the sink. I imagined the row that would have followed and my sister-in-law reminding my brother of her condition. He would have felt obliged to choose between his wife and his mother. He had chosen his wife. My sister-in-law sometimes walked off during a meal at a hawker centre because she did not like something I had said. I would be left with my half-eaten dish, wondering what had happened. After a few days, I realised this was not a happy home. However, I had committed to the stay and looked forward to my Darwin break. The experience left me searching for what our faith had taught us through the Bible. Our faith taught us to look after the widow and her orphans. Did that not mean anything to them? The mother occupied a position of great esteem in the Indian household.

The eldest son and his wife were expected to look after his parents till their death. And to that end, Mum had given my eldest brother preferential treatment all his life. She had signed the home ownership papers as head of the household, permitting him to buy the flat though he was single. It was the same flat to which he brought his wife home. My sister-in-law brought a Bible when she moved into their home; they read it daily. It all just did not seem right. I felt that he had betrayed our family. I had hoped my Bible-reading sister-in-law would help heal the family's hurt. Instead, she was the final rent in its fragile fabric, ripping us apart. We were never the same again.

Darwin

The flight from Singapore to Darwin was short, thankfully. It meant I could return to Singapore frequently; I had been away from my family for 14 years. I had only planned a brief four-day stay. My main aim was to acquaint myself with the local hospital and the town I planned to live and work in soon. I visited the hospital and toured the unit. At the time, Australia's employment policy demanded that all job applicants live in the country before applying for a job. I could not do much more than wait it out when I arrived. I returned to Singapore for a few more days before leaving for Saudi Arabia to work off the rest of my contract.

Bedouin Souq

"Have you been to the desert Bedouin souqs, Lilly?" My colleague asked me. I shook my head in reply, and she resolved to arrange for me to join the group on their next trip. Bedouin souqs or markets occurred as needed. The dates were known by word of mouth. Any journey for expatriates had to be carefully planned with permits and special transportation; attending a souq was no different. I managed to go to one, which was well worth the effort. How the driver knew where to go was a mystery. We were bussed into the desert to a pop-up market in the middle of nowhere near an oasis. The nomads converged from different settlements, displaying their goods on carpets over the sand. There were preserved dates and baskets made of palm leaves, elaborately wrought brass and stainless-steel pots and pans, Arab coffee pots with their characteristic long spouts, pottery and even camels and goats for sale. Slaughtered meat buzzing with flies was laid out in the open.

The expatriates went there for one particular purchase: Bedouin hand-made rugs. These were small pieces that were easily carried under the arm. They were exquisitely woven with tribal patterns and were undoubtedly a good buy as they were unavailable outside the Kingdom. For me, the experience of just being there was good enough. I could not carry much out of the Kingdom. I had sold all the furniture in my house in England. All I had were in boxes in transit between England and Australia. These would go into storage once they reached Australia, awaiting my final address.

Gold Souqs

"Come on, Lilly, let's go to the gold souqs in the next town," beckoned a fellow midwife. She had lived and worked in Saudi for more than ten years and was well acquainted with Saudi life. We took the local bus, a first for me. We travelled for about 40 minutes before alighting at our destination, not far from a mosque. There was no air conditioning, and it was in dire need of maintenance. My colleague offered advice as we walked towards the souq alongside the mosque.

"Don't come here on a Friday. It is where they chop off the limbs and behead lawbreakers. They will push you into the mosque to make you watch if they find you anywhere near here!" she said this very casually in a matter-of-fact tone.

I lost interest in the outing and could not wait to return home. The gold souq was no different to the jewellery shops in Little India in Singapore, only more opulent. Gold jewellery was worn to make a showy display of one's wealth here. Some of the designs were downright ugly. It looked like the goldsmiths would do anything to get as much gold on one item as possible. The hair on the back of my neck stood up when we had to pass the same mosque on our return to the bus station. I was glad to return to the refuge of my flat. Later, colleagues recounted how many Filipino workers had lost limbs and heads. There was also the infamous incident of an Indian man beaten to death on the streets by the *Mutawah*, the Saudi religious police. His wife's *abaya* had revealed too much of her ankles.

Hashing

During winter, the desert temperatures abated a little giving the expatriate community a chance to indulge in the sport of hashing. I had the opportunity to attend one of the events. It was an adult form of treasure hunting held on the outskirts of the desert. Markers had been set a few hours before. A leader who knew the area led the organised groups to ensure no one got lost in the desert. The trek was 5 km long. We were briefed before setting off to stay with the group for safety and ignore anything suspicious-looking emerging from the sand. The organisers were referring to the many honour killings in the desert. These were unmarked graves. Most victims were women who defied Saudi conventions and expectations, killed by their fathers, brothers or husbands in honour killings. The Saudis also eliminated anyone who was deemed a problem in the desert. Thankfully we did not see anything untoward. However, we missed the prize and returned to the base, where the evening entertainment consisted of a campfire, spit roast, music, song and dance. The Saudis were too far away to bother us, and a permit was granted for the event. Despite the dreadful events that were said to have taken place in the setting, I had a wonderful time.

All that glitters
"Everybody gets a chance to see it," Anna said of the Royal Suite. Whenever the King's wives or female relatives were admitted to the hospital, they stayed in the Royal Suite.

"One of the other midwives will accompany you to monitor the King's wife. So don't worry about it," Anna reassured me.

We pushed the cardiotocograph machine to the suite. My colleague knocked on the door, and we entered a large room with a plush interior. Several other Saudi women attended to the royal patient sitting on the bed. After we had recorded the necessary vital statistics, I went to the bathroom to wash my hands. To my astonishment, I was in a room where all the hardware was made of yellow gold. Everything glittered under the lights and reflected off the mirrors on the walls. On the way back, I remarked upon the gold in the bathroom. I was told the gold was real, not just gilt. Anna confirmed it when I asked her about it back in the ward.

Last days
Time flew by in the last few months of life in Saudi Arabia. I went on a final shopping spree to buy a meaningful souvenir to commemorate my time in Saudi. I settled on a tourist version of a Bedouin camel seat. The Bedouin seat is more rustic, made of small branches cut and lashed together into shape before being placed on the camel's rugged back. When bound this way, the components flexed as the camels moved, preventing the twigs from digging into their flesh. The tourist version consists of two fixed A-frame pieces joined laterally by two bars. The frame was topped with a leather seat and featured a seated camel head at each end. The A-frames are ornately carved with brass inlay. The entire contraption came flat-packed for ease of transportation.

I decided to return to England for the last time to see some friends and booked one-way tickets from Saudi to London, then to Singapore and finally to Australia. Despite being prudent, I found that my baggage was still overweight. Paring my possessions to the bare essentials, I engaged a freight company to transport the excess to Singapore. My elder brother agreed to store some of my things at his Singapore address till I had a permanent address in Australia. The staff at the birthing unit gave me a *Masalama* party; Anna gave me a Polish doll from her homeland as a parting gift. There were last hugs and well wishes from the staff. I took a taxi back to the flat to pick up my bags. Taking off my *abaya*, I laid it on the bed with a note to the next occupant, wishing her well and saying that she could have my *abaya*. After one last look around the flat and a brief check, I shut the door and took the lift to the ground floor. I returned my keys to the manager and thanked him for his help. He wished me well and laughed at the girl he had had to rescue from the window box just two days after her arrival! I watched the Kingdom disappear from the aircraft window. Never come back, I vowed. I had achieved what I wanted. My bank balance was much healthier, and I had a new life waiting for me in Australia. God has opened that door for me, and I could step out in faith, knowing He was by my side.

One Last look

Staying with a friend back in the town of my midwifery training, I hired a car and drove down memory lane to some of my old haunts. I was still waiting for a closure letter from Davis and Warren to inform me of the settlement of my divorce proceedings. Ultimately, I rang the office to find out what was happening.

"Hello, Davis and Warren," said the familiar voice of the receptionist.

"This is Lilly. I'm ringing to see if anything is left to do with my case," I said.

"Hold on, let me check with David," she replied.

"He'd like you to have lunch with him," the receptionist said after a few moments.

"No, I can't do that. David's a married man!" I cried, alarmed.

"No, no, it's a business lunch. He does this with all his clients," she clarified.

I thought about it for a moment, unsure, before finally agreeing. The next day David and I went to a Chinese restaurant at lunchtime. It was on the opposite side of the square in front of his office block. After we had ordered the meal, he told me about his wife.

"That will teach me to go to meetings. Her name is Janet. I call her Jan," he said, sounding almost angry. They had met at a local meeting.

I felt uncomfortable as he told me she had had a miscarriage before falling pregnant again with their present baby.

"She tried again so soon," I stated, the midwife in me kicking in.

"And for me!" he chimed in, pointing to himself.

My midwife maths was buzzing in my head. In May, when I was asked to ring him while in Saudi, he told me he was married. It was the beginning of July now. That was quick work! David agreed that I could take a photo with him in the restaurant. The waitress took the picture. We left the restaurant after he paid the bill. Stopping outside the square, we stood facing each other in front of his office block.

"Give me a hug," David asked unexpectedly.

And I did. Looking up into David's face towering above me, I noticed the question on his face. He seemed to want to ask me something, but could not say it.

Finally, I said, "Bye."

He nodded, and I let go of him. Turning around, I walked away with my head held high. I willed every bone in my body not to break down.

Farewell England

Once again, I peered out of the aircraft window, watching England disappear. I was still trying to understand why David had asked for a hug if I did not mean anything to him. Or did I? I had waited for him to make his move all those years before. The chasm between us had widened even more. I was glad to be moving to Australia without an encumbrance from England. All I had to do was concentrate on making my life in the land "Downunder".

"Oh God, help me!" I sent a silent plea heavenward.

I remembered my favourite bible verse:

> No test or temptation that comes your way is beyond the course of what others have had to face. All you need to remember is that God will never let you down; he'll never let

you be pushed past your limit; he'll always be there to help you overcome it." (1 Corinthians 10:13)

CHAPTER 7 – "DOWNUNDA"

My move to Australia was a leap of faith. Standing at the departure gate at Changi Airport, I said to my brother,

"I don't know what lies ahead of me. I have two pieces of paper saying I am a nurse and midwife. I have no job to go to, no roof over my head and £20,000 in the bank with which to make my future."

My brother replied, "Nothing ventured, nothing gained."

The flight took only four hours.

"Welcome to Australia," the immigration officer at Darwin Airport said. "Where are you heading?" he asked.

"I hope to find a job at the local hospital," I replied.

"You'll find something. The hospital is always looking for staff," the officer said confidently and smiled.

I took a taxi to the hotel I had booked for the next three days, checked in, and headed to Darwin General Hospital. On reaching the hospital, I headed to the maternity unit to see if I could find a manager. She sent me to the administration department to get information on registering with the local nursing board. Per her advice, I filled out application forms for a job and the Nursing and Midwifery Board registration. Mission accomplished; I headed out to meet John. John had worked at the same time as me in Saudi Arabia.

"Come and stay with us when you arrive in Darwin. You can have our spare room for as long as you need it," he generously offered.

After meeting his wife and having dinner with them, I took him up on his offer. They were warm and friendly, making me feel very much at home. I stayed with them for two weeks, making daily visits to the hospital's administration department to determine how my job application was progressing. There was none. They had to wait until I was on the roll of the Northern Territory board before making me an offer. I began to worry. The Australian government did not permit a job application while the applicant for permanent residence was not living in Australia. Not having a job made things difficult because I would have to live off my savings. I was glad I had spent that year working and saving; I could depend on that nest egg to see me through for a while. After three weeks had passed, I began to get anxious. I approached a local nursing recruiting agency which proved to be a good move as they soon secured me a position in remote Queensland. Trusting it would be the right job, I headed out, asking for a month's grace to get there, pleading my reliance on public transportation. I also wanted time to visit my ex-midwifery colleagues from England who had moved to Australia. I booked myself on the Greyhound bus with breaks of two days in every major city on the way, except for Melbourne, where I had a week to spend with my friends. The bus started its journey in the evening after a dinner break for the driver. The first break was at Alice Springs. As night darkened the skies, I made myself comfortable using the vacant seat next to me to spread out and fell asleep. It was a restless sleep, so I looked out the window.

"Must be dark now," I thought. It was, but I was astonished by what I saw—a vast array of stars twinkling like sequins in the pitch-black night sky. The sight was mesmerising. I had never seen anything like it before. I gazed at the sky for as long as possible, marvelling at God's creation. Settling back into my seat, I fell asleep again. When the bus stopped at a town called Katherine midway through the journey, I had seen intoxicated Aboriginal men and women outside the local watering hole, which was not a pleasant spectacle. At Alice Springs, I booked into a hotel for two nights and went to an Aboriginal music night. I also toured the Flying Doctors Museum. My next stop was Adelaide, where I visited the Barossa Valley wineries. At the hotel, I remembered Sam's younger sister had moved to Adelaide. Finding her in the phone book, I called her.

"Congratulations, your annulment has come through," she informed me.

"Really! I did not know that," I replied.

"It came through nearly six months ago," she said.

"I was in Saudi Arabia then. I'll have to check and see if any correspondence was sent there," I replied.

We spoke for a few more minutes, and she told me Sam had returned to Singapore at his mother's advice. He was living with his new Thai wife, whom his mother had introduced to him. We promised to stay in touch.

"You will always be my sister-in-law, no matter what," she assured me.

In Melbourne, I met with my former colleagues and stayed with them for a week. It felt like we had never been apart. I realised that I had missed them more than I had known. They showed me around Melbourne. All too soon, I boarded the bus for Sydney and on to Brisbane, where I took a smaller bus to my final destination.

The hospital

The instructions were to report to the emergency department, where the receptionist asked me to wait. A nurse eventually turned up.

"Hello, Lilly, my name is Nick Peters. I'm one of the nurses here. Call me Nick. Welcome to the Top End hospital. I'll take you to your lodgings. As it is Saturday, I won't show you around. On Monday, you'll meet the Director of Nursing at the admin office at 8.00 am. He'll get you fitted with uniforms and do your orientation," he informed me.

We walked a short distance from the main building towards the accommodation block, and Nick led me to a unit. He opened the door and handed the key to me.

"Thank you, Nick," I said and put my hand out to him, which he took in a handshake.

"The kitchen staff have put milk and bread supplies in the fridge to start you off. The pub just down the road will serve an evening meal from five. There's a fish and chip takeaway as well. The supermarket closes at eight and has a fairly good stock of groceries. I'll see you on shift. Have a good rest tonight," Nick smiled, waved and headed to another flat I assumed was his.

"How many deliveries do you have a year?" I asked the director of nursing.

"Difficult to say ... about 10 or 20," he guesstimated.

"Who does the antenatal care and the antenatal classes?" I inquired.

"Oh, the early childhood nurses do that. You don't have to worry about it," he said.

"When was the last delivery?" I asked as alarm bells began to ring in my head. What had I let myself in for?

My first week on the job was barely over, and I already sensed that it was not a match for my skills. I had not worked in general nursing for over 14 years. The director told me that the last delivery had occurred two months ago and none was booked for the future. I did not say anything and decided to wait a bit, thinking it was better to give myself time to think and re-evaluate. But it soon came back to me. The hospital was a thirty-bed, mixed-sex cottage public facility. The local GP was also the hospital resident doctor. On the weekends, a locum from the city provided cover.

Settling in

Looking around, I found I had a one-bedroom flat with a small kitchen, living-cum-dining area, toilet and bathroom. The building was typical of Queensland: made of wood, appointed with basic modern furniture, well-maintained and clean. I quickly unpacked and headed to town to get groceries and look around. The bus driver was only too happy to fill me in on the way. It was a small seaside town with only about 2,500 permanent residents. This number doubled during the holiday season. While there were significant local services for residents, most regularly drove to the next big city to do major shopping. The walk to the town centre was short, and I soon reached the waterfront, which was quite beautiful. After shopping, I returned to my flat. Someone had left some novels and brochures for local tourist attractions in the living room. I dived into them to see what I could do on my days off. I settled down for the rest of the week, walking along the streets on Sunday to take in my surroundings.

A crisis of faith

I did not look for a church. I wanted to rethink and evaluate my faith which had taken a downward turn after the divorce and my departure from England. I felt let down by the Catholic Church. Yes, I had attended Sunday mass, but my heart was not in it. I did not feel the love I was reading about in the Bible. Indeed, my Bible reading had tapered off in the last few months. It saddened me to think about my marriage to Sam. He called me a hypocrite and did not care for me as a faith-filled husband should have. The demise of my marriage after a childhood of homelessness and poverty made it hard for me to keep up my unquestioning faith in a loving, paternal God.

Initiation

After a few shifts, I met all the nurses and settled down in my job. The staff were friendly and helpful. I soon had offers to be shown around the town and advice on the do and don'ts of small-town living. The nurses gave me an initiation to the country.

"Seeing that you are new to Australia, you must try our national dish," a nurse said during a tea break.

She placed a plate of savoury crackers smeared with butter and some brown stuff before me.

"You don't have to eat it if you don't like it," she said kindly. Everyone in the staff room was watching me.

I looked at her offering and thought the brown stuffed looked like Bovril. When we were ill, my mother used to mix some of it in rice porridge. I quite liked Bovril. Picking up a cracker, I popped it into my mouth. Big mistake! It was bitter and salty all at once. I found it hard to continue chewing but kept going and eventually swallowed the mouthful. My distaste must have shown on my face as everyone burst into laughter.

"That's Vegemite, Australia's number one spread. You have just passed your initiation. Welcome to Australia," the nurse who had made the plateful of goodies said, laughing. "Don't worry. We won't hold it against you if you don't like it, Lilly."

I grabbed the nearest glass of water and downed it.

"That was pure salt! I'll be sure never to have it again," I gasped. They must have liked it because the rest of the crackers soon disappeared.

We spent the remainder of the afternoon chatting. Everyone was kind and concerned about ensuring that I was settling in. I was warned against wandering the town's streets alone after dark. The local thug was known to kidnap women on their own after dark and rape them. The police knew him well, but somehow, he evaded prosecution. He would steal the residents' dogs and demand they pay a ransom for their safe return. Pet owners who failed to pay found their dog hanging from a tree in his front yard. And I thought I had left Saudi Arabia!

On the ward

For the first time in my 24 years of nursing, I experienced dispatch, retrieval and arrival of patients from the city via a medical helicopter service. We received them and sent them to the larger city hospital on the landing pad outside the main hospital building. On one occasion, an Aboriginal man was admitted with acute gastrointestinal bleeding. He had to have one-on-one nursing care while waiting for the retrieval service. I was one of two nurses on duty that day, and it fell to me to care for him. The patient had two intravenous drips, one in each arm. One was for blood, while the other was for maintenance fluids. I had my hands full and was relieved indeed when the retrieval team arrived, and I was able to dispatch my patient to a facility that was better equipped. At the rate that he had been bleeding, I had feared losing him. I was glad to return to the rest of my patients. The desk phone started ringing, and my colleague Joanne answered. It was personal. She spent the next 30 minutes chatting with her friend, feet on the desk.

Meanwhile, the call bell board was lit like a Christmas tree. I was outraged. What kind of nursing was this? I was seething as I attended to the needs of my allocated patients. I refused to help my colleague with hers. Unchristian of me, I know, but my anger got the better of me.

"It's hospital policy in the bush, Lilly. You must go in the ambulance with the Doctor to retrieve the body. It's a payback shooting," Nick, who was in charge, briefed me. I was working the night shift, and it was sometime after midnight.

"What does that mean?" I asked the Doctor on the way out. He explained that amongst the Aboriginal tribes, there were tribal "payback" killings. This form of customary law killing is still practised, though at odds with white Australian law. It is an essential aspect of settling grievances amongst Aboriginal communities. Acknowledging the right to punish prevents the outbreak of revenge killings. After an incident, the elders and victims meet to negotiate to restore balance and enable the families and tribes concerned to continue their relationships. The victim party states its demands, and the offending party agrees to settle the debt incurred. The process prevents conflict from escalating, promotes healing and restores peace in the community. It was still dark when we arrived. A local pointed the house out. The ambulance driver and the Doctor carried the stretcher into the house. I followed them into a house that had gone to wrack and ruin. There were holes in the plasterboard walls. Furniture that had seen better days was strewn around. Clothes and other items were scattered across the floor or piled into small mounds. No wonder; there were no cupboards for storage. Nor were there beds, just dirty mattresses strewn on the floor or leaning against the walls. Graffiti was scrawled across the walls. Lying on the floor in a bedroom was the body of a woman. Blood splattered the wall behind the body. Next to her was a rifle. She had placed the gun in her mouth before pulling the trigger. The Doctor did a cursory check to confirm that she was dead. He asked an older man sitting in the room about the time of the suicide. We lifted the body onto the stretcher, loaded it into the ambulance and headed to the mortuary. I returned to the ward with the Doctor to sign the death notification as a witness.

"How often does this happen?" I asked.

"Often enough," he replied, not looking at me as he continued writing his notes. I returned to work, resolving to look for another job in the city!

Fruity Joe

"Everybody knows Fruity Joe," Nick claimed. "We all know to look out for him when we drive home in the dark. If he's drunk -- and that's often -- he walks down the middle of the road, using the dividing line to guide him home. He lies on that line and sleeps when he's too drunk to keep walking. We skirt around him as we drive! He's called that because he makes moonshine with mangoes. In summer, there are more mangoes than anyone knows what to do with. Waste not, want not, I say. He's also a frequent flyer at the local pub." Nick elaborated.

As intriguing as Fruity Joe was, I was more interested in the local fruit. Shame that it was not mango season. I saw a tree just outside my flat. I imagined all the lovely mangoes I could feast on and the many preserves and dishes I could cook with them. On a day off, another colleague Anita took me to the botanical gardens. Looking around, I stopped in front of a big tree about 30 feet high, nearly as wide as it was tall. I was astounded. It was a curry leaf tree. I had only seen curry leaf shrubs back home, at most five to 10 feet tall. Perhaps they did not reach such lofty heights because they were constantly harvested for their leaves. South Indian recipes call for curry leaves in almost every dish. This tree had probably never been harvested and had grown to its full magnificent glory. It was beautiful. I stood gazing at it in awe, plucked a few leaves to taste them and confirm that it was a curry leaf tree. Anita, who had lived in the town for some years, reckoned that no one would mind if I took a few leaves for cooking. She suggested I cook a curry for the staff, so I picked a handful. The excursion included a trip to the lighthouse's highest point in the area. It overlooked the river. The estuary meandered on one side and the town to the other, with the buildings slowly merging into the wilderness in the distance. Anita and I then went for a walk on the beach.

"Never come here during the monsoon season. You might bump into Old Salty," she said.

"Who's Old Salty?" I asked

"Old Salty is a cunning crocodile. He comes when the waters are high and lives in the mangrove swamp. He is known to wait in the swamp for the unsuspecting or foolish person who decides to swim in the river despite the "No swimming" signs. He comes out and waits on the road cutting off the only escape route for them. There's no chance of escaping him. All the locals know not to swim here," she explained.

"Shall we head back home?" she asked. I could not agree fast enough.

Decision

Two weeks after arrival, I decided I couldn't continue working in this hospital. There were just not enough maternity hours for me to keep my midwifery qualifications viable. Scanning the national newspaper, I noted and responded to jobs advertised by hospitals in the city and received prompt replies. Two hospitals offered me a job, but neither came with accommodation. An ex-colleague from my stint in Saudi Arabia worked in one of them and kindly contributed to helping me find a house. I accepted the job at the hospital where she worked and informed the director of nursing of my impending resignation. A few days before I left, I found the atmosphere at the hospital thick with tension and fear.

I learnt there had been a murder the night before, near the hospital. Two brothers were involved in a shooting incident, and one had killed the other. The brothers were well known for being like chalk and cheese. The rowdy brother had turned up at the responsible brother's doorstep and made a ruckus. A local thug, this sibling was the same one who terrorised the town and hung kidnapped dogs on the tree in his front yard. Despite his brother's repeated instructions to leave, he had refused. He was shot when he attempted to breach the door and enter the house. The police arrested the brother who pulled the trigger. But the gossip was that he had done the town a favour and ought to be released on the grounds of self-defence. The town drew people seeking a gateway to the wilderness. It was undoubtedly an exciting town. The staff of the hospital gave me a little farewell party. We enjoyed a potluck meal at my flat. I cooked a curry with the last curry leaves from the botanical garden. A Taxi would arrive at 6.00 am to take me to the bus depot.

"Would you like a joint?" Joanne asked.

"A what?" I said, confused.

"A joint, weed, Marijuana!" she expanded; I was lost for words.

"Joanne, thank you, but no. I'm from Singapore, where they hang you for possessing narcotics!" I told her, alarmed that a nurse would indulge in drugs.

Why was I surprised after all I had seen and heard in the short month I had been here?

The early morning bus ride back to the city was a beautiful trip through the tropical forest along the coast, different from the one the bus had traversed on my arrival. Once in the city, I had to book a train to the next town where I would work on the outskirts of Brisbane.

"We have no economy seats on the next departing train, which is mid-morning tomorrow. And even then, you cannot afford it because only first-class seats are available," said the arrogant and presumptuous ticketing clerk. My blood began to boil.

"What is the price of a single first-class ticket?" I demanded.

"Four hundred dollars," he intoned slowly and clearly, relishing every syllable.

"I'll have it!" I replied sharply.

Not looking at me, the ticketing clerk sorted out the ticket and accepted my credit card for payment. He did not deserve my gratitude, I fumed, not with that attitude! I left without thanking him. The train journey was an overnight trip covering some 400 km. It departed mid-morning and arrived late in the afternoon the following day. My single first-class cabin lived up to expectations, though it was not overly luxurious. I made myself comfortable and waited till the train pulled out of the station before exploring the rest of the carriages. I found a lounge and bar and the restaurant car. Settling in the lounge, I tried to read with no success. The rolling views outside were just too distractingly beautiful. I decided to watch it go by as I would not be likely to come this way again. A few more passengers joined me in the carriage, and we chatted casually. Soon it was lunchtime, and we headed to the restaurant. Crisp white napery, crystal glasses and silverware adorned the tables. The menu featured Australian bush foods. It was my first-time tasting Moreton Bay bugs, wattle seed ice cream and kangaroo fillets dressed with a lemon myrtle dressing – all worthy of the hefty price tag. Back in the lounge, cocktails were served during happy hour till dinner, which was as tasty as lunch and followed by after-dinner drinks. The evening's entertainment was a piano recital. I called it quits at 10.00 pm, heading back to my cabin for a shower. It was a moving experience indeed! Passengers seeking a shower stand on a perforated raised metal platform that responds to the train's every jolt and turn as it hurtles at over 100 km per hour. Settling in for the night, I looked out at the sky, hoping for a repeat of the previous bus night's dazzling display of stars. Unfortunately, the light pollution from the towns along the route obscured the stars in the night sky. Fortunately, lulled by the train's movement, I fell asleep effortlessly. Refreshed after a good night's sleep, I headed to the restaurant carriage for a hot gourmet breakfast and a repeat of the previous evening's proceedings of drinks at the lounge while watching the countryside roll by before another delicious lunch. The wonderful experience ended when the train stopped at the town in which I was going to work. The train journey reminded me of a first-class flight I had enjoyed when Sam was with the airline; I was upgraded on a staff ticket. Oh well, all good things must come to an end.

Starting anew
"Lilly, Lilly!" I heard my name called. Standing on the train station platform with my bags, I turned to find Di, my old friend from Saudi Arabia. She was waving and hurrying towards me. We gave each other a big hug.

"Welcome, Lilly. It's so good to see you. Can I help you with your bags?" she grabbed one of them.

"Oh, Di, you don't know how good it is to see a familiar face!" I smiled at her.

"I'll take you to your flat. It's not very far from here. I hope you like it. The estate agent made me promise you won't throw wild parties!" She giggled.

"I think I'm past that, Di," I reassured her.

We walked about 500 m before turning into a complex of single-story units. Most of the residents were retired. It suited me well because I wanted a quiet place to sleep on night duty. The flat was a stand-alone one, with a designated car park. I found a small two-bedroom furnished unit with an open-plan living, dining and kitchen area. The bigger bedroom featured a double bed; a single bed was in the other. The flat had a dual heating and cooling system, for which I was thankful. Di left me to settle in, handing me the keys and making arrangements to meet me again the following day to show me around the town. She had thoughtfully bought milk, bread and some spreads, which she had put into the fridge. It was enough to start me off and a nice change from all the rich food on board the train. I spent the rest of the day unpacking and settling in. The kitchen had basic crockery and cooking utensils, which would do for now. I made a mental note of what I needed when shopping. A music system was a priority buy. I can't live without music. I walked around the complex and nearby streets in the evening and turned in early. The following morning Di and I roamed about town. The real estate agent was my first stop. I signed my rental contract, and we made for the shopping strip to find the supermarket and local stores. We had lunch together before we parted company. I was to report to work the following day. Back at the unit, I listed what I needed to do to settle into the country. Transferring my British driver's licence to a local one was a top priority. I had to be mobile to live in this big country. The bulk of my money was still in England. I would transfer it to Australia as soon as possible to buy a car and perhaps a deposit for a unit. My third 'first day at work' in some 15 months felt like groundhog day. Once again, I underwent orientation: a tour of the hospital, uniform fitting, and the usual administration procedures to finalise the details of my employment at the hospital.

I was on a contract for casual work with a view to a permanent position when one became available. The maternity unit, as expected, consisted of antenatal services, birthing, a postnatal ward and a sick baby nursery. There was no community midwifery service. Birthing was by conventional methods with no provision for water births. Home births were frowned upon. Midwives who engaged in home births were demonised. Many worked alone and feared being disbarred from registration if something went wrong with the delivery. It was obstetric nursing, not midwifery, as I had trained and experienced. Nevertheless, it was a job, a source of income, and a good starting point.

Seeking

On the first Sunday, I attended mass at the local Catholic Church. I joined the stream of people walking into the building; there was no one to welcome people at the door. The service was no different from what I was used to since childhood. The congregation consisted mainly of Caucasians and Filipinos. We stood, kneeled, sang the hymns, recited the prayers and heard the readings and the sermon. When the service was over, I walked out of the church. No one had said a word to me. My soul and spirit did not feel nourished at all.

It was time to find another denomination. In the depths of my heart, I felt a stirring that there was something more than what I had just experienced and had been experiencing as faith all the past years. I did not feel nourished spiritually or see any form of love or fellowship that demonstrated the love of God. That evening I surfed the Internet with the laptop I had bought in Singapore. I was hoping to find my old friends and reconnect. While in Saudi Arabia, many of my colleagues found friends from all over the world to communicate with, sometimes forging long-term friendships. A number even found marriage partners. After toying with spending the rest of my life alone, I decided I wasn't cut out for it. My faith told me that God had not meant for us to manage on our own when he created Adam and Eve. Instead, a man and woman would thrive together in the marriage covenant. I still firmly believed that God heard and answered my prayers. He had brought me thus far. My search on the Internet brought me to a dating website with a free ten-day trial, so I selected it and added my profile. The site requested a pseudonym and a description of the qualities I sought in a man. My request was for a gentleman seeking a committed relationship. He had to be a practising Christian, attached to and actively serving in a church. He would have to be employed and aged between 40 and 50. Before I hit the 'send button', I prayed fervently.

"Almighty God, find me someone right for me. I tried to do this myself and failed miserably, as you know. I turn to you now and place my trust in you. His Christian denomination does not matter to me. All I ask is a man who is committed to you and will be committed to me. He must take the Bible to heart and do what the book of Ephesians says: love his wife as Christ loved his church. In turn, I will submit to him as a Christian wife must. Whatever denomination he is attached to will also be mine," I prayed.

Challenged

"Why do you have to come and change things? Who do you think you are?" A midwife challenged me in the staff room during the lunch break.

"We are not trained to do it and are not paid to either!" said another.

The Saturday before, I had worked in the birthing suites and, after attending a delivery, had performed an episiotomy repair. The Doctor on call was in the operating theatre performing a surgical procedure for a miscarriage. It would be some time before she could return to birthing to repair the episiotomy. I was trained and had done over one hundred repairs in the past. My training had taught me that a delayed repair would mean exposing the patient to a higher chance of infection. With that in mind, I picked up the phone, rang the theatre and informed the Doctor that I had the training to repair it. She could check with me and assess my work when she returned to birthing. She agreed, and I started suturing. While I was still working on the procedure, she returned and watched me for a while. Satisfied with what I was doing, she sat in an armchair reading the papers while waiting for me to finish. When I had completed the procedure, she checked the repair and said she could find no fault with it. I did not think any more of it. On Monday, the staff was buzzing with what I had done at the weekend. They were firmly against a nurse doing episiotomy repairs and stated their position loudly, clearly and somewhat aggressively. They did not like that I had repaired an episiotomy.

"I have been trained to do such repairs and have been doing it for many years. I will not de-skill myself because you have not got the skill," I replied.

No more was said about it after that. I informed the midwifery manager of what I had done at my earliest convenience. She told me that procedures had to be followed, adding that midwives in the unit were not trained to do episiotomy repairs. She finished by firmly forbidding me to do any more such procedures. Her admonition knocked the stuffing out of me. Would I have to find another maternity unit that would allow me to practise as I had in England so I would not lose my skills? Once again, I found myself doing some serious thinking. Transferring my British driver's licence required that I be re-examined. The driving test was odd, with the assessor more interested in why I came to Australia and my job. He asked me to do a three-point turn on a hill crest. I obliged even as I stated that it was not the ideal place for such a manoeuvre and promptly hit the curb! I passed despite this. A fellow midwife was selling a second-hand car; I went to view it. It was just what I wanted: an aqua-blue Ford Laser costing some $10,000. I had to withdraw the amount from my English bank account to pay for it. To my surprise, the bank demanded proof of identity first. The only way I could get that evidence was to call Davis and Warren, speak to David, and ask him for help to release all my money and transfer it to my Australian account.

"Hello, Davis and Warren," the familiar voice of the receptionist said when I called the firm. I explained what I needed, and she put me on hold.

"Hello, Lily. You're not in trouble, are you?" David said when he came on the line.

"After all this time, you should know me. I did not go to work in Saudi to keep my money in England," I raged. "I have a car waiting for me in the car yard. I want to buy it with the money I earned. I will also need to pay my flat bond and month's rent. Why is the bank withholding my money? It's mine!" I ranted.

"Leave it with me. I'll sort it out for you." David assured me

I rang off, having given him my Australian bank details. It did not take long for the transfer to happen. David did not bill me for his services. I picked up my first car and paid for it in full.

Replies

It was exciting reading the replies from the dating agency. An Indian man wrote in ungrammatical English, saying he did not mind an older woman. Having just kicked one Indian man out of my life, I told him in not too many words what to do with himself! Another reply came from a man with six children—not going that way! His note read like he wanted a babysitter. Yet another wanted only to meet once a week and on a Wednesday! That suggested an affair. I was not interested in being the side piece of a man who would complain about his wife and expect understanding and sympathy from me; it certainly was not my cup of tea. One reply stood out, though. He was a Swiss immigrant living in New South Wales who ticked all my boxes. He was an active and practising Christian looking for a lasting commitment, not a fling. Something about him felt different. I sent him a reply. Buddy responded the following day. And so, we began.

Buddy

At 48, Buddy was eight years older than me. His marriage of 25 years had just broken up, much to his heartbreak with his wife finding another partner. He had two children; the eldest, a girl, had left home and was studying for her degree. His son was sitting for his school-leaving exams. He did not know of his parents' breakup yet. Buddy had decided to keep the separation from him until after his exams. Although Buddy did not reveal where he worked, he told me he was an Information Technology (IT) Manager. The dating agency had advised us not to reveal our true identities until we were comfortable with what we read in the emails we exchanged. Telephone numbers and photos were also withheld. We wrote to each other every day. To test Buddy out, I suggested we write our own love story. I wrote the female part and he, the male. It turned out to be a good move. We discovered much about each other's mindsets and attitudes as the story progressed. I soon became fond of this chap. Reading his replies to my part of the story was exciting, and I looked forward to reading them. After a month, we exchanged phone numbers and scheduled a call. We also gave each other our actual names. Buddy's name was Gian, meaning God's precious gift. Was this a sign of God's generous provision for my future? I wondered.

The call

"Hello, Lilly," the soft masculine voice said.

"Hello Gian, how are you?" I replied.

"I'm well. The Swiss accent was quite evident. It's lovely to hear your voice at last," Gian said.

"The same here. Where are you calling me from? I can hear cars in the background?" I inquired.

"I am calling you from the bush. I must drive through it to get home. The highway cuts right through it. I've just come off it and am in my car," he explained.

It was just past 5.00 pm in the late afternoon. We talked about our day at work. Gian knew I was a midwife, but I wanted to learn more about his job. He told me he was the area health service's manager for information technology—a position he had held for over ten years. We talked for a few more minutes before ringing off, planning to call each other whenever I was home between shifts. We called each other every day after that. After a couple of weeks, we decided to exchange photographs.

"You are not going to send me one of those glamorous ones, are you?" Gian teased.

"I have one of those if that's what you like," I teased him.

I had a set of photographs done in a studio a few weeks ago. I decided to boost my self-confidence and capture youth bloom while I still had it. I had recently turned 40 and was aware of the advent of middle age. I sent Gian a number of these shots. There was one of me in uniform at work holding a baby and a second one of me in a saree. The third was a portrait, a "glamorous one." His photos showed a trim man of average height with a broad smile, green eyes and a head full of dark hair. I thought Gian was good-looking with a kind face. We had a lot more to talk about from then on. Our story-writing stopped as talking was more exciting! Christmas was around the corner, and we decided to meet on the 27th of December. Gian was living in the next state and suggested we meet somewhere in the middle, in a seaside town. I had the day off, but he would work in the morning that day. We made plans to meet. Gian would drive the 500 km that separated us.

Christmas Day
What a difference from England! Although the wards were decorated with Christmas decorations, there was no special Christmas lunch for the mothers. The Christmas baby did not have a special cot. The summer heat made it like a hot Christmas in Singapore; I missed the English Christmas. It just was not the same. I worked a morning shift, went home to my favourite grilled mackerel meal and waited for Gian's call in the evening.

"Merry Christmas, Honey." Gian wished me over the phone. He was calling me after the family dinner, their last one. His ex-wife would soon be leaving the family home with her new boyfriend. It had been an emotionally charged day for Gian.

"Merry Christmas to you, my Darling," I replied.
"What did you have for dinner?" He asked.
"Grilled mackerel," I announced.
"Grilled fish on Christmas day!" He sounded astonished.

"Why not?" I dodged, "It's my favourite meal. I had a beautiful salad and a roast potato to go with it. Now I have a full belly."

"And you are all by yourself on Christmas day. I am sorry I can't be with you, Lilly, but I will make it up to you when I see you the day after tomorrow," he promised. He seemed concerned that I was alone.

"Don't worry; I have spent many a Christmas alone in England. I'm used to it," I hastened to reassure him.

We chatted for a while, and Gian gave me the hotel details. He would arrive late in the afternoon. While it would take him three hours to arrive at the destination, it would only take me two. When he rang off, I felt both excited and anxious. Was he the right one? Was I doing the right thing meeting him? It was too late to pull out, and I would never know if I did not go. I had asked God to choose for me, so I must trust Him and step out in faith. I had not given up on my faith yet; I just had to find a congregation that met my spiritual needs. Perhaps Gian would lead me there.

The drive

After lunch, I drove the 200 km to our seaside town. As I turned into the hotel driveway, I spotted Gian standing by his white Holden Commodore. He was dressed in a white business shirt, tie and black trousers. I watched him as he dragged a black briefcase out of the back seat. He looked up at me as I pulled up.

"Gian?" I asked when I'd wound down the window.

"Yes, Lilly, it's me," he replied, dropping the briefcase into the boot.

I jumped out of my car and ran straight into his arms. Gian greeted me with a big bear hug and a long kiss. I fit snugly into his frame: the top of my head stopped under his chin. He smelt of a pleasant spicy aftershave. His green eyes sparkled, and he had a big grin.

"Oh, it's so good to see you. What beautiful brown legs you have!" He exclaimed.

I was pleased that he had noticed my best asset. I had chosen to wear shorts to show them off.

"Thank you, it's lovely to see you, too," I said, squeezing him around the waist.

"I'd better park my car before someone else comes in," I told him. Releasing each other from our first embrace, I parked alongside his car. When I got out, Gian put a large, soft, cream-coloured teddy bear into my arms and gave me another kiss.

"Merry Christmas, Honey," he said, smiling at me.

I hugged it tightly. It was the first teddy bear anyone had ever given me. What a precious gift! I gave him his Christmas gift: a silk tie with a red and blue pattern. We had dinner in a steak house, and Gian ordered a red wine to go with the meal.

"About an inch is enough for me," I said as he poured me some.

"You said you were a social drinker in your portfolio!" Gian reminded me.

"Yes, I am more of a cocktail person though I do have the occasional Scotch or brandy," I told him.

"This is unusual for me, taking a bottle of wine home after dinner. Usually, we would be on our second or third bottle with dinner if I was out with my ex. It has made the meal very cheap." Gian informed me as we walked back to the hotel with the half-full bottle in his hand.

We talked into the night and most of the next day at the beach, getting to know each other better. On Sunday morning, Gian asked if I wanted to attend a church service. He was happy to participate in any service I chose. We wound up going to a Catholic Church for the late morning service.

"I attend a happy-clappy type of church. It's Pentecostal," he said.

After church, we headed to a restaurant for lunch. At the waterfront, we talked about our relationship. The beautiful coral-white beach lay before us, and the aqua-blue, crystal-clear waters curled up into waves crashing onto the beach as the tide came in.

Gian took my hand into his and asked: "Would you commit to a permanent relationship with me?" he asked.

"Yes, I would," I confirmed.

"Do you want to have children, Lilly?" Gian asked.

"No," I replied. "I'm 40. My time for having babies safely is over. I couldn't bear to be told that the child I carried was likely to be born with Downs syndrome and that I ought to have the pregnancy terminated. I had come to terms with that long ago when I was going through my divorce," I said, my voice thick with emotion.

"I am sorry," Gian said. "I had the snip soon after my second child. A reversal is going to be difficult at this stage."

"Well, that sorts things out for both of us then…though our babies would have been beautiful with our mixed blood. Don't fret. It was just not meant to be Gian," I reassured him. "We have each other."

"What do we do with the distance between us?" he asked.

I have just come into the country and still feeling my way around. I thought aloud: "It is common sense for me to move down and join you where you live. You have a more stable job and a home. I can get a job at the local hospital where you live."

"Visit me first for a couple of weeks and see if you can adjust to living in the bush," Gian suggested cautiously.

"I'll check my roster and book a flight down to you. We'll take things from there, shall we?" I asked.

"Yes, I'll look forward to showing you my home," Gian said, smiling at me.

We sat and watched the waves for a while, enjoying being in each other's company until it was time to check out and make our way home. As I drove home, I felt at peace with the last two days spent with Gian. There had been no emotional highs or lows. Just a quiet reassurance that felt right.

The visit

In mid-January, I flew to Gian's hometown. He met me at the airport. He had booked us into a hotel as his ex-wife was still packing and had not yet moved out. She was due to leave that day, and they had planned a farewell dinner at their home the day after she moved out. I offered to cook that meal for them. Gian was pleased to let me do it, although he could cook a meal. The following day he drove me to his house.

"I got the CD you sent me in the post a few days ago. And I listened to the track you wanted me to," I said, looking at him. "Thank you."

"Well, that tells you how I feel about living in the city because my heart is in the bush ... you know, surrounded by nature," he said. He looked concerned as he drove home.

A famous Australian vocalist sang the song in question. The track was aptly named *A Bushman can't survive*. The song is about the emotional turmoil a country boy felt because the city girl he loved had a life in the city, and he could not survive there. The city's promise of "lights, opera, rock and roll and party pies" did not match his beloved bush. The drive lasted some 15 minutes, and Gian's anxiety was palpable. I did not say anything, waiting to see his home before speaking. We were both silent, each absorbed in our thoughts.

"Here we are," Gian announced after a while. "This is the start of the dirt road to my home. It is a five-kilometre stretch through the bush. There are just five homes, and mine is on 120 acres. My ex-wife and I share this with her brother. We have separate houses within the acreage. So, you won't be living with them if you decide to live with me," he explained.

Gian drove past two houses, finally turning into a long driveway before stopping in front of a large bungalow. No one was home. His son had gone with his mother as he was moving into town with her. Two dogs greeted us: a female border collie and a blue heeler. The house was simple, built of Besser block with a tiled roof. It was about ten years old but still appeared in need of completion. The walls required rendering; curtains were hung on a string. Gian had laid the parquet floor himself. There were four large bedrooms, an ensuite, a family bathroom, a modest kitchen and an underground cellar that was flooded! It certainly needed some loving and a woman's touch; neither worried me. Outside, Gian had planted an orchard. There was also a sizeable vegetable garden and a large chicken coop for about 30 chickens. A three-bay shed stood by the side. It housed a tractor and a trailer. A large water tank collected rainwater for the household. There was an independent sewerage system. Ten heads of cattle of various breeds occupied the rest of the acreage, with the house within a fenced-off area of about five acres. Some distance away was a significant 40 megalitre dam. The rest of the place was bush. There were no other houses seen. Only the call of various bush birds broke the silence. I had only ever seen something like this in Australian movies! As I surveyed the scene before me, Gian crept up behind me. Putting his hands on my shoulders, he asked,

"Well, what do you think? Good enough to call home?" He asked, trying to sound casual.

"More than good enough," I said, thinking of the shoe-box-sized flats in Singapore. I recalled the squalid one-bedroom flat we had lived in when we were rehoused after being homeless. What would my family say if they saw this? Even my house in England could not come close! But Gian did not know all of that. There would be time enough to reveal all in the future.

"Yes, plenty good enough," I repeated, turning around and giving him a big hug. "I am home," Gian smiled. His eyes twinkled, and he planted a kiss on my forehead.

"I have a dinner to cook tonight," I reminded him of the final get-together we would have with his ex-wife, her boyfriend and their son.

"What do you need for the meal? I've got a full vegetable garden of produce for you if you want it," he offered, pointing to the vegetable patch.

We went through this, and Gian picked various vegetables for our dinner. Then we drove to the local supermarket for meat and spices. Back in the kitchen, I cooked a chicken *kurma* accompanied by *biryani* rice with nuts and raisins, a mixed vegetable stir-fry, papadums and *raita*. Much to my delight, the meal went well with the family, and we all parted in good spirits. Gian drove me back to the hotel. The rest of my visit was spent touring his home town and talking -- lots of talking.

"So, Lilly, what do you want to do about coming down here?" Gian enquired.

"Well, first things first. I have to quit my job. Then I'll pack up my stuff and drive down once I've completed my notice," I replied.

"I'll fly up and drive you down. It's a long distance, and you shouldn't do it on your own," Gian offered.

"Oh, thank you, that would be such a help!" I grabbed the offer.

We decided that Gian would fly up and drive me down to his home on the first weekend after my contract ended. I flew back to my little unit with wings on my feet.

A perfect start
It was a coincidence that the day after Gian arrived to drive me to his home was Valentine's Day. Realising this, I planned a big surprise for him. I wanted an impressive start and found a

couple of events celebrating Valentine's Day. At the airport, I watched him disembark and walk pensively across the tarmac towards the arrival hall, where I met him. It was so good to be in his arms again. I had not realised how much I had missed him during our three weeks apart. On the drive back, I told him we had to go to a particular town tonight as I had planned a special to start our life together.

"So where are we going?" he wanted to know.

"Not telling you!" I teased as we drove to the hotel that was further inland.

Dinner was a basic affair at the country pub. We turned in early as we had to be up at 4.00 am to catch the transport to our destination. Whilst waiting for the coach in the early morning cool, Gian tried again.

"Still not telling me?"

"Nope!" I said, feeling very cheeky. "You'll see soon enough."

It was still dark when we boarded the bus and set off. After a while, the bus stopped beside a farmhouse opposite a large barn, floodlit with spotlights. A coupe utility drove out when the large barn doors were pulled open. On it was my surprise.

"It's a hot air balloon! You are taking me on a balloon ride!" Gian exclaimed. "You are full of surprises, Lilly!"

I just looked at him and smiled. There were two balloons, soon inflated with powerful gas burners. About six of us and the pilot climbed into the basket and quickly ascended into the sky. The sun was rising, and we saw that the property we had taken off from was a sugarcane plantation. When we reached maximum flight height, the morning sun shone on breathtaking farmland dotted with small towns. In the distance was the Great Dividing Range. The glass-adorned skyscrapers of the nearest city glistened as they reflected the sun's rays. The view was spectacular. The two balloons flew side by side, and the other climbed higher. After a while, it started to pass over our balloon. Gian held onto me rather tightly, and I sensed he was agitated.

"Are you OK?" I asked.

"Yes, yes, I'm fine. I want this balloon going over ours to get to the other side," Gian said, peering up out of the side of the basket. But it took a while. Eventually, we saw the other balloon float away from us. Gian settled down to enjoy the rest of the flight, still holding on to me. The hour-long flight ended, and we descended onto a large field before being transported to the farmhouse. We were greeted by caterers who served us champagne pink with strawberries. They directed us to our Valentine's Day breakfast. This meal consisted of bacon, eggs, sausages, cold meats, prawns, caviar, loaves of bread, cheeses and cakes. A choice of luxury cereals was also available. The champagne was free-flowing, along with strawberries, cream and chocolate.

"Better watch the champagne flow!" Gian said, thinking of the drive home.

"Don't worry; you enjoy it. I'll drive us back. We still have the evening event to attend." I reminded Gian.

"Are you going to tell me what that is?" He asked.

"Nope, a surprise is a surprise." I insisted. I had told him to bring a suit, so he had an inkling that it was a formal event.

"I need a new suit. Let's stop in town so you can help me pick one out?" Gian enquired.

"Yes, there are gentlemen outfitters in town. We'll stop and get you one," I agreed.

After breakfast, we returned to the hotel to pick up our car. We drove into town, where Gian settled on a suit in midnight blue. On the way home, Gian told me of a recent event where two hot air balloons collided and went down. Several people were killed. No wonder he had been tense on the flight! We spent the afternoon resting before getting ready for the evening. I donned a saree of black silk with gold embroidery and a shocking pink border. My long black locks hung loose down my back. I finished the ensemble with a black clutch bag and high-heeled court shoes.

"You're looking lovely, Honey," Gian complimented me. He had put on his new suit and wore the tie I had given him for Christmas.

"You brush up well for a bushman," I teased him, adding, "I do like that tie."

"Are you going to tell me where we are going now?" He asked.

"All in due course," I replied, smiling as he faked a frown.

We drove towards the city and pulled up at the Sheraton Hotel. Walking towards the ballroom, I produced the tickets for the event.

"Cat's out of the bag now," said Gian reading the notice board in the hotel foyer.

"I hope you enjoy it. I found the ad on the hospital notice board and thought it would be a nice end to our first Valentine's Day," I explained. I looked at him and smiled, hoping he felt the same.

"It's for a good cause, so I approve," he said, hugging me as we walked to our table for an evening of fine food, wine and entertainment.

The event was a fundraiser for the Regional Woman's Hospital, an evening show featuring a mix of professional and hospital staff efforts. The three-course dinner featured Australian native fare. A good-looking female doctor with a fabulous figure and voice performed one act, a Cabaret item.

Beauty and brains!

"She has to be a fraud. It's just too much to have so many gifts in one person," I whispered to Gian as the Doctor strutted out her number in a skimpy outfit.

"Doesn't do anything for me; I'd rather have this than that." He said, squeezing my shoulders as his arm rested on the back of my chair.

"Thank you," I said, kissing his cheek. I revelled in his attention. It had been a long time since a man had treated me well and shown me so much love. Tomorrow, my new life in Australia will begin. I had slowly fallen in love with this gentleman who sat by my side. I reached out my hand and placed it on his thigh; he covered it with his. I felt peace in my soul and turned my attention to the stage. We were restless and had trouble falling asleep after an exciting day. At 3.00 am, we rose, packed up my things and made for Gian's home. He drove the entire distance, and we reached our destination by late afternoon. I entered the living room and found a large banner with the words "Welcome Home Darling" hanging across one wall. It was so very thoughtful of him.

At the farm

Now that I finally had a permanent address, I had all my boxes from England and Saudi Arabia, which had been in storage, delivered. Yet another new application for my nursing and midwifery registration had to be made. It was a hassle to apply for enrolment in each state; the process took several months. However, it gave me plenty of time to adapt to my new surroundings. I asked Gian to teach me how to drive his old two-and-a-half-tonne tractor. It gave me a buzz to use it. On the weekends I got to know the neighbours. They came over Saturday afternoons to enjoy drinks in the yard and have a yarn. The vegetable garden was producing far too much for the two of us. Getting Gian to reduce it to half did not take much persuading. The dogs became friendly with me, and I felt protected by them when Gian left for work every morning, leaving me alone on the homestead. Gian would take me bushwalking whenever he could. We walked along the perimeter of the property, taking the opportunity to check fences and repair them as we went along. I learnt the name of each piece of equipment: fence post hammer, ratchet, fence stretcher etc. When summer came, the Australian Wattle surrounding the property burst into bloom. To my delight, the pretty, sunshine-yellow pom-poms did not trigger my hay fever.

The cattle soon recognised my voice and answered when I called. Big boy Banjo, an Angus bull all of 800 kg, took to standing close to me whenever I ventured into the paddock. He would stroll up behind me so quietly that I nearly jumped out of my skin the first few times I turned and found him at my shoulder. It was hard to imagine that he had come home as a milk calf lying in the back of the station wagon some years ago. Rejected at the cattle sales yard, the gentle giant enjoyed it when I scratched his forehead. He never missed a beat servicing his ladies and always had them in calf. The neighbours often called to ask if they could borrow him. Banjo seemed to know he was on to a good thing as he trotted happily alongside Gian to a neighbouring property to service a different bevvy of bovine beauties. The many chickens knew when 'Daddy' came home from work and would all gather at the chicken coop gate, waiting for Gian to give them a treat. Now and then, I would find feathery little yellow puff balls flipping about in the 'maternity wing' of the coop. The label was penned on a piece of packing cardboard and tacked to the door. We sold the abundant supply of eggs to an older woman in town who hated the answering machine. When she needed more eggs, she would yell, "Gimme some eggs", down the line and abruptly hang up by way of a message. She once complained that our eggs were too clean, making her customers doubt that free-range hens indeed laid them. She asked for some poop to be left on them. It was hard for this city-born-and-bred, hygiene-obsessed nurse not to clean the eggs, but I eventually came to terms with it.

Making a home

I found cleaning the house and putting my stamp on it most gratifying. It also made me feel more at home. Gian's wife had left several personal items in her haste to leave. She and her boyfriend had gone straight on to a fruit-picking holiday together. I was only too glad to pack up the last of her things and send them to the address she had given us. Gian and I went shopping for fabric I made into curtains with lace trimmings. He put up some proper rails for me to hang, taking down the old make-do pieces of fabric held by a string. To my great satisfaction, my efforts made the house look like a proper country farmhouse. I enjoyed the peace and tranquillity of living in the bush and looked forward to Gian's return from work every evening. He always noticed my efforts and thanked me for making his home beautiful and comfortable. He now looked forward to returning home every evening to a delicious dinner, lovingly prepared, and I would be waiting to hear how his day had gone. Gian's attitude and reciprocal expression of his love for me starkly contrasted with Sam's. It soothed the hurt and pain from my first marriage like a healing balm.

"Here you are," Gian said, pressing a $50 note into my hand.

"That's your weekly pocket money to spend any way you like," his eyes twinkled as he added, "It's my job to look after you."

Two months had passed, and I was still waiting for my registration to come through. I felt uneasy not earning a wage for the first time since I started working at sixteen. I was dependent on Gian for everything though we were not yet married. Most of my previous earnings were in the bank, untouched and ready for a rainy day. But his words, "My job is to look after you," triggered my memory of my dream eighteen years ago in Singapore. God had shown me in that dream that a Caucasian man dressed as Gian had been when we met for the first time, and he would look after me. The various clues come together like puzzle pieces: our first meeting at the seaside town, Gian wore a white business shirt, tie, and black trousers. He had been holding a briefcase when I first saw him as I drove into the car park. God had fulfilled his promise to me. I had prayed for so many years to be delivered from Sam's cruel hands and find my one true love. And here he was, Gian. Correspondence from the Catholic church in London about my successful application for annulment of my marriage to Sam arrived with a bill for A$800. Although they did not request payment, Gian paid the bill without hesitation.

Sight

I accompanied Gian to the church that he attended on Sundays. Though it was a Pentecostal church and they did things differently from what I was used to, I felt at home. The congregation was happy and welcoming, and the music was modern. Best of all, the Bible was preached from the pulpit, so it came alive. I found the chosen scripture relevant, pertinent and meaningful. I was beginning to understand my faith for the first time in 40 years. I took to reading my Bible more diligently and was gratified to find this scripture:

"Then he opened their minds so they could understand the Scriptures." (Luke 24:45)

It made sense to me. I had to wait 40 years for God to open my eyes to his word, just like Jesus spent forty days in the desert meditating on his father's plans for him and was tempted by the devil. Moses led the Israelites through the desert for forty years before settling in the Promised Land. The Pentecostal church had seminars and women's groups to attend. All this was new to me. But there was a problem which my growing faith had enabled me to see.

"Gian, you must commence the divorce proceeding if you are serious about our relationship," I urged. "It's not right for me to live with you like this as technically you are still married."

"I'll make an appointment with the local solicitor and get things going ASAP," Gian promised. "But Lilly, you must know that you are my wife in my heart. You have been my wife from the moment I set eyes on you," Gian said earnestly, looking into my eyes.

"And while you're at it, make sure you get your Will sorted out, too," I added.

"Why?" he asked, looking at me, concerned.

"Don't you have one?" I queried.

"No, Lilly, I never thought I needed one!" came the astounding reply.

It was time. God had opened the door for me to tell Gian about my life. I sat him down at the dinner table and told him what had happened to my family and the consequences of my father dying without a Will. Though he found my sorry tale hard to believe, he realised he had a responsibility he needed to attend to urgently. His divorce took just five months, and he also made a Will. The process starkly contrasted my divorce proceedings in England, which had taken well over six years. I still had not received any communication that the case was over! With his divorce now finalised, I felt more at ease living with Gian.

"Lilly, would you marry me?" Gian asked as we sat down to dinner one evening on a short holiday.

I was not expecting the question, although I knew it would have to come soon enough to make our relationship right in God's eyes. Our faith dictated that we shouldn't be living together unmarried. I was giving him time before I drew the line.

"Yes," I replied and kissed him.

Made new

My journey of faith had well and truly begun. I realised the falsehoods the Catholic Church had taught me as a child and young teen. I learned that my Catholic baptism as a baby would not help me see the Kingdom of God or enjoy eternal life. Daily, I delved deeper into my Bible for direction, meaning and understanding. In the quiet of the day, I pondered its words, meditating on its lessons. Jesus taught Nicodemus about being born again.

> "Now there was a man of the Pharisees named Nicodemus, a member of the Jewish ruling council. He came to Jesus at night and said, "Rabbi, we know you are a teacher who has come from God. No one could perform the miraculous signs you are doing if God were not with him." In reply, Jesus declared, "I tell you the truth; no one can see the kingdom of God unless he is born again." "How can a man be born when he is old?" Nicodemus asked. "Surely he cannot enter a second time into his mother's womb to be born!" Jesus answered, "I tell you the truth, no one can enter the kingdom of God unless he is born of water and the spirit. Flesh gives birth to flesh, but the spirit gives birth to spirit. You should not be surprised at my saying; you must be born again. The wind blows wherever it pleases. You hear its sound, but you cannot tell where it comes from or where it is going. So, it is with everyone born of the spirit." (John 3:1-8)

It was almost six months since I met Gian and began attending the Pentecostal Church with him. I was ready to be water baptised and asked the church pastor if he would perform the ceremony for me. The baptism occurred on a Sunday afternoon after church at the local beach, where I was fully immersed.

CHAPTER 8 -- UNION

Gian and I married. To our vows, we added the promise, "To pray with and to serve God until we join our Lord Jesus Christ in Heaven" I wore a saree of gold and cerise. In Mum's memory, I held my bouquet draped over my arm with its ribbons long and flowing down to just before the hem of my saree.

Our relationship grew in strength from day to day. The challenges of a mixed marriage did not seem to affect us. Perhaps this was because I had spent most of my adult life in Western society. Admittedly, Gian was easy to live with and enjoyed Asian meals. He started growing Asian herbs and vegetables for our table. On one occasion, he took me to a Chinese restaurant. The food was adapted to the Australian palate and did not taste authentic. When the meal was over, he asked if I had enjoyed it. Not wanting to hurt his feelings, I said I had. Some months later, we visited Melbourne so I could introduce Gian to my old nursing friends from England. The gang, largely Malaysian Chinese, booked a table at a well-known Chinese restaurant for dinner. Gian experienced authentic Chinese fare that night. My friends decided to test him by ordering chicken feet. It did not faze him; Gian ate it with relish. When he was a child, his family often ate offal and cheap cuts of meat; they also bred rabbits for the table. Having come from Singapore, the meals I cooked tended to be a mix of South Asian, East Asian and Southeast Asian cuisine and standard British fares such as a roast of a joint of beef or lamb or an entire chicken. It would have challenged the palate of any man, but Gian was open to anything I plated up for him. Throughout this combination of meals, sometimes featuring very simple dishes, Gian recounted his life story. His family of origin had not been well-to-do. He wanted to impress upon me that he was not unfamiliar with a simple life. His mother drowned when he was five, and his father remarried soon after.

Gian's life became a nightmare as he suffered abuse at the hands of his stepmother, Doris. He ran away from home several times, sleeping on park benches until the cold and hunger drove him back home. So, he knew firsthand the trauma of homelessness. Despite these challenges, he did well in school and secured an apprenticeship to train as a scientific tool-maker. As soon as he turned 21, Gian left home, migrating to Australia. Neither of us had had a comfortable childhood. These challenging experiences brought us closer. We felt like two peas in a pod: compatible and in agreement on most things. Even our values were aligned, which delighted us to be equally yoked. We knew we could survive any hardship. Harrowing childhood experiences put grit into our bones. Gian had come to Christ through a Swiss fellowship a few years after moving to Australia. It amazed me that my efforts in the kitchen encouraged him to open up to me. Gian reassured me he was not afraid of being poor, having experienced poverty and homelessness just as I had. He would eat anything I put before him, though he was glad I was a good cook. When we entertained, friends chose anything from Indian, Swiss and Chinese to Malay, English and Australian fare to enjoy at our table. Gian is also a good cook. He makes many Swiss dishes, especially handmade Knoepfle or Spaetzle, a drop noodle made from egg noodle dough.

God's plan

I now know that this was God's plan. God had put a chasm between David and me. He had silenced me when I would have spoken up about my affection for David because He had a plan for me. God had chosen Gian for me. I could have had another lawyer offer a very impersonal service with no prior knowledge of me through his mother or sister-in-law. Instead, God had sent David to care for me in a very personal way over the years and often at a great distance. Yes, I would have enjoyed the high life had I pursued a romantic relationship with

David; lawyers make a lot of money. However, David would not have led me to Christ. Gian did. David would not have given me eternity. Gian has. I have eternity in my hands. Such is God's wisdom and plan. If we wait on Him and trust Him, he will make our lives beautiful. The wait has been worth the while. This scripture sums things up for me:

"Be joyful in hope, patient in affliction, faithful in prayer." (Romans 12:12)

God has answered my prayers and kept me safe from harm, ensuring my life partner and I also have a rich spiritual life together. It is captured in the following scripture:

"Do not be yoked together with unbelievers. For what do righteousness and wickedness have in common? Or what fellowship can light have with darkness?" (Corinthians 6:14)

Upon reading the Book of Psalms, I felt this one, of the 150 poems it contains, had been written specifically for me:

"I cried out to him with my mouth;
his praise was on my tongue.
If I had cherished sin in my heart,
the Lord would not have listened;
but God has surely listened
and has heard my prayer.
Praise be to God,
who has not rejected my prayer
or withheld his love from me!"
(Psalm 66:17-20)

Forgiving

Gian and I visited Doris in a nursing home on my first trip to Switzerland. We were both taken aback when we saw her. We had expected the robust, burly woman captured in Gian's old photographs. Instead, the woman who greeted us was a small, fragile figure bent over a wheely walker as she inched towards us.

"Why did you marry this black woman?" She asked Gian in Swiss German as she looked me over.

She did not speak English, and Gian translated for me. I just smiled at her. Gian asked me to wait for him outside her room as he needed to talk to her. I knew what he was going to say to her. It was to ask her why she had abused him as a child. More importantly, he had resolved to forgive her for what she had done. They talked for a long while. The door finally opened, and Gian and his stepmother were smiling. He had indeed forgiven her. As we bid her goodbye, she handed me a little package. It was a table runner that she had embroidered. Today this runner graces the top of the dressing table in our guest room. A cut-glass tray that belonged to my mother sits atop it. Doris died a few months after we returned to Australia.

I saw a different Switzerland as a wife of a Swiss national. We spent time with Gian's family, living with them at first and then in accommodation away from the main drag of the tourist routes. We lived in small towns like Alstetten and Appenzell, renting apartments in homes and farms. Gian took me for walks in the Alps and to beauty spots just outside villages with lakes like Seealpsee and gardens with impressive mountain views of the Swiss Alps. Seeing the Matterhorn was breathtaking, along with an ice cave carved out of a glacier with various ice figures lit with coloured lights. Cable car rides up the snow-capped Alps were magnificent. It amazed me that no matter how high the cable car ended, there was always a restaurant to enjoy food and drink.

Living my best life
My Catholic approach to giving to God had been to drop a dollar or two into the collection box when wardens came around during mass. Gian's was an entirely different approach. He did what the Bible instructed us to do:

"Bring the whole tithe into the storehouse so that there may be food in my house. Test me in this," says the Lord Almighty, "and see if I will not throw open the floodgates of

heaven and pour out so much blessing that there will not be room enough to store it." (1 Malachi 3:10)
and
"Give, and it will be given to you. A good measure, pressed down, shaken together and running over, will be poured into your lap. For with the measure you use, it will be measured to you." (Luke 6:38)

We have been blessed in one way or another by Our Heavenly Father as we walk through life with Him. Gian responds to the church's requests for offerings and generously supports children in third-world countries through aid agencies. We have never looked back.

Unfinished business
I did hear from Davis and Warren once more.

"There's a letter from your English solicitors," Gian informed me, handing it to me. The postal service does not deliver directly to rural properties. Gian picked up our mail from a mailbox we had at the post office in town on his way home from work.

"I wonder what they want?" I said, opening the letter.

The letter requested that I contact the firm as there was still an outstanding matter about my divorce. It had been more than five years since I left England!

I rang the firm and spoke to David.

"We are going through old case notes before destroying them, and I found some money in your account that should have been returned to you," he explained.

"How did that happen?" I asked.

"An oversight, I think," David replied.

"Well, send it to me. You have my address," I instructed.

"I'll do that," he assured me.

We chatted briefly, and then David's voice changed and sounded different. Gone was the official tone of a solicitor. In its place, a more caring tone asked how I was doing.

"What does your husband do?" He wanted to know.

"He is the area IT manager for the local health service and a hobby farmer," I told him.

"What's a hobby farmer?" David asked.

I explained that we lived on 120 acres, had cattle, chickens and dogs, and grew our vegetables. David sounded astonished at my lifestyle.

"And did you have any babies?" He inquired after a pause.

"I can't have babies!" I replied.

"I am sorry," he said and hung up abruptly. With the handset still pressed to my ear, all I heard was the beep of the disconnected line.

Workplace bullying

"Are you a Filipino mail-order bride?" Paula, a fellow midwife, asked with a face like thunder.

She had a sour disposition and appeared less than approachable. The question shocked me; I could have had her guts for garters! I bit my tongue. The knowledge that Gian worked in the same hospital made me cautious. Any waves I made were likely to have an impact on him too. So, I just let it go. There were also covert hostilities. I would turn up at the hospital to find some of my shifts on the roster allocated to another midwife. The other midwives seemed to dislike me because of my association with Gian.

"Who do you think you are? You come into this country, get a good job and hook a good man!" a colleague who was the sister-in-law of the nurse unit manager raged.

"How come you speak English so well?" was another oft-heard remark.

Where did they think I came from? A tree house in the jungle? And because of the colour of my skin? Obviously, these women were not well travelled. They lived blinkered lives in a tiny world. The small country hospital we all worked in appeared to be the centre of their universe. On my first shift, I accompanied a mother for a Caesarean section, as I had done countless times before. When the baby was born, it developed respiratory distress. I did what I had been trained to: attend to its needs, place it in an incubator and give it oxygen therapy. Then I called the paediatrician from the district hospital to attend to the baby as this unit was in a small country hospital. Together we inserted an intravenous line and worked on the baby till it was stable. At the end of the shift, I handed the case over to another staff member, only to find out later that my competence had made her feel threatened. As with the previous hospital, there was no midwife-led care, antenatal midwife clinics, home births, and community midwifery. I was not allowed to run parent education classes despite my ten years of experience. The position was reserved exclusively for a particular group of midwives. Midwives were not allowed to deliver the baby of a mother they looked after. This task was reserved for the on-call doctor, who was called to deliver the baby when the mother was ready. He was paid for each baby he delivered. Midwives falsified documents, claiming that a doctor had attended to a patient at the given time though he had not. After the baby had been born, the doctor arrived late but demanded that the midwife sign the document.

"We have to work with them," was their reason. I refused to sign the document.

Gian and I used to work the same day shifts. It raised eyebrows. After a year, I could not take the bullying any longer and applied to the district hospital in the next town for a job in their maternity unit.

"You will never be allowed to work in the birthing unit there. Only the doctors' favourite midwives are allowed in," a friendly midwife who had tried the same move warned me.

Despite her warning, I switched hospitals. Things did not improve. Indeed, they got worse: senior staff, even the manager, gave me a hard time. I missed going to work with Gian. Most of my skills were not recognised. As I was warned, I could not work in the birthing unit. Junior staff were given preference. I discovered later that some of the midwives who enjoyed preferential treatment were involved with the doctors. When I applied for the parent educator position, the job was given to another midwife, despite her lack of training and experience. The unit funded her training before officially installing her in the post. She quit the position two months later because she did not enjoy the work.

"Oh! You're a Pommy!" declared a midwife I was working with. I set her right by informing her of my Singaporean birth.

"We don't want your Christian attitudes here," sneered another.

Turning the other cheek became the norm for me. It was not possible to respond civilly and rationally to these daily aggressions. Gian was very supportive of me.

"Just look at their private lives," he said. Gian was not far wrong.

There were marriage problems and breakdowns. The husband of one of my colleagues walked out while she was still pregnant with his child. Others had children with challenging behaviours. It was unsurprising given the children's role models. Their unprofessional and unethical behaviour and poor work attitude beggared belief. Swear "F" words were freely spoken in the staff room, and a patient was called a "bitch."

I challenged the unit manager to carry out a staff satisfaction survey. The results shocked the whole hospital and were reported to the CEO of the health authority. Compulsory team-building exercises brought in did not change the working environment much. The bullies had learnt to bully at home. They had likely been schoolyard bullies and eventually grew into adults who brought their bullying behaviours to the workplace.

"Please attend the surgery," said my GP's receptionist. She also asked that my husband accompany me.

Worried, Gian and I attended the appointment. We both expected to hear news of an adverse diagnosis.

"What is going on in your life? Your cortisol blood levels are going through the roof!" my GP asked. Gian and I looked at each other.

"It's most likely to be work-related," I told her.

Dr Saunders asked for evidence. I gave her a file thick with my complaints and documenting incidents. At the next appointment, she said she was not surprised. The hospital was known for its toxic work environment. She advised me to leave and get another job. However, this was not an option. We needed my wages as Gian, and I was subdividing our property. In self-preservation, I gave up all thoughts of career advancement and opted to work in the postnatal ward. I secured a teaching parent education position when the manager could not find anyone to fill the position. A mother voted me in for a Midwife of the year award. The correspondence went to the manager, who handed the envelope to me. Nothing was mentioned in the unit about my nomination. Throughout this ordeal, I relied heavily on Gian and my faith to feed my soul and prevent further deterioration of my health. The following are but two examples of scripture that gave me the strength to endure this ordeal:

> "Moses answered the people, "Do not be afraid. Stand firm and you will see the deliverance the Lord will bring you today. The Egyptians you see today you will never see again.

The Lord will fight for you; you need only to be still."
(Exodus 14: 13-14)
and
"For the battle is not yours, but God's."
(2 Chronicles: 20:15)

Countless verses in the Bible told me to leave it all to my Lord and Saviour, Jesus. He would sort it out for me. Eventually, faithful to His promise, my perpetrators were sorted out one by one: some resigned, and others were told to change or be sacked. One was killed in an accident. Although the unit improved somewhat, the issues were not entirely resolved. There was always an underlying tension, and I often went to work feeling apprehensive. But I left it all at the foot of the Cross, and God worked it out for me – as the scripture cited below promised.

"No trial has overtaken you that is not faced by others. And God is faithful: He will not let you be tried beyond what you are able to bear, but with the trial will also provide a way out so that you may be able to endure it." (1 Corinthians 10:13)

I could not have asked for a better way.

Toastmasters International

"My boss has advised me to attend a Toastmasters course for public speaking to help me with my presentations at work. There's one starting up soon in town," Gian informed me one evening at the dinner table.

He had had his annual appraisal and admitted he disliked giving presentations to community health workers.

"It's called a speechcraft course," he added.

"That sounds interesting. How about attending it together?" I suggested. And we did.

My years of teaching parent education have given me a strong lead in public speaking. I enjoyed it tremendously, although it challenged Gian. We got excellent end-of-course evaluations and joined the club to continue improving our skills by completing the essential communication and leadership skills courses. I progressed to the Advanced Bronze Communication level adding leadership and public relations to my skills. But it was the speech competitions that I excelled in. I won the 'Table Topics' prize the first time I entered a club-level competition. Unfortunately, I could not defend it at the next area competition as Gian, and I had booked a holiday in Singapore that weekend. It was the start of an exciting time in my life. I entered competitions at club, area and district levels, collecting a folder full of certificates. Gian declined to compete but drove me around the state to attend the competitions. We often took short breaks at the same time. The experience with Toastmasters boosted my spirit and confidence, which had taken a beating at work. The area Distinguished Toastmaster was very supportive and recognised my skill.

On Air

One Sunday, a couple from a local Christian radio station visited our church and told us about their radio ministry. With Gian's blessing, I became a volunteer. After being trained, I began live on-air broadcasting. Friday was a full working day at the station, and eventually, I was awarded my own program. My love for cooking was the impetus for my hour on air. I shared recipes, cooking methods and ways to use ingredients. I also organised competitions and gave away cookery books and Australian timber chopping boards purchased from a local carpenter. Winners came to the station to pick up their prizes and meet the members.

"You have a following, did you know that?" the station's boss informed me one day while allocating more hours to my program. I worked 'live' on a three-hour show on Friday morning, then pre-recording the contents for Monday through Thursday. It was another confidence booster for me. I called my cooking program *Love in the cooking pot* because it took love to produce all those meals every day of the year to feed a family. These affirmations of my worth were exciting and wonderful. However, the cherry on top of the cake was the enrichment I got for my faith. Two half-hour programs fed my soul and spirit as I sat and listened to them in the studio. They were from "Derek Prince Ministries" and "Focus on the Family" Australia. Prince's preaching gave insight into why things had gone so wrong in my family. One episode called 'The sins of the father' was pivotal in my understanding of scripture concerning how my father's, brother-in-law's, and sister-in-law's behaviour affected my family. It drew on the following scripture:

"I am the LORD your God, who brought you out of Egypt, out of the land of slavery. You shall have no other gods before me. You shall not make for yourself an image in the form of anything in heaven above or on the earth beneath or in the waters below. You shall not bow down to them or worship them; for I, the LORD your God, am a jealous God, punishing the children for the sin of the parents to the third and fourth generation of those who hate me, but showing love to a thousand generations of those who love me and keep my commandments." (Exodus 20:2-6)

I began thinking about my family. Had my ancestors been among those whom God charged with hating him, bowing down to idols and false gods? I knew that my ancestors were of the Hindu faith. Was this why my family had seen such hardship? Was this why my father did not carry out his responsibility of writing his Will and setting his affairs straight? He had chosen to die a slow and painful death from septicaemia rather than allow the doctors to amputate his gangrenous leg to save his life. Why had he made that choice? Why had he and my brothers-in-law and Sam been given to alcoholism? Was Sam under the curse of gambling and alcohol? Were they under the demonic influences that Derek Prince had mentioned? Why did my sisters and I suffer physical, emotional and financial abuse from our husbands? My sister-in-law, an avowed follower of Jesus, threw my mother out of her home.

Is my family under a generational curse that would last about one hundred and forty years? The last two generations had been observant Catholics. Has Catholicism failed us? But the rest of my family remains Catholic. I am the only one who rejected its teachings and has been water baptised. I now understood that the gods they worshipped were alcohol, gambling, adultery, pursuing higher education and perhaps many more, at the cost of family responsibility. Sadly, all marriages of the next generations have fallen foul, mainly in divorce or single parenting. Domestic violence continues. Try as I might, I could not find the "Fruits of the Spirit" in the book of Galatians that set the living standards for all believers, with my in-laws of the same ethnic background.

"But the fruit of the Spirit is love, joy, peace, forbearance, kindness, goodness, faithfulness, gentleness and self-control. Against such things, there is no law." (Galatians 5:22-23)

The entire law is fulfilled by keeping this one command:

"Love your neighbour as yourself." Galatians 5:14

I pondered my marriage to Sam and how sharply it contrasted with my marriage with Gian. Prince explained much about the demonic realm working in our lives. He delved into many things my family still practices: astrology, superstitions and remnant Hindu practices persist alongside the Catholic doctrine and all its paraphernalia. Some members are still Hindu. Finally, Prince spoke about forgiveness of those who had wronged me in my past and present. He reminded us of this scripture:

"If you forgive others when they sin against you, your heavenly Father will also forgive you. But if you do not forgive others their sins, your Father will not forgive your sins." (Matthew 6:14)

I had to learn to forgive and let go of the hurts of the past. I grappled with this as I still harboured resentment toward Sam.

It remains a constant battle to this day. Understanding my brother and sister-in-law's treatment of my mother remains challenging. Eventually, Gian pointed out the following scriptures from Timothy:
> "Give proper recognition to those widows who are really in need." (1 Tim 5:3)

and
> "Anyone who does not provide for their relatives, especially their own household, has denied the faith and is worse than an unbeliever." (1 Tim 5:8)

and
> "Religion that God our Father accepts as pure and faultless is this: to look after orphans and widows in their distress and to keep oneself from being polluted by the world." (James 1:27)

I had to repent for not looking after my mother and forgive my father for his lack of responsibility. In 'Focus on the family', Dr James Dobson explained aspects of family life that brought to light the many issues that occurred and continues to trouble my family. Because my two brothers still endure past hurts in unforgiveness, I remain estranged from them. However, I still speak to my remaining sister and half-sisters. Gian and I have tried to bring the family together with no success. We have had to leave it all at the foot of the Cross. Another secular station in the next town asked me to produce a breakfast show for them. I hosted a live hour-long show early Sunday morning called *Soul breakfast*. My time on both stations spanned six years, during which I sat on the board of directors at the Christian station, formally trained at TAFE, and attained a Certificate 4 in radio broadcasting with distinction.

Gideons

"I have joined the Gideons," Gian said one afternoon upon returning home from a morning coffee for men at church. A year later, I joined as an auxiliary. We served in the ministry as visiting officials to churches around the area, informing them of the work of the Gideons putting bibles in prisons, doctors' surgeries, and police graduation ceremonies. Our Toastmasters training in public speaking was put to good use. I was kept busy between Toastmasters, radio broadcasting and Gideon auxiliary work, my job and household responsibilities. I did mourn the loss of the autonomy I had enjoyed as a midwife in England, but I knew that what I had on a personal level now was far better. My career in England had been wonderfully fulfilling, but my marriage had died. Things in Australia were the opposite: my marriage soared while my career had stalled. I was genuinely grateful to have Gian by my side and God at the helm.

One last encumbrance
As happy as we were, Gian and I still had one final battle. Gian and Rod, his former brother-in-law, were partners in the ownership of the land on which we lived. As part of Gian's divorce settlement, I bought his ex-wife's share of the land for $75 000. The funds for this had come from my pension in Singapore. I withdrew these savings as soon as I became Australian. It made me one of three owners of the 120 acres. We approached the local Council seeking the division of this land parcel into two sixty-acre parcels. Council deemed us developers and demanded that we build an 800 m public road through bushland to connect our subdivision to the highway. It would do away with the 5 km dirt road through the bush we currently use. We fought Council on the issue. We felt that they were attempting to unload the cost of a public road onto private citizens rather than request federal funding. Negotiations went back and forth, with Council refusing to budge. They threw the book at us. What made it worse was that Rod, who was supposed to help us, abdicated from his role. A morbidly obese heavy smoker who was drunk by 10.00 am, there was no getting any sense out of him. He was often abusive when we approached him. It put a lot of pressure on

Gian, who handled the reams of paperwork and attended Council meetings to dispute their claims and demands while working full-time throughout the process.

Intercession

After five years of this, we were ground down. We had constantly prayed for Council to have a change of heart to no avail and concluded that perhaps this was not part of God's plan for us. He likely had a different vision for us. Gian and I decided to call it quits and live on the property as we had all along.

"Gian, why don't we bring in the Intercessors to pray over the property?" I suggested.

"I don't know, Lilly. If that is what you want to do, try it. I am at wit's end with all of this!" he declared, exasperated. Gian's stress levels were so high that he worked holes into the bedsheets with his feet while he slept. The following Sunday, I approached a member of the Intercessors and spoke about our issues.

"I will take it to the next meeting and return to you. We approached all matters as a group. The group consist of several of us from all the Evangelical churches in the area. Keep praying," was the advice

A few weeks later, the member returned and informed me that the intercessors had agreed to perform a biblical cleansing of the property. A congregation of Intercessory ladies descended on our property on a Saturday afternoon. One woman in the group suggested that things may not have gone well for us because Aboriginal blood was spilt on the land. They walked through our home, praying. They asked me to show them everything we had bought overseas and proceeded to examine them closely. They asked that we remove souvenirs we had bought while on a Bali vacation. Muslim Balinese artists prayed over their products before selling them to unsuspecting tourists. When brought into the home, the deities and spirits they had invoked in their prayers moved in too. My artist brother had made a mask of his face, of which they disapproved.

"It's a death mask. You have to destroy it!" They informed us. I had kept it because the mask was the spitting image of my father. Everything was removed into the paddock and set alight while Gian prayed for God's protection from spirits that might be released. The whole house was anointed with oil. They then walked the perimeter of the entire property. They prayed and cleansed the land, sprinkling cleansing salt and anointing the surveyor's post at the corners of the property. They anointed three of these posts before time ran out. It was an enormous undertaking to walk the boundaries of 120 acres.

He hears us
A few weeks later, we informed Council that we would not proceed with the subdivision. As we sat in the meeting room waiting for council officials, Gian and I prayed fervently for God to intervene. The official that arrived was different from the one we usually dealt with. The lady said the former officer had been taken ill and would be away for a while. She asked that we talk her through our application. The new official seemed to be much more sympathetic. Though we were tired of repeating our arguments, we presented our case clearly and respectfully.

"Would you agree to construct the public road as a dirt road and pay a contribution to the council for it to be built up to a tar road in the future?" She asked.

"Yes," Gian agreed promptly.

She would take the new proposal to her seniors and inform us of the outcome. A few weeks later, we received a letter from Council. We had its approval to subdivide the land into six blocks of twenty acres each if we agreed to contribute to the public road. We were obliged to clear a dirt road connecting our property to the highway. We also had to put in

an 80 m tarred road in front of the first block of land and construct the internal roads to access each 20-acre parcel. We accepted the offer, and the subdivision commenced. True to his promise in the Bible, God had answered our prayers:
> "And if we know that he hears us -- whatever we ask -- we know that we have what we asked of him." (1 John 5:15).

Another scripture we relied upon during this time is:
> "Do not be anxious about anything, but in every situation, by prayer and petition, with thanksgiving, present your requests to God." (Philippians 4:6)

We gave up our Toastmasters positions, my radio broadcasts and our work with the Gideons to put all our efforts into the subdivision. Gian sold all the cattle as the internal fences on the property had to be brought down. Without these fences, they could not be corralled. It was a sad day for him when he said goodbye to his pets.

Subdivision

The lands department allowed landowners to clear a maximum of five acres each year, which gave us time to do the subdivision at a manageable pace. Gian brought in bulldozers to create a clearing for homes and to build large dams. This work took the next four years to complete. He spent weekends clearing the fallen trees, making windrows and setting them alight to remove the timber. We gave away firewood to anyone who wanted it. Working with surveyors, we submitted plans that gained Council's approval. To fund the subdivision, we borrowed $250,000 from a commercial bank. The roads were built, and the parcels of land formalised. After putting in a day at the office, Gian worked several hours more, often doing labour-intensive tasks. He would return home exhausted. I would massage ointment into his back and limbs to relieve his pain. He did not get any help from Rod, his ex-brother-in-law. I had the once-in-a-lifetime opportunity to name the public road we had constructed. The town's streets were named after local soldiers who had died in wars while in service. We did not have any such relatives. So, I christened it after a biblical warrior. We found many uncanny similarities between the biblical warrior and us. We had gone up against a large and powerful adversary, Council. We triumphed with God's intervention. So, the street name was particularly apt and especially meaningful to us.

Only one parcel of land was sold when we put all the blocks on the market. This lifestyle block had been my favourite. The little hill at the back of the subdivision had views of the Great Dividing Range. With that one sale, we repaid the commercial bank loan. We bought the remaining pieces of land from Rod with our savings. It finally freed us from him. The three remaining blocks were unsold for nearly two years. Real estate agents brought interested parties to inspect the property, but most did not know what to do with 20 acres of land. Eventually, Gian decided we would develop the individual parcels of land ourselves. We put our house on the market. It went in a week as an investment property for the new owners allowing us to rent it from them. God had provided us with the right type of buyer. Living in the same house and managing the subdivision that was our backyard was a luxury. We ploughed the proceeds from selling our home into building a new four-bedroom house and a four-bay shed in one of the three remaining blocks and moved into it on completion. I quit my hospital position with no more loans or mortgages to service. Instead, I became a GP nurse, ending 38 years of shift work; no more night duty and workplace bullying. Hooray! Gian sold his old tractor, which had seen better days and bought a new one. The day it was delivered, he had a broad grin that reminded me of a Cheshire Cat. He was in such a good mood and so gracious that he let me be the first to drive it.

Trouble

Our neighbour Ray was a real estate agent. A right of carriageway on our land fronted his property. Ray had sold a plot of land behind our property and granted the Robertsons the right to use this carriageway. However, as the carriageway was not on his land, this right of way was not his to give. It meant they gained access to the road by opening a gate on a corner of our property.

This gate was used exclusively to maintain high-power electricity pylons that ran along the carriageway. It was the one surveyor post that had eluded the Intercessors. The Robertsons enjoyed this carriageway's convenience, saving them the 5 km drive through the bush. It was the drive we had to take before the subdivision. We were outraged as we had built these roads for our subdivision, not their use. We eventually took Ray to court and waited four years for the case to be heard in the State's Supreme Court. In the meantime, Ray and the Robertsons turned all our neighbours against us. I walked the right of carriageway whenever possible, reading the Book of Psalms aloud. Once, I decided to cleanse it by sprinkling salt as I did the readings. As I walked the road, a neighbour drove up alongside me.

"What are you doing?" The driver asked.

"Praying and cleansing the road with salt," I replied.

"Don't you know that that's bad luck," he claimed.

"Well, it all depends on which God you pray to," I replied.

Without another word, he sped into the driveway of the house he was renting. His dog came out to greet me as it did each time, I walked the road. He screamed at his dog to get back into the house. He must have thought I was a witch! I continued with my walk, praying and salting the road. A few weeks later, the man moved out of the property.

Divine knowledge

"A man is trying to steal your land!" The woman said.

Gian and I were in India visiting the orphanage that we supported. At the end of each visitor's stay, the pastor's mother, regarded as a prophetess, would speak to the visitors in prophecy. She was well-known in the village and surrounding areas for the accuracy of her predictions. She spent her time praying and fasting. Gian and I realised that she must refer to our pending court case. We had not told anyone about it.

Moreover, the prophetess did not speak any English. Her daughter acted as an interpreter for her. So how did she come to know about it? We attributed it to divine revelation.

"Do not worry. You will win the case!" she said through her daughter. She also advised me to commence a monthly women's Bible study group.

Our court case was heard in the Supreme Court over two days. God blessed us with a decision that went our way. Our neighbour had to pay our court charges, some $80,000. We instructed our lawyers to advise the surrounding neighbours that if they continued to use the carriageway or harass us, we would not hesitate to see them in court. We never saw or heard from them after that. Ray kept to himself. I commenced the women's Bible study group, and Gian initiated one for the women's husbands because they did not want to miss out. God had answered our prayers.

Once again, the Bible had sustained us through challenging times, the promises of the Lord's support for the faithful:

> "I sought the Lord, and he answered me and delivered me from all my fears." (Psalm 34:4)

The following is another particularly heartening scripture that many lovers of God draw strength, courage and peace:

> "Do not be anxious about anything, but in everything, by prayer and petition, with thanksgiving, present your requests to God. And the peace of God, which transcends all

understanding, will guard your hearts and your minds in Christ Jesus." (Philippians 4:6-7)

Still building

Moving into our new home left us with two more blocks of land to develop. Gian retired from his job and used his pension to commission the second house and a two-bay shed. His retirement did not last long. The health service re-called him as they could not find anyone to replace him. Gian agreed to work from home. With the second house completed, we again put the home we had lived in on the market. It took three years to sell, and we moved into the second build. Gian then started on the third build on the last remaining block. He commissioned a sizeable four-bay shed with a two-bedroom unit within the shed. It sold off the plan bringing the subdivision work to a close. Gian was busy repairing the dirt roads as no one else cared about them. We now had just the house in which we were living. We breathed a sigh of relief that the stress of building and moving was finally over. During this time, we were sustained by the following scripture:

"If my people who are called by my name humble themselves and pray and seek my face and turn from their wicked ways, then I will hear from heaven and will forgive their sin and heal their land." (2 Chronicles 7:14)

Long wait

"Lilly, I have always wanted to live in Tasmania. Gian had asked me on our first date 20 years ago. How do you feel about that?"

"I'm a bit of a nomad. I'll live anywhere as long as I don't suffer from hay fever the way I did in England," I informed him.

Over the next 20 years, we visited Tasmania every two to three years, touring the Apple Isle of Australia to get to know it and find the best place for us to settle down. Gian was constantly looking at the Tasmanian real estate market and making a short list of the places which appealed to him. He updated the list regularly. We had placed our home on the market in anticipation of moving to Tasmania. But after four years and no interest, we pulled it off the market. I started hanging up our paintings and pictures from the storage, thinking we would stop here for good. Quite unexpectedly, the house sold privately and expeditiously. We were surprised and thus utterly unprepared to vacate in two months. I quit my job immediately and started packing. Gian arranged to continue to work remotely wherever we chose to move. We attended farewell parties at my workplace, church and with our Bible study groups. All our possessions were packed into a container for storage in Tasmania. On the last day, we drove out of the subdivision with a huge sigh of relief. We were glad to leave behind 20 years of trials and tribulations that had stretched us to the limit. Through it all, we had grown in our marriage and faith. Once again, we were heartened, and this gem from scripture strengthened our faith,

> "This is the confidence we have in approaching God: that if we ask anything according to His will, he hears us." (1 John 5:14)

We boarded *The Spirit of Tasmania* in Melbourne to cross Bass Strait to our new life. Gian had rented an apartment long-term, anticipating a wait before we found a home. God blessed us again. We met two real estate agents on our arrival to Tasmania, the first Sunday we were in church. They showed us a beautiful property on sixty acres of land that Gian had on his shortlist. I was less than sure about it.

"It's too opulent; I have never lived in a house like this in all my life. No!" I objected.

Gian and I had made a pact with each other. If one did not like a property, it was a no-go. So, we viewed fifteen other old, shabby properties that required significant renovations.

"Lilly, I am tired of building. We have been at it for 20 years. I am too tired to go through another round of council negotiations if we do another build." Gian pleaded with me. We were back in the living room of the opulent house for a third viewing.

"Can we afford this?" I asked him. All our wealth had come from our work and the subdivision.

"By the time we pay for a new build and cover the expense of the rental and storage of all our possessions, we can afford this comfortably. Everything else we have viewed is not suitable. This house is live-in ready, being only seven years old," Gian reassured me.

I agreed. We signed the papers, and the contracts were exchanged on my birthday. What a gift! It has now been more than six years since we moved in. I retired from work and deregistered my nursing and midwifery qualifications. Gian continued working for the first two years of our life in Tasmania until the health service found a program to replace the one he had written. He upgraded and converted our property from an equestrian holding to a cattle farm. We had new wallaby-proof fences replace the old ones on the boundaries. More gates and fences went up internally to create grazing paddocks for the cattle. Two old barns were replaced with one large new one to store the year's hay and silage crop. Gian pulled down the old, wooden cattle race and replaced it with a modern, galvanised steel race. He built a large greenhouse for his vegetable garden to cope with the long, cold Tasmanian winter. As for the house, we enclosed an external area into a conservatory, so we had an entertainment area. The house itself needed minimal adjustments. Our property is on the top of a plateau overlooking a valley. There are broad-acre farms on both sides of the valley. In the backdrop is another hilly range. The river in the valley is a favourite for trout fishing. Gian and I are pleased with where we are. Farms of various sizes surround us. There are cattle, dairy, crop and hobby farms. Large bay windows in the front of our home showcase views of the valley that constantly change with the season, time of the day and weather.

The community has welcomed us warmly, and we have settled in well, making friends with other farmers who have become a fountain of knowledge for us. Church life continues, and we are blessed to have an active role in it. We run a social club at our church which meets weekly for ten months of the year. Orphan and widow support in India is still maintained; I have lost count of how many we have supported. Recently one of our orphans married and left the orphanage. She had her first baby and asked us to name her baby. We gave her two choices: Abigail and Hannah. She picked Hannah. We were so pleased that she remembered us. A pastor found her wandering the streets, homeless after the death of her parents. She would have been easily picked up by pimps and placed in the prostitution trade. We will continue to be involved with missions till we leave this earth. The church we now attend planned a mission trip to Uganda to reach out to young girls. I travelled with the Wings of Love Ministry. The team consisted of our pastor, the leader and me. Girls in Uganda do not go to school during their periods because they have no sanitary pads. We visited three village schools and gave out over a thousand washable fabric pads that could be used repeatedly. We held workshops on self-respect and the dangers of pre-marital sex for young women.

Traditionally girls here are married off at puberty. Many die in childbirth because their young bodies are not ready for pregnancy. Girls aged thirteen were married to any man who would take them off their parents' hands because they are seen as a burden to the family. We held education sessions to dissuade mothers from continuing with this traditional practice. With my midwifery background, I spoke to traditional and hospital-trained midwives. The pastor organising the trip informed me that women were beaten in labour. The midwives confirmed this barbaric practice. I told them the practice had to stop immediately as it ran counter to everything midwifery stood for. Since then, a group of international obstetricians has published an article in *The Lancet* addressing the issue and commencing a change in the hospital training of midwives in Africa. Traditional midwives were amazed at the birth charts I showed them about the birth process of a baby. They had never seen anything like it. They had learnt their craft from their mothers and aunts. I spoke to them, sitting under a mango tree in a field! Truly, Africa was an experience.

A journey

I am now over sixty years old. I would never have dreamed that the twelve-year-old little girl who wore a tattered uniform and walked to her exams would travel, work and live in all the countries I have. I have cried my mother's tears and walked in her footsteps. I can only praise God and thank Him for delivering me out of poverty and all my life's troubles and getting me to where I am today. He has held my hands through my trials and given me such happiness in my marriage to Gian.

Most importantly, He has chosen me as His child, and I have the gift of forgiveness and eternity in heaven with Almighty God. My heart is at peace. My faith continues to grow and enrich my life with the wisdom of God's word. I have but one regret: not meeting Him at the start of my life. But God knows what he is doing. He has taught me a great many things. My eyes continue to be opened with each encounter I have with Him through his word in biblical education, church attendance and sharing with my evangelical fellowship.

My darling, the best is yet to come! Thank you, Gian, my husband, the love of my life, confidant and soul mate. You are the best thing that has happened to me. Thank you for choosing me to do life with you, understanding and caring for me, and standing by my side. Where would I be without you?

Thank you, my reader, for coming on this journey with me. I pray that it has enriched your soul and encouraged you that all things are possible in Christ Jesus.

With abundant blessing in Jesus' name,
Lilly.

"For I know the plans I have for you, declares the Lord. Plans to prosper you and not harm you, plans to give you hope and a future." (Jeremiah 29:11)

"You will know the truth, and the truth will set you free." (John 8:32)

"If it is possible, as far as it depends on you, live at peace with everyone." (Romans 12:18)

www.ingramcontent.com/pod-product-compliance
Lightning Source LLC
Chambersburg PA
CBHW020318010526
44107CB00054B/1895